Advance praise for My Wilderness Life

Inspired by a spirit elk, John Fraley has been able to live the dream of many a Montana boy confronted by ever-encroaching civilization—devoting his life to wilderness, or what's left of it. The wilderness can be glorious and it can be unforgiving, as his account of the loss of a friend confirms: the friendship was glorious, the loss brutal. Fortunately for us, he takes us along in a readable account of his many decades in the field as scientist, hunter, trapper, fisherman, and devotee of the backcountry. The underlying message is that the struggle to preserve the wild is a never-ending and necessary one, for the spirit as well as the land.
> — **John N. Maclean**, author of *Home Waters: A Chronicle of Family and a River* and other books

My *Wilderness Life* is a remarkable work based on John's extraordinary experience and career working in wild places with wild creatures. It's a story about kinship that endures like wilderness. We are fortunate that John shares his journey with us.
> —**Tim Love**, Seeley Lake District Ranger, U.S. Forest Service, retired

My *Wilderness Life* overflows with Fish and Wildlife biologist John Fraley's formidable adventures in and around Northwest Montana's Bob Marshall Wilderness, Bitterroot Mountains, and Idaho's River of No Return. This is an articulate and insightful work compelling readers to keep turning the pages. John's story is seasoned with humor, self-deprecation, and larger-than-life accomplishments that are all true. (For purpose of full disclosure, I have known John since meeting at the University of Montana, five decades ago. Even then I regarded him as an expert angler with a boundless physical constitution and probing intellect.) Among John's myriad accomplishments are epic backpack and snowshoe trips; a torturous 35-mile, three day trek to haul out over 200 pounds of elk meat; the first snorkeling surveys of fisheries habitat in many Flathead River tributaries; fighting a forest fire; hunting; fur trapping; rafting wild rivers; researching, and authoring pieces for scientific journals and books documenting the lives of early settlers and pioneers. John's legacy is substantial comprising his love for his wife and their three children, scientific studies that establish the baseline for future research, and enduring allegiance to others, including putting meaning to his friend Terry McCoy's premature death while participating in an elk study project.

— **Bob Krumm**, history author, retired newspaper owner and publisher, nationally recognized reporter, columnist, editorial writer, photographer.

-o- **John Fraley** -o-

MY
WILDERNESS
LIFE

*One Man's Search for Meaning
in Montana's Backcountry*

ISBN: 978-1-56037-822-8

Text/Photography © 2022 by John Fraley unless credited otherwise.

Design by Steph Lehmann

Front cover photo: John Fraley atop Kevan Mountain in the Bob Marshall Wilderness. PHOTOGRAPH BY KEVIN FRALEY.
Back cover photos, top left and middle: Self-timer photos. PHOTOGRAPHS BY JOHN FRALEY;
top right: John Fraley with backpack. PHOTOGRAPH BY BOB KRUMM.
Page 199: Photograph of William "Bud" Moore. PHOTOGRAPH © VICKI MOORE.

For more information about our books, write Farcountry Press, P.O. Box 5630,
Helena, MT 59604; call (800) 821-3874; or visit www.farcountrypress.com.

Library of Congress Cataloging-In-Publication data on file.

Produced and printed in the United States of America.

26   25   24   23   22   1   2   3   4   5

Table of Contents

Acknowledgments

I thank my daughter, Heather, my sons, Kevin and Troy, and my wife, Dana, for sharing many wilderness trips over the years that helped shape this book. I also appreciate the support and companionship of my co-workers and friends who joined me on many backcountry treks. Montana Fish, Wildlife & Parks allowed me to reference my past reports and journals. Conservationist icon and mentor Bud Moore allowed me to use his notes from a sixty-mile trek he made across the Bob Marshall and proposed Great Bear Wilderness, which my son and I later retraced and I wrote about for this book. Les Marcum, professor emeritus in the wildlife program at the University of Montana, helped me study the wilderness plane crash and tragic death of my college classmate and hiking partner, Terry McCoy. Members of the U.S. Forest Service and the smokejumper fraternity helped me sort out details as I put the story together. Their names are mentioned in the text. The friendship of Terry's family was very important to me for years in the aftermath of the tragedy. I also appreciated discussions I had with Dr. Cathy Ream regarding Terry's life. Will Harmon served as editor and guided me through the process of completing this book. Finally, I thank my late parents, Richard and Barbara Fraley. My father had the wisdom to raise us in a home along the banks of a creek, setting the course of my life; and my mother, who was my soulmate, rarely said a bad word about anyone.

This is a work of nonfiction. I did my best to be accurate, relying on personal and written sources whenever possible. Some information is based on my imperfect memory, and I take full responsibility for any errors. ◄◦►

CHAPTER 1

My Wilderness Life

I feel lucky to have lived a wilderness life. For a half century, I've fished, hunted, fur-trapped, skied, snowshoed, trekked—and worked, as a fisheries biologist—across eight designated wilderness areas, almost exclusively in Montana. If you add it all up, I've spent about 750 days, or a couple years of my life, in wilderness. If your time is where your heart is, then my heart lives squarely in wilderness.

We have wilderness icon Bob Marshall (1901–1939) to thank for our precious, protected wildlands. Bob gushed enthusiasm for wilderness preservation, and through his force of personality, he evangelized many thousands to answer his call. In his short life and after, he blazed a trail for establishing primitive areas and on to congressionally designated wilderness as we know it today.

In his two early seminal articles, "The Wilderness as a Minority Right" (1928), and "The Problem of the Wilderness" (1930), Bob set the stage and laid out what is still the best case ever argued for its advocacy. Amazingly, he published both articles before he turned thirty, and they still stand as beacons today. In "The Problem of the Wilderness" he called for formation of the Wilderness Society, and then went on to co-found it. That article appeared in *Scientific Monthly*. Read it alongside the 1964 Wilderness Act and you will see how his words inspired the language later enacted by the U.S. Congress.

When Bob died of a heart attack at age thirty-eight in January 1939, the conservation community was stunned. He was known for his long hikes and superior physical condition (see my 2018 book, *Rangers, Trappers, and Trailblazers*, for a description of his 182-mile, five-day dash through the "Bob"). His life loomed so large that on August 16, 1940, U.S. Forest Service regional forester Evan Kelly combined three primitive areas and named the 950,000-acre Bob Marshall Wilderness in Bob's honor.

Bob Marshall was one of my big inspirations as I trekked around the Bob as an eighteen-year-old. My 1972 U.S. Forest Service map featured a photo showing him with a huge pack on his back. Yep, this was someone I wanted to emulate. As a teenager, I had the enthusiasm but no crystal ball revealing just how important a role wilderness would play in my life.

I'm honored that you've picked up this book. In it, I've pulled together some of my best times, worst times, most challenging times, and fun times in the big open of wilderness. These pages also explore the natural history of important fish and furbearers that thrive in wild areas. Maybe you can learn from my experiences and mistakes; I hope you'll at least be entertained.

The author, John Fraley, with his daughter, Heather, and son Troy at the boundary of the Bob Marshall Wilderness.

One overarching theme of the book is my search for meaning in the short wilderness life of my University of Montana classmate, Terry McCoy. He and I shared great wilderness trips together until an airplane crash in the Welcome Creek Wilderness ended his life at age nineteen while he was radio-tracking elk. Terry died young and didn't get the chance to have a long wilderness life like I've had. His life, and his death, have haunted me in more ways than one. Chapters 2 and 14 trace the story of the crash and try to find sense and solace in the tragedy.

Some stories are from my work as a state biologist in the wilderness, and others bring you along on my own hunting, fishing, trapping, and trekking trips, in summer and winter. You'll join me on sketchy winter river crossings, backcountry elk hunts, and fishing expeditions, sampling native cutthroat in headwater streams and even snorkeling to count them, and on my own dash through the Bob. We'll ski into the Scapegoat and the Selway-Bitterroots and retrace the steps of conservation guru Bud Moore on a sixty-mile journey through the Bob and the Great Bear.

You'll share my work and philosophy about the native bull trout in the Middle and South Forks of the Flathead, and thrill to a helicopter trip on furbearer surveys across snowy landscapes in the heart of the Great Bear. Along the way, there are tense encounters with grizzly bears and moose, and a trip through the "impassable" canyon of the Middle Fork of the Salmon River.

Hopefully, you'll laugh with me about some of the backcountry mistakes I made. And find food for thought in my ideas about the evolution of cutthroat trout and pine marten, among other wild critters.

These stories span five decades of my wilderness life. I'm anxious to bring them alive for you, so please sit back, read on, and share these fun and often poignant times with me. -◦-

CHAPTER 2

Spirit Elk of Pyramid Lake

When I feel the wind blow in the wilderness, I think of whispers from the past. And I wonder: do traces of past travelers remain on the landscape?

Visitors from long ago have left their DNA behind, and their elements cycle through the landscape. Couldn't their spirits linger too?

I sure think so.

A Big Bull Elk near Pendant Cabin

In late September 1973, at age nineteen and accompanied by a friend, I drove my Volkswagen Bug northeast from the University of Montana to the Holland Lake Trailhead, a gateway to the Bob Marshall Wilderness. Carrying cheap backpacks, we hiked about six miles, up the switchbacks to Upper Holland Lake, a pretty tarn where we camped for the night. I caught a few nice cutthroat trout that I baked in aluminum foil over coals in the fire. My area of study at UM was Wildlife Biology, Aquatic Option, so of course I was really interested in these high-country trout.

The next morning, my friend stayed at camp while I climbed another set of switchbacks 1.5 miles up and over Pendant Pass. Atop the 7,000-foot alpine pass stood a rustic, weather-beaten sign marking entry into the Bob Marshall Wilderness. I felt a rush of excitement—I'd read

John Fraley at the Holland Lake Trailhead in late September, 1973, headed into the Bob.

about Bob Marshall, and the new 1973 wilderness map that I carried featured Bob's picture and an inspirational essay about his wilderness passion and exploits. I was finally following in his footsteps.

I sped past Pendant Lake, down into the Big Salmon Creek drainage. Although I would travel this route many times in the future, on this trip it was all new country to me. Yet it felt like I'd traveled through it for years, the alpine benches, shallow lakes, and rivulets strangely familiar.

As I neared Pendant Cabin, about four miles below the pass, I saw movement on the trail's edge just ahead. A huge bull elk in the wilderness is an impressive sight, especially when it's only thirty yards away. The bull sized me up, then spun and slowly trotted off across a little meadow and into the timber. "Wow," I thought, "I hope I have an encounter like this during big game season."

At the Big Salmon Trail junction, I swung southeast and continued six miles, leaving Big Salmon Creek, crossing a low divide, and following Shaw Creek to its mouth on Gordon Creek. I hiked downstream along Gordon Creek and set up my camp at Shirttail Park, which features a pretty little meadow surrounded by conifers right on the streambank. The next morning, I fished downstream on Gordon Creek and caught some of the biggest cutthroats of my life, up to 16 inches and a couple of pounds. For an avid angler, this was heaven.

Good Advice from a Ghost

The next morning, I pulled camp, reversed course, and hiked six miles up Gordon Creek and over Gordon Pass. I felt like I could have walked all day and night, I was so excited. What spectacular country! I made up my mind then to do a fisheries study of all these waters someday, a vow I eventually kept.

Striding down from Gordon Pass, I again reached Upper Holland Lake and closed the loop. And that's when the spookiness began. I ran into an aging Forest Service ranger who said he was staying in a cabin at the upper end of the lake, and we chatted for quite a while. I got the impression that he was stationed there. He could see I loved covering ground in the backcountry. I told him about the cutthroat I caught and the pre-hunting season bull elk I'd seen, right on the trail, and he seemed interested.

"Well, kid, hunting season's open in this district within the wilderness right now," he said. "In fact, it began a few weeks ago on September 15."

I was crestfallen. If I'd known about the early season hunt, I could've taken a big bull elk. Then the old hand shared a secret. He told me of a pass to the south where the wilderness hunting district was only a five-mile hike in. He said it was great elk country, and most hunters, traveling with outfitters, ride past it, farther into the wilderness. "Try that spot," he said.

I thanked him and hiked away, back down the switchbacks to the trailhead. I had already begun to plan my hunt for a week or so later.

Funny thing, I later asked a few people about that old-timer. They said there wasn't any ranger actually stationed at Upper Holland Lake. I later learned that, in September 1948, Art Whitney and Scoop Scovel had built a cabin on stilts there as a base for snow surveys, but it wasn't really habitable by the early 1970s. This tiny cabin was later stabilized and rebuilt in August 2000.

Terry Kills His Spirit Elk

About a week later, on October 5, I was following the mysterious old-timer's hot tip, heading back to the Bob with my good friend, Terry McCoy, who was a terrestrial wildlife student at the University of Montana. The year before, we had lived in the same dorm and discovered we both loved the backcountry. Together, we had done a dozen backcountry ski and hiking trips in the Scapegoat, Bob, Salmon River, and Bitterroots. Terry was living his dream to come west and find his place in wilderness and wildlife. At only eighteen, he had an enviable work-study job using an airplane and radio telemetry to locate elk for Dr. Bob Ream, who was studying the effects of logging on elk in the Sapphire Mountains. I figured Terry knew a lot about elk. He did, but not in a conventional way. From his hunting and fishing roots back east, Terry had established himself in the bigger-and-better wilderness landscapes of Montana. His wilderness future looked bright.

We reached the trailhead late that evening and trudged up the switchbacks. Past the wilderness boundary, we walked into a big mule deer buck. I had him in my scope, but the light was too low for a good shot. We continued over the South Fork Divide and down to a little alpine lake to camp for the night, wildly excited for what the next day might bring.

The next morning, we scampered out of our sleeping bags before dawn and were about to start a fire when Terry stood stock still and said, "Did you hear that elk bugle? Come on, let's get going before he moves." I hadn't heard the call and wondered if Terry had just imagined it.

We grabbed our packs and hurried up the shelf-like alpine benches as dawn broke. "There it is again," Terry said, as we climbed. "It's coming from the other side of that ridge." I'd never had problems with my ears, but I couldn't hear that elk bugling. "That's great," I thought, "Terry's so enthusiastic. But we're not going to top that ridge and see a big bull just standing there, bugling away."

We climbed one more bench and then up to the ridgetop where Terry insisted this monarch's call was coming from. We sneaked up to the crest overlooking a little alpine basin. There, about 150 yards away, stood a big bull elk, head down, feeding on the beargrass slope.

I was astonished. First off, I'd never heard a thing. Second, not only had Terry "heard" the bugle several times, he had led us right to the spot through country neither of us had ever set foot in before.

From a kneeling position, Terry took aim at the bull through his scope and pulled the trigger on his Winchester bolt action .308. But the firing pin just slapped harmlessly against the shell, a dud. He levered in another shell—same thing. At this point I was thinking that I should take the shot, then "Boom!" his rifle fired on the third attempt.

The bull seemed as surprised as I was. He backed down the slope a few steps, swung around, and stood there, wobbly. Terry fired again and the bull went down. Terry McCoy had bagged himself a six-point bull elk that had bugled a tune that only he could hear.

I hunted an hour or so across the alpine benches toward Marshall Mountain. I remember hearing the "thunk, thunk" of Terry's hand axe as he chopped the skull cap and removed the antlers. After a while, I rejoined Terry to help him on his elk. We pieced up the elk and packed it down to our camp near the alpine lake. We boned out part of one rear leg. We planned to pack out that meat, the skull cap, and the antlers on our backs

Terry McCoy butchering his elk at Pyramid Lake, October 1973.

the next day. We hung the three remaining legs and some loose meat in bags on subalpine firs around our camp.

As we drove back to Missoula with our loaded backpacks, we stopped for gas at Clearwater Junction, and several people complimented Terry on the elk rack in the back of his pickup. The next day, Bob and Cathy Ream accompanied Terry and hiked back up the trail with their horse, Dusty, to pack out the rest of the meat. Cathy later told me that she carved more meat off the neck and ribs of the carcass so nothing was wasted. They returned to Missoula that evening. Packing out his elk inspired Terry to learn more about horsepacking, and that winter he took Smoke Elser's packing class at Smoke's barn, not far from the Reams' house up the Rattlesnake in Missoula.

Then and now, I've never quite figured out what happened on that hunt. I'm sure that I didn't hear any elk bugle, and I couldn't figure out any way Terry could have known where that elk was feeding. Maybe someone put that elk there just for him.

Terry's Plane Goes Down

Less than a year later Terry was dead, killed on August 31, 1974, in a small plane crash a few miles southeast of Cleveland Mountain in the Sapphires while charting elk locations using radio telemetry. I was supposed to be on that flight, but the day before they had to switch planes, so Terry and a contract pilot flew in a smaller, two-seater craft. Terry and I had planned to leave on a backpack trip into Big Salmon Lake later that same day when he returned from the flight. I slept in his trailer the night before, and on his way out the door at 5:30 A.M. I heard him say that he would just grab an apple for breakfast. You don't want a full stomach on a flight in the mountains, that's for sure.

I was supposed to meet him after his flight at the Forestry Building on the UM campus. I waited in my Volkswagen with our backpacks, but Terry didn't show up at 11 A.M. as planned, and the tragedy unfolded from there.

Terry and I had talked about going back to the little spirit elk valley in a few weeks when the early rifle season for elk opened up. But sadly, Terry never got back to that alpine slope in the Bob where he shot the bull elk meant only for him. Or maybe he did. In fact, I'm pretty sure a part of him did.

Ten Years Later, A Spirit Whispers in My Ear

One early August, a decade after Terry killed his bull, my wife, Dana, and I hiked the five miles from the trailhead over Pyramid Pass and down to Pyramid Lake. We set up camp and fished for the non-native Yellowstone cutthroat trout that dominated the lake, catching a few for dinner. Thinking of the spirit elk hunt, I felt a little melancholic, but I looked forward to climbing the peak and looking around the alpine shelves where Terry had shot his elk.

The next morning, we made our way around the east side of the lake, passing the area among the boulders and subalpine fir where Terry and I had camped. I could recognize the big block of rock along the shore near where Terry had carved away on a rear quarter of the elk, and the spot where we'd hung the elk quarters in the subalpine fir.

From the edge of the lake, we headed north and west up the rock shelves where Terry and I had climbed and stalked back in October 1973, drawn by the elk bugle that only he heard. Now a profusion of snow-white beargrass blooms and ruby-red Indian paintbrush decorated the slopes.

We passed the general spot where the elk went down in the beargrass basin at about 7,200 feet and aimed for Pyramid Peak. A few hundred feet in elevation later, the slope steepened as it jutted the next 700 vertical feet up to the peak.

The day was calm and the sun beat down on us as Dana and I sat on top of Pyramid. We looked straight west toward Morrell Falls and the Seeley Lake Valley. The view to the north featured Marshall Mountain, the head-waters of Marshall Creek, and the upper Youngs Creek drainage.

Downslope to the east, we could see the basin we'd hiked through on the way up, what I remembered to be the elk kill site. The day was already warming up. I left Dana on the peak and walked north along the ridge to a little saddle, a beautiful spot overlooking the beargrass basin. I sat down and contemplated how I'd been allowed a decade of great living since the hunt with Terry. I had a dream job with the state studying fisheries in and out of the wilderness. I was so blessed, and I felt sad for my friend.

As I enjoyed the sunshine and still air just on the Bob side of the ridge, I heard a swoosh rolling up the slope, as loud as a moderate wind. The pulse of air spun up the gap, rattled the low alpine vegetation, and hit with a rush. The gust sped past, through the saddle and over the ridge of Pyramid Peak. It struck me as a dust devil without the dust. Then it was calm again, absolutely calm.

I thought to myself, *Is this what a spirit feels like?* I hadn't imagined it; the gust blew strong and loud, then died. There was no other air movement. It was as spooky as anything I've experienced, and I believed.

I hiked back along the ridge and met up with Dana again. She hadn't heard or felt any wind; it had been calm on her side of the peak. I'm not sure what she thought about my story. But it didn't matter. I knew that, some-how, it was real. Or surreal.

Returning to Pyramid to Search for Meaning in 2019

Over the years, I've been back several times, walking by Pyramid on my way into the Bob, heading for the headwaters of the South Fork to conduct westslope cutthroat studies. In my head, I often tried to sort out the mysteries of the elk that only Terry heard, the plane crash that took his life, and that breath of air on an otherwise still morning. But I never got around to scaling the shelves and locating the exact spot where the spirit elk died, and it kept gnawing at me. I knew I would eventually have to try, but life kept intervening. It was always on my mind.

Then in 2019, sorting through some old boxes, I found the photograph: eighteen-year-old Terry McCoy with his elk that sunny October day in 1973. Terry stares proudly at the camera, looking earnest, pleased, and happy. He poses with his untrusty .308 rifle spanning the fine rack of the five- or six-point bull, framed by beargrass and alpine surroundings. My rifle and our gear sits to one side. He wears the standard outdoor garb of the 1970s: red chamois shirt, white long underwear top, jeans, square belt buckle, waffle stompers. With this photo to orient by, I believed I could stand at that spot again, and I promised myself to do it.

On the slopes above Pyramid Lake, Terry McCoy poses with the elk only he heard, October 1973.

It had been forty-six years since that spirit elk hunt defined my friend and me. In 2017, a violent inferno, the Rice Ridge Fire, had swept over the top of Pyramid Pass. The fire had almost reached Seeley Lake and scorched much of the Youngs Creek drainage on the Bob side. It burned red-hot up to Pyramid Lake and up and over Pyramid Peak. But armed with the photo, I hoped to compare the terrain and stand on and contemplate the exact spot. I figured that fire doesn't burn rock, so landmark rocks could guide us.

My daughter, Heather, and I returned to Pyramid Lake several times in 2019 to look for the spot. The first time, in late June, it was too wet, socked-in, and miserable to climb the shelves to the peak and find the spot, so we went only as far as the lake. I hadn't been over the pass since the fire, and it sure made me sad. I know that fire is a renewing and natural part of forest and alpine ecosystems, and I agree that it plays an important role. But this fire burned so hot and so nearly complete that I have to say it was downright ugly after only one growing season, with charred black logs on the ground and dead conifers standing on the slopes.

On July 28 we hit a great day for the pilgrimage. We carried with us an enlarged copy of the photo of Terry with his elk, and also a photo of him boning out a rear elk quarter along the lake. We felt hopeful and excited. As the goal of the pilgrimage, using the photos, I hoped to locate the lake campsite, butcher site, and most importantly, the exact point where the elk went down in the little alpine valley below the peak.

Who knows what might happen if we did?

At the Pyramid Pass Trailhead, Heather and I readied our packs. It was a blue-sky day without a cloud, and it promised to be hot. I didn't know what to expect, didn't know how difficult it would be to locate the spirit elk spot, but I was optimistic.

We hiked the four miles to Pyramid Pass in the bright sunshine; the burn wasn't nearly as ugly on a beautiful day. After another half mile, we reached Pyramid Lake and looked across to the point where Terry and I had camped.

I thought it would be simple to find our camp location using a photo of Terry cutting up an elk hind leg. Big rocks on the shoreline were like guideposts to help us locate the butcher spot. But it wasn't so easy. The lake was about three feet higher than during our October hunt in 1973. So the actual butcher rock was submerged, and when Heather stood on it, the water was over her knees. Also, over the decades, some sizable rocks had moved, perhaps from snowslides, gravity, and maybe wind-blown waves. Finally, by lining up the photo with landmarks across the lake, we located the exact spot and walked up the bank right into the old campsite. It's the only flat spot at that end of the lake. This was it: the spot where Terry and I had climbed out of our bags and headed up the shelves above the lake.

It looked different, of course—the fire had claimed the timber and burned the site, but the topography made clear this was it.

So, we had found the butcher rock and the old campsite, and that gave us the starting point from which Terry had followed the elk bugles. Maybe the search for the final site was going to be a cinch.

Heather and I began climbing the alpine shelves and across little valleys, re-creating the route Terry and I had taken. Just shy of a mile from camp, we reached a long, prominent shelf or reef. It overlooked a small, gentle valley and, about 150 yards away, a partly timbered beargrass slope. I was pretty sure this was the promontory that Terry shot from. We walked down the shelf and across the flat, toward the beargrass slope. Amazingly, even though thousands of acres of the surrounding landscape had burned in 2017, the fire had spared this little valley. I was elated because it would be much easier to find the kill site if it hadn't burned. Eagerly, we studied the photo of Terry posing with his elk, comparing it with the ledges, rocks, and vegetation surrounding us.

After exploring for a while, and based on topography, we figured the kill site was within about a 100-yard circle of where we stood. Everything seemed about right. We then looked more closely at the landscape, comparing details to the photograph. Beargrass meadows now supported krummholz trees of various ages. Some fairly large rocks seemed to have moved. Depending on how we angled the photo, it could line up to a few different possible kill sites. Some of the rock ledges were obscured with alpine brush. The photo's field of view was pretty tight, and that made it difficult to line up clues in the background. After a lot of looking around, we identified three possible flat sites that might have been it. Narrowing it down was much harder than I thought it would be.

After marking the area, we decided to take a break and head for Pyramid Peak, our next goal. I wanted to see if anything like the spooky wind gust that swept over me in 1983 would happen again. We walked up the little valley and skirted the lower slopes of the peak, following the same route that I did when I hunted the area for a few hours after Terry downed his elk.

We climbed the steep face of Pyramid and soon reached the 8,320-foot summit. The fire had burned hot and swept over the ridge, wiping out any alpine timber. The burned-out remnants of twisted alpine trees clinging to the ridgeline evoked black skeletons in various poses. From the peak, I could line up the kill site, shooting point, and Pyramid Lake far below; it offered a perfect overall view and perspective. Then I walked to the saddle and stood where the wind gust spooked me in 1983, half expecting a repeat. This time, all was quiet. After taking in the vast scene, so changed from nearly half a century ago, we headed back down the steep ridge to the little valley.

We combed the area and again looked at photo angles. Heather picked up a bleached elk vertebra. Searching, she found six more. Could they be

Pyramid Lake in 2019 from the flank of Pyramid Peak.

from Terry's elk? I'd seen bleached bones persist on a bench along Ole Creek in Glacier Park year after year for more than a decade when I surveyed the stream annually for bull trout redds. Once a bone with little or no marrow is bleached and dry, it seems pretty inert. The skull with brain matter and the ribs would be spoils for scavengers; the vertebrae less so. An elk has a dozen thoracic vertebrae. Heather found seven, apparently all from the same large elk, and all bleached and old. We couldn't be certain, but the convergence seemed to be more than mere chance.

We eyed the vertebrae for butcher marks but found none. Terry and I had filleted the backstraps from each side of the vertebrae, so we might not have nicked the bones.

I had packed in a metal detector, thinking that we might find one or two of the .308 slugs that killed the elk or some other scrap of metal Terry or I had inadvertently left behind. In this remote, pristine place, any signal would most likely be something from our long-ago hunt. Heather and I took turns sweeping the ground with the detector. After a half hour of no hits at the likely sites, we gave up. We realized that, even though we had to be very close, with three probable spots, we just couldn't positively locate the exact kill site. Sometimes the landscape guards its secrets.

This beargrass slope is likely the area where Terry McCoy shot his elk in 1973.

Heather dragged me away and we headed back down through the alpine swales and benches to Pyramid Lake. As we walked along the rocky lakeshore and past the campsite, a few things dawned on me. First, memory is imperfect, at best a bare-bones accounting of what really happened; the details smooth over and the actual complexities of landscape are forgotten. Most surprising were the changes over five decades in what I considered solid features: rocks had moved; vegetation and even trees grew in some places and were swept away in others. The photograph helped a lot, but it also illustrated the rate at which the landscape had changed as the decades marched along.

I'm not sure what I thought would happen when we retraced the trip. Spooky things had been part of that hunt long ago, and I thought maybe that mood would continue. I still think that spiritual things can happen in the mountains, but not necessarily when you want them to.

I was sure glad that Heather accompanied me. She's been my principal advisor since she was about nine. Finding the vertebrae was a good example of her powers of observation; the bones were scattered among the gravel and rocks, so they weren't obvious. I would have missed them.

More Details on the Plane Crash

I couldn't shake the burden of Terry's tragic death. I kept thinking about the whole thing and wondered how I'd ever put it to rest. I knew I'd have to visit the remote site of the plane crash in the Welcome Creek Wilderness, and a monument left for Terry on a lonely ridge on the game range below the top of the range. Maybe I would gain enlightenment and comfort if I did.

The day that Terry died still haunted me. Back on the last day of August 1974, I had sat in my VW Bug in the UM Forestry Building parking lot and waited for Terry to show up after his survey flight. Our backpacks were in the back seat. It was a gorgeous day, and I looked forward to our trip to Big Salmon Lake in the Bob.

Terry didn't show as planned at 11 A.M. and I was worried. I called Bob Ream, the UM study coordinator; his wife, Cathy, in her journal that day, wrote that I was "frantic." The flight had focused on the rugged Sapphire

Mountains, about twenty-five miles southeast of Missoula, so I feared the worst. Ream and others began the air search that afternoon.

The ground search began Saturday afternoon in the heavily timbered mountain ridges in the Sapphires, in what is now the Welcome Creek Wilderness. I joined the ground party and spent that evening searching until dusk. That night, I stayed at the Reams' place up Rattlesnake Creek in Missoula.

On Sunday, as the air search proceeded, we mounted an extensive ground search, combing the Welcome Creek Trail up to Cinnabar Creek and on up the Cinnabar drainage. I'd collected aquatic insects in the drainage, so I knew it well. After many hours, I was hoarse from yelling Terry's name; it felt hopeless, but it seemed like the only thing I could really do.

I hoped against hope that he was still alive but perhaps injured. If he survived the crash, I reasoned, he could be dragging himself down the mountainside and we might run into him.

Late that afternoon, we returned to Missoula to regroup. Most people thought the intensive air search, including eight planes and a helicopter, offered the best chance of finding the plane. Sunday's search, after nine hours, had turned up nothing. But at 4 p.m., Ream had finally spotted a trace of the crashed plane as he looked down from a helicopter in upper Carron Creek's thick timber. Word spread rapidly, and I headed to the airport.

At 6 p.m., a plane carrying four smokejumpers approached the site to attempt a rescue or salvage operation. It took the plane's pilot nearly an hour of searching to relocate the crash site because Terry's plane had entered at such a steep angle it didn't create a break in the trees.

The jumpers dropped into the steep, thickly timbered terrain. They floated down, and each one of them landed high in a tree, suspended above the crash site. Two chutes of gear were also dropped, including tools and a chainsaw to cut a makeshift heliport.

I was at the smokejumper center at the Missoula airport when the jumpers reached the plane about 7:30 p.m. They radioed to dispatch and to planes circling above them: "No joy on the ground, no joy on the ground." That's the way I remember it, either hearing the transmission or someone at the center repeating it to those of us waiting.

The news article in the *Missoulian* the next day quoted the jumper as saying, "No Joy, no joy. There's no life here." Terry and the pilot were reported dead just after 7:30 P.M. The news article reported that Terry's plane had crashed sometime Saturday afternoon, but actually it crashed Saturday morning. His plane left the airport that morning at 6:15 A.M. The paper noted that the plane crashed on the east slope of the Sapphire Mountains in the Carron Creek drainage about 1.5 miles southeast of Cleveland Mountain.

I couldn't have known it while we'd been combing lower Cinnabar Creek, but Terry had been hanging, dead, upside down in his seat belt in the wrecked plane high above Carron Creek.

I drove away from the airport, disoriented and shocked. I'd known that if Terry was out of contact for two days, he was probably dead, but now reality set in. Small planes are not made to withstand a crash in the mountains. From my VW Bug's radio floated the new Carole King song, "Jazzman," which had just been released as a single the week before. The long saxophone solo contributed to my melancholy as I drove away. The song grabbed me. Since then, I think of that moment whenever I hear the song.

Terry's crumpled airplane in thick lodgepole, fall of 1974.

In the dense forest, wreckage of the plane is wedged against trees.

The smokejumpers cut a rectangular clearing in the forest on top of the ridge for a helicopter landing site; the bodies of Terry and the young pilot from Lolo were transported out. I felt so bad for Terry's family, whom I'd just been getting to know. I would come to know them much better in the aftermath.

The next day, the *Missoulian* ran a photo of the four parachutes hanging in the thick lodgepole on the ridge, with the headline, "Two Killed in Plane Crash." A short article in the *Great Falls Tribune* reported that search coordinator Jack Hughes of Missoula said the plane was not carrying a federally required emergency locator transmitter. But little information was offered about the circumstances of the crash.

I visited the remote crash site a few times that fall. It seemed that any time I was involved with Terry or his memory, something noteworthy happened. In my second foray to visit the crash site, just two weeks after the tragedy, a mutual friend, Bob, accompanied me. But we never made it to the saddle to start the cross-country trek down Carron Ridge through the timber into the site. I got waylaid by a black bear instead.

On Friday, September 13, 1974, we were driving up the access road to the top of the ridge in the Sapphires. I had my 6mm Remington rifle and a bear tag just in case, as the season had opened some days before. When a medium-sized black bear ran across the road and up a timbered ridge, I quickly pulled over, and my friend and I carefully walked up the slope. Looking ahead through the timber, I saw the bruin standing broadside to us. I made the shot and the bear dropped, but he rolled and half-stumbled down the ridge right toward us. I was pretty sure it was mostly a roll, but my friend turned around and sprinted back downhill, thinking that the bear was charging us. The bear stopped stumbling and just rolled down toward me, then lay still. My friend noted that I had "stood my ground," but really, I knew all along that the bear was dead on its feet.

I field-dressed the bear and examined the stomach contents, which consisted of a gallon of fairly pristine huckleberries, so obviously we'd interrupted his last meal. It was my first and last bear. I never wanted to kill another one.

Bears were on my mind only because I'd been looking for some way to stay connected to Terry. In another radio-tracking project, Terry had been monitoring a black bear for Dr. Chuck Jonkel on the Threemile Game Range. Dr. Ream suggested that I meet with Dr. Jonkel and offer to finish out the tracking until the bear entered its den. Dr. Jonkel gave me an antenna and receiver and told me to have at it. I drove around the game range in my Bug and got some locations over the next month, but I really didn't know what I was doing.

Terry's Family

The next summer, in 1975, I spent a few days with Terry's family at their home in Harmony, Pennsylvania. I arrived just in time for dinner and sat in Terry's chair. We all agreed that I fit right into the rotation. We shared a strong emotional tie and a genuine affection for each other. I immediately felt close to Terry's sister, Cindy, who was about the age of my little sister, Beth. I gave the McCoys a smoked ham from my black bear.

The McCoys came out to Montana that fall. Terry's dad, Chuck, had drawn an antlerless elk permit in the Sapphires and hunted there with Bob Ream. Chuck was successful, bagging a young antlerless elk.

The McCoys—Chuck, Beverly, and their remaining children, Bob and Cindy—didn't have a lot to remember Terry by, and he had been away at UM for a few years. I guided them into the plane crash site. We hiked from the road's end high in the Sapphires, and I led them a few miles from the top of Carron Ridge down to the spot that held the crumpled plane. They didn't say much as they knelt by the cockpit; you could see from how it had burrowed partly into the ground the speed the plane must've been traveling. The plane had only broken the very top of a few lodgepole as it plunged straight into the ground.

Terry's family took some comfort in the great work Terry had done on the elk study; and they were proud when Dr. Ream told them that Terry urged the establishment of wilderness status for the Welcome Creek area, which also became a project of noted conservationist Bud Moore at about the same time. But kneeling by the destroyed plane, it couldn't have been much comfort to them. We didn't talk about the circumstances of the crash or the deaths or condition of Terry and the pilot. I didn't feel comfortable bringing any of it up, but it bothered me because so little information was

Dana Fraley, left, visiting with the McCoy family in Pennsylvania.

available. I assumed that, as family, the McCoys knew more than I did. But looking back now, I'm not sure. We kept in touch and visited each other off and on over the years.

I hiked to the site a handful of times; I kept small pieces of the plane and part of one of the tracking antennae but eventually got rid of them.

In the early 1990s, the McCoys came to Montana again and we went onto the Threemile Game Range to Grayhorse Point to visit the monument that had been built for Terry. My wife, Dana, and young son, Kevin, came along. On that visit, Beverly showed the pent-up anguish of outliving a son. Now with a son of my own, I felt terrible for her loss. We spent time at the monument, then all headed north to our home in Kalispell.

We toured Glacier Park on that trip. Beverly brightened as she gathered mountain goat hair from alpine firs along the Hidden Lake Trail near Logan Pass. Being an outdoorsperson, she really liked Montana.

In July 1998, a friend of Terry's from back east came to visit. We hiked into the crash site, along with Dr. Les Marcum, who had been working on the elk-logging study and writing his dissertation at the time of the crash.

Les went on to become a respected, long-term wildlife professor at UM. We gained Carron Ridge and headed down toward the site, about two miles down the ridge. There was more blowdown than I'd seen in the 1970s, and it required some bushwhacking, but we finally found the crash site. After twenty-four years, the heliport the smokejumpers had cut on top of the ridge hadn't seen much tree regeneration; the clearing looked about like it did when they cut it in 1974. The plane didn't look much different either, just lonely and piled up among the lodgepole and fir.

Over the years, the crash site continued to drag at my conscience; I needed to go back again and sort out my feelings. Les and I saw each other from time to time; as a representative of Montana Fish, Wildlife & Parks, I gave occasional presentations to his wildlife class at the university. More than twenty years after we'd last visited the plane, I contacted Les and we agreed to meet to go over aerial photos of the ridges near the crash site. Because of the remote location, likely blowdown, and possible burns, I wondered whether I could find it again.

On August 9, 2019, we met at a park in Missoula. Les was now retired, but he hadn't changed much since I'd seen him last. He still harbored some of the same feelings as I did about the tragedy of Terry's short life. He told me a couple of stories about time he spent with Terry. Once, when driving along in the study area, he and Terry had a conversation about the state of the 1970s and the concepts put forward by Paul Ehrlich in his 1968 book, *The Population Bomb*. In the book, Ehrlich predicted worldwide famine and chaos in the coming decades because of overpopulation, and he urged population control. Terry was worried about this and other events that marked the era. Les lamented that Terry felt anxiety about it, and that it turned out to be misplaced. To Les, this showed the depth of this young man. "The world would have been a better place if Terry had lived," he said. Les still treasured memories of watching a bugling elk with Terry in the study area.

Les loaned me a copy of the *Elk and Timber Management* final study report that he and seven other authors completed in 1985. In it, the authors thanked Terry for his work tracking elk on the Sapphire Mountains portion of the work, and noted his tragic death. The landmark report made a series of recommendations to reduce the impact of timber harvest on elk habitat, movement, and distribution. Les and the other authors found that above all else, elk focused on shelter and security in their use of the habitat; forage was secondary. Elk sought tree cover on summer and winter range. Researchers also found that logging caused short-term displacement of elk and that they avoided open roads. Terry's flights and his elk locations were key to these findings.

Hunting for the Old Plane Crash Site in 2019

The day after I met with Les, Saturday, August 10, 2019, my daughter and I mounted our attempt to relocate the plane. Les didn't think he was up to the bushwhack, so he stayed in Missoula. I was apprehensive and wondered what it would feel like to see the crash site again, if we could find it. But I wanted to see the plane again, pay my respects, and maybe find some meaning or closure.

Early that morning, Heather and I drove from Missoula down the Bitterroot, but access to the Sapphires had changed due to logging sales and spur-road closures. When we reached Cinnabar Saddle, a gate blocked the way. Adding three miles each way seemed to rule out the already challenging trip, especially since an intense thunderstorm was forecast to hit that afternoon. But Heather was enthusiastic about trying, so, armed with our packs, maps, and GPS, on past the gate we hiked. Heather might have been thinking that this thing had been gnawing at me for a long time, and, at sixty-five, I might not get many more chances to complete the tough trek.

We walked and jogged on the closed road to the former trailhead, then continued along the top of the ridge that forms the boundary of the Welcome Creek Wilderness. A few small metal national forest wilderness signs marked the perimeter. It was uplifting to know that Terry's plane rested within a wilderness that he'd advocated for.

The 28,000-acre Welcome Creek Wilderness was designated in 1978, just four years after the crash. Conservation icon Bud Moore, who'd retired from the U.S. Forest Service about the time of the crash, also advocated for wilderness designation of the area. Bud had hiked into Welcome Creek and Carron Cabin to demonstrate wilderness hunting and furbearer trapping as values to preserve in the drainage. I don't think Terry and Bud ever met, but they were kindred spirits. Maybe Bud was meant to take up where young Terry had left off. Wilderness designation protected the watershed that fed Rock Creek, a storied blue-ribbon trout stream. It also protected habitat for the extensive elk population studied by Terry and Les.

After another mile or so, Heather and I reached the 7,100-foot flat of the ridge dividing Carron and Welcome Creeks. I'd been there probably five times before, so I thought at this point we had it made. Everything seemed familiar. We checked the GPS and headed down the ridge through relatively open lodgepole, whortleberry, and beargrass. There were elk rubs everywhere, the weather was holding so far, even sunny, and the day seemed promising.

Then things began to go south. The first mistake I made was using my memory to guide us. Heather had the GPS and said we needed to stay closer to the Carron side of the ridge as we descended. She turned out to be right. After a misplaced mile down a side ridge to 6,500 feet, which was roughly the elevation we were shooting for, we had to backtrack and then stay closer to the Carron side. After that, we followed the GPS, sticking as close to the top of the dividing ridge as we could. I knew that we had about two miles in a straight line to go down the ridge from the top, which doesn't seem that far. But with the deadfall and blowdown we ran into, we knew it would be nip and tuck to find the crash site and make it back out before the storm hit. We encountered much more fir and brush and much less open lodgepole than I remembered.

About a mile down the ridge, the blowdown and brush began to make us wonder. I just couldn't remember this much clutter, and it shook my confidence. But the GPS showed us on the right track, just not far enough down the ridge. At 1:30 P.M., with the storm due at 3 P.M., we realized that given the fact we had to balance on logs and break through sticks and brush, not knowing specifically how much farther the site was, we would have to quit. We looked down into the thick timber and debris, studying the maps and the GPS. We guessed that we were probably less than a mile from the site, but without knowing it wasn't wise to push farther until we did more research and could mark the crash exactly on a map or GPS. Heather seemed particularly reluctant to turn around.

Disappointed, we marked a waypoint so we could tell exactly where we were, and started bushwhacking back up the ridge. I'd been to the site about five times and I had photos of it, but the conditions and our worry about the approaching storm repulsed this attempt. My memory seemed wiped clean of much of the route. The overall trip felt familiar, but many of the details were smoothed over or just gone. It's amazing how selective memory can be.

On the way back up the ridge and out of the worst of the blowdown, we found remnants of a solidly built old cabin, sinking into the earth. Finding this on a trail-less, remote ridge raised our spirits and made us wonder who would have built it here long ago. On the walk out to the car, Heather was enthusiastic about trying again. I guess the mystery gripped Heather, too. She'd seen my photos, been down the ridge, and she wanted to see the plane.

Cell service kicked in near the trailhead, and we saw that Les had left a message to warn us that the severe storm would soon hit. We hightailed it down the dirt road while storm clouds enveloped the Welcome Creek divide. We stopped on campus back in Missoula for a pop, and Heather suggested we grab a picnic table at the old Forestry Building, the same spot where I'd parked to wait for Terry the morning of the plane crash.

Sure enough, the skies grew dark and then came a pounding rain mixed with hail. I drove back to Kalispell through 120 miles of incredible thunderstorms and hard rain with the wildest lightning I've ever seen. It was as if something was telling me I didn't need to come back to the crash site. Maybe I'd paid my respects and anything more was pure obsession.

I was fine with turning back from the site for the last time. But knowing my daughter, I suspected we would try again.

Gathering More Information on the Crash, NTSB Report

Heather and I needed more information and guidance if we were going to mount another attempt to locate the crash site. I looked to my son, Kevin, who is a brilliant guy and skilled with modern orienteering technology. He worked for the State of Alaska as an environmental scientist. If anyone could help, it would be him.

Kevin and I spent a day going back and forth over the phone as he used Google Earth to search for the old heliport clearing or the plane. He put our

GPS waypoints of the old cabin and our turnaround point on the Google Earth image. I would need to consult with Les again, now that we had the new images, and I sent him prints of the Google Earth images and photos that I'd taken of the plane crash site from 1974, 1975, and 1998.

Les and I agreed that the larger clearing on the image was not the right spot. We both felt that the heliport was farther down the ridge and on the Carron side. Looking at 1966 and 1995 aerial photos that Les had, we could see the two clearings; maybe the one on the Welcome Creek side was created by blowdown. We could make out a smaller, more rectangular opening farther down the ridge and in more open lodgepole where we thought it should be. This search in itself was turning into a mystery.

Now, armed with better knowledge of the terrain, Heather and I thought we had a decent chance of finding the site, if we could just get through the downfall. It felt a little crazy or obsessive, but we agreed to try again in two weeks.

I'd always wanted to find out more about the circumstances of the crash, the plane, and everything associated with it, including what the smoke-jumpers had found when they reached the plane. Offhand, Kevin had said to me that since we had the specifics of location and date on the crash, we might be able to find more information on the National Transportation Safety Board (NTSB) website. I was doubtful based on my previous attempts to find old government information, especially regarding this crash. The county no longer had any accident report or coroner's report; they said it had been lost or discarded.

A half hour later, the brief NTSB report popped up on my phone. Kevin had done it again. The report confirmed many of the things I'd heard at the time of the crash. First, it noted that the plane was "destroyed." That's for sure. It listed two fatalities.

The pilot was young, in his early twenties, with a total of 274 hours of flight time and only 64 hours in terrain. He was not instrument trained. The plane, an Aeronca Champion 7GC (N8092E), may have been underpowered for the task. No flight plan was filed.

The plane had a maximum speed of 95 miles per hour and a stall speed of 38 miles per hour. The pilot and passenger seats were in tandem; maximum capacity was a pilot and one passenger. The fuselage and wings were formed from welded metal tubing covered with fabric; light wood formed part of the floor of the cockpit. Clearly, the Champion was not made to survive a crash in the mountains.

Everything was against Terry when he walked out the door of his trailer that morning on the last day of August 1974. I've always felt guilty that I didn't get up and see him off and wish him luck when he walked out the door munching his apple. I was thinking more about sleeping a bit longer before our trip into the Bob later that day.

According to the report, Terry and the pilot lifted off from the airport in Missoula at 6:15 A.M. Their flight must have been grand at first. Unlimited visibility and scat-

This image, taken on a return trip to the crash site in July 1998, reveals how the violent crash compacted the flimsy Aeronca Champion.

tered clouds provided excellent flying conditions. The pair flew up the Bitterroot Valley past Florence and over the Welcome Creek divide and began surveying the thickly timbered Cinnabar, Carron, and Welcome Creek drainages. They must have reveled in the beautiful weather, the scenery, and the elk they were locating. Terry was living the life that day: flying for elk at only nineteen, and looking forward to a trip into the Bob after the flight.

The antennae that Terry had mounted on the wing struts picked up signals from a number of radio-collared elk, according to the recovered data sheet. Individual elk could be identified by their unique signal pulse.

After flying past Cleveland Mountain and down the Welcome Creek drainage, the pilot swung the little plane up the Carron drainage, presumably from its confluence with Welcome Creek, at about 5,000 feet. The plane climbed as the ridge to the north rose steeply. Terry was noting elk locations probably on both sides of the drainage. The two young men continued flying upslope and into the fairly open lodgepole, maybe both of them visually sighting elk that were showing up on the receiver.

We don't know exactly, but likely the pilot looked up suddenly and saw Carron Ridge rising more steeply than he'd anticipated. He tried to muscle the plane through a sharp turn to avoid hitting the ridge, maybe even trying to top the ridge at 6,800 feet. He lost control of the plane as the flight speed on the Champion dropped, and the plane stalled, rolled, turned upside down, and dove nearly straight down. How long the two men knew they were goners is hard to say, but at least a few seconds. I'll always wonder about that; Terry's day had abruptly gone from wonderful to terrifying to fatal. What thoughts must have raced through his mind at the end when the plane plummeted through the timbered canopy and slammed into the ground? The plane hit the ridge at an elevation of 6,392 feet according to my GPS.

According to the NTSB, the plane went down at 7:45 A.M., one and a half hours after takeoff. The investigators must have been able to determine the time of crash from the instruments on the plane, or they estimated it.

The report noted that the crash was due to stalling via pilot error. The pilot had failed to "obtain or maintain flying speed; attempted operation beyond experience/ability level; failed to follow approved procedures, directives, etc.; and diverted attention from operation of aircraft." Given the last issue, perhaps the pilot was looking at the elk as Terry located them.

The lack of a legally required locator beacon caused a couple days of additional pain for everyone, especially the families, and danger to people in the nine or so aircraft involved in the extensive, low-flying search. We heard that Terry and the pilot didn't suffer; everything indicated that they died on impact. When you look at the crash and the obvious violent impact, this seems likely. But, unable to unearth the coroner's report, I have always wondered.

Oddly enough, according to NTSB records, this same plane was involved in an accident ten years earlier at an airport in Collegeport, Texas.

The landing gear had collapsed and the plane swerved and rolled over, all due to improper operation of the craft. The thirty-eight-year-old pilot, who had only fifty hours of flight time, was injured, and the plane sustained "substantial" damage. Terry's crash wasn't the Champion's first rodeo.

I was gratified to learn so much more about the plane and the circumstances of the accident. But before we made another attempt to find the crash site, an opportunity arose to visit the monument constructed for Terry on the Threemile Game Range.

I contacted Bob Beall, another PhD student who had worked on the elk logging study. He'd gone on to a stellar career as a forestry professor, and retired as a professor emeritus at Flathead Valley Community College. I taught a wildlife class for him for years, and he served as a mentor. Bob spent most of his time studying elk use on the Threemile Game Range on the lower slopes of the Sapphires. He had worked on the study through the fall of 1973.

Bob had a winter elk observation site on 5,487-foot Grayhorse Point, which overlooks the game range; from the point you can look up to Cleveland Mountain and the summer range that Terry had surveyed.

A Pilgrimage to Terry's Forgotten Monument

In 1975, UM established a monument on Grayhorse Point to honor Terry's contributions to the elk study. The monument consisted of a vertical gravestone-like marker mounted with mortar in a cairn of native rock gathered at the site. The stone bore the simple inscription: "Terry L. McCoy, 1954–1974, U of M elk study." Aside from a brief ceremony at the installation, the remote site has probably since been visited only a handful of times.

I felt drawn to visit the monument again to see if it still stood, to experience it, pay my respects, and see if it needed any maintenance. I wondered what kind of shape it would be in after weathering all those years. I talked to Les to refresh our memories on how to access it. I also contacted folks from the local Forest Service office, but they weren't familiar with it. I called the FWP game range manager, but she wasn't in. In the decades since I'd been there, my memory seemed to have seriously faded, but I decided to just go for it armed with a map and my GPS.

Dr. Bob Ream, center, gave a brief reading to a gathering of Terry McCoy's friends and colleagues when the monument was installed at Grayhorse Point in 1975. PHOTOGRAPH COURTESY OF ROBERT KRUMM.

My sister, Beth, was visiting in August 2019, so she accompanied me on the trek. Beth was in great shape, having been an All-American collegiate gymnast and a bike racer, and she loves the heat, so she was particularly suited for our trek on this 92 F. day.

The access roads proved to be rough and rutted, and we ended up parking at a locked gate a couple miles short of the old trailhead, but it still seemed the most direct route. In the distance, four humps rose along the ridge. The first three had openings on top, and we hoped that the third one was Grayhorse; our planned direction seemed correct. I had some misgivings about finding the monument in such oppressive heat, and it was already past noon. But the elevation gain would only be about 1,000 feet, and for relief we had some partly frozen water bottles with us.

As we started the climb on an old trace across the hot meadows and scattered ponderosa pine, I was so focused on finding the trail and the monument that I was oblivious to the natural wonder unfolding in the air around us. My sister's comments finally caught my attention. We were walking through literally clouds of light-colored butterflies. I've always been interested in bugs, and spent part of my career studying aquatic insects, but I'd never seen anything like this. Beth said she felt like she was being swarmed and slapped in the face by them. I looked more closely; at first, we thought they must be moths. But they bore the clubbed antennae of a butterfly, distinguishing them from moths. They were nearly pure white, with small black stripes. They flew everywhere as we walked along through the ponderosa parklands and up a small ravine that became familiar to me as we went along. Decades ago, I had driven up this little trace that had then been an access road.

Once again, pursuing Terry's story had led me into another realm. The butterfly swarms struck us as a sign. Beth and I later researched the phenomenon of this mass butterfly emergence and figured out, based on its periodicity, that it was a very rare, crazy coincidence that it was happening the exact day of our pilgrimage.

The butterfly clouds persisted along the entire route to the saddle between Threemile Point and what proved to be Grayhorse Point to the south. We strolled from the saddle down the ridge toward what we hoped would be Grayhorse and the monument. Oddly, Grayhorse Point did not show in my GPS map. I began to have doubts that we were headed to the right spot. When we reached a double knoll, the elevation on my GPS read 5,487 feet, the exact elevation indicated for Grayhorse on the topo map that I carried. I felt guarded enthusiasm.

On the first knob, we found a pile of rocks but no monument stone. I wondered if it was just gone or had been vandalized. Then I looked ahead and saw a larger pile of rocks on the next knob.

I ran ahead, hoping against hope that this was it, and swung around the rock pile. There, on the grassy knoll, facing the valley far below, stood Terry's carved stone. Emotion, memory, and fulfillment overwhelmed me.

I felt that we were closing the loop in my search for Terry's ghost or spirit, or whatever this quest had become. I realized then that Terry's story had been with me all my adult life.

The large directional tracking antenna, left as a memento, was nowhere to be seen, apparently removed when the elk study was closed down later in the 1970s. Due to gravity, weathering, and failing mortar, the rock cairn arrangement around the carved stone had deteriorated some over the forty-four years it had stood there, as compared to an old photo. But it still looked great. And the stone itself appeared nearly pristine.

The monument knob afforded almost a 360-degree view of much of the elk study area; we looked over the game range and to Cleveland Mountain in the distance and the top of the ridge between Welcome and Carron Creeks. Terry's plane rested a few miles down the east side of that

The Terry McCoy monument on Grayhorse Point.

ridge. The scene was profound and calming. No casual visitors would trek the two miles of cross-country, unmarked route to stand here. The monument was obscure, largely forgotten, hard to find and hard to reach, but situated in a fitting place.

Beth called me over to the back side of the ridge to feel a gentle wind that was coursing back and forth across the saddle. It wasn't eerie or scary, just peaceful. A blue grouse with three or four young stood under the pines for what little refuge the trees offered from the intense sun and heat. Everything seemed right on Grayhorse Point.

After contemplating everything, paying our respects, and taking lots of photos, we were ready to begin our trek straight back down the face of Grayhorse. Beth had pocketed a few little stones for memorabilia. I was reluctant to take such a memento; in my experience, when you remove things from their context, they lose most of their value. But I finally put a small stone in my pocket.

We headed down the face of the ridge and rejoined the old trace we'd walked up earlier. As we strolled back down the trail, the butterflies swarmed us again. Some of the photos I took of Beth contained thirty or more of the whitish, black-striped butterflies. They were thick all the way back to the starting point near the exit of the game range. On bare ground, dead butterflies looked like fallen snow.

Back at the car, Beth pulled out the three small rocks she had saved from Grayhorse Point. I reached in my pocket for the one little rock I'd saved.

"Hey Beth," I said, "my rock is gone and my pocket is inside out. What the heck? And my favorite shirt and hat are gone."

Beth said, "You'd better cut it out or people are going to think that you're crazy."

I told her that if anyone had followed the story this far, they'd already think I'm crazy.

The butterfly phenomenon seemed even more mysterious as we further researched it. About every three or four decades, "outbreaks" of the pine butterfly (*Neophasia menapia*) can persist in an area for a few days, then peter out. This can happen in a series of about three years, with a long time span between outbreaks. The adults mate, then lay strings of emerald-colored eggs along the length of ponderosa pine needles. The eggs overwinter, then the green larvae emerge in late spring and start chewing on the needles, even causing defoliation. Also, the trees can become weakened enough to attract pine bark beetles. In August, the larvae pupate, attach to needles, and emerge as adults in huge swarms like the one we ran into. This mating swarm lasts only a few days. Forest Service information shows that the last large outbreak reported in this area for these bugs ended in 1973, during the year Terry killed his spirit elk, and the year before his plane went down. We just happened to run into this swarm on the particular day we had chosen to trek to the monument many decades later.

As we scanned through information on butterflies, a few things about butterfly lore attracted my attention. In legend, butterflies are the most common sign of "after death communication." As the theory goes, the lost individual is making a guiding sign, saying that his or her spirit is at rest and to offer comfort and relief. In some societies, the life cycle of the butterfly, with transition from egg to larvae to pupae to adult, signifies resurrection.

The whole experience seemed to be a sign that, although Terry's life was cut short, he has influenced my life in a powerful way. I was determined to anchor my life in Montana. I've relished its wilderness for a half century, in part because Terry couldn't. So in this sense, he's lived on, especially in people who care enough to remember him. At the least, Terry's short and tragic life inspired me to tell his story and the stories of others before they are forgotten. I believe the human spirit longs to be remembered, and memory is so temporary and fleeting.

So just like the rest of my search for the meaning of Terry's life and death, our hot day at Grayhorse Point ended with wonder and revelation. But another trip to Grayhorse may be on the agenda: I have to go back to get my hat, my shirt, and my rock.

Finding the Plane Crash Site, Leaving a Memorial for Terry

The plane site kept calling us; I now knew that I had to visit again to get closure. Heather and I scheduled our next attempt for September 1, 2019. We began preparations to make it a slam dunk.

I visited again with Les to pinpoint the plane's location on a map. My son Kevin sent me the coordinates for a small knob that we believed sat upslope from the site. He also passed along the coordinates for what we thought might be the small helipad clearing cut by the smokejumpers on September 1, 1974. FVCC Professor Tim Eichner, an expert on GPS and orienteering, helped me load the points and provided tips on navigation. Armed with coordinates, more maps, aerial photos, and Les' encouragement, along with knowledge from our previous scouting trip, we were ready to go.

And we decided to roll out the heavy artillery. We asked my youngest son, Troy, an officer with the Bozeman Police Department, to come along and bolster our search crew. How could we miss with Troy? He's a backcountry expert, and he'd just completed a stellar cross-country and track career with Gonzaga University, with a special talent in steeplechase. In fact, he became the only athlete in Gonzaga history to achieve Track and Field Division I NCAA All-American status, finishing seventh in the nation. In the 3,000-meter steeplechase, you leap over barriers and water jumps as you dash around the track. Given all the downfall on our route, Troy was the perfect search partner.

Kevin put our waypoints of the old cabin and the point where Heather and I had turned around on the Google Earth image. It looked like we had stopped about a mile short of the little helipad in a sea of downed timber. Les and I again studied the maps and photos. A small, irregular clearing showed on Google Earth less than a half mile down the ridge from the 6,628-foot point. This looked like the spot. Kevin sent the coordinates for what we now thought was the helipad location, and our best estimate of the plane crash location. Looking at aerial photos from 1966 and 1995, we noticed that the small clearing appeared on the later photo but was not on the 1966 photo. This seemed to confirm that it was the helipad.

Armed with all the advantages for navigation, better knowledge of the terrain, and led by an All-American steeplechaser, we thought we could find the little clearing, now forty-five years old, and the crashed plane, which I remembered being just off the ridge at the far corner of the clearing. I wondered how much regeneration filled the former clearing, but I felt pretty good about it because the Google Earth image (from 2014) still showed a remnant of the little swath. And I knew that if we found the clearing, we would find the plane.

On Sunday, September 1, 2019, the forty-fifth anniversary of the discovery of the location of the plane crash site by the smokejumpers, we all rendezvoused at Heather's apartment in Missoula. Then we headed south down the Bitterroot and into the foothills of the Sapphire Range, up to Cinnabar Saddle where the road was gated. We left the gate at 9:30 A.M. and hoofed it from there. It was a sweltering hot day, but we had some frozen water bottles and they helped a lot.

After about three miles of closed road and informal trail, we reached the head of the Carron Creek ridge on the flat of the Bitterroot-Welcome Divide. Following the GPS in part, we began hiking down the complex Carron Ridge, hopping over downed trees and pushing through areas of brush. We saw lots of elk tracks and sign; elk rubs were common.

About a third of the way down the ridge, Heather received a gift. She walked right up to a fine moose paddle, shed a few years before by a bull who had wintered in this lonely spot at an elevation of nearly 7,000 feet. Again, something special happened on every trip in this quest.

We followed the GPS and the path of least resistance through the brush, and entered into the middle mile of thick, downed timber. This complex ridge kept us on our toes, offering tricky side ridges to lure us in the wrong direction. Troy's route-finding skills helped us stay on the best route, and he eagerly led the way and hopped over any "barriers" that we encountered.

The trek through the blow-down and brush seemed to go on and on, partly because we had to snake back and forth across the ridge to get through. We probably

On the bushwhack to the crash site, Heather found this weathered moose antler.

Heather and Troy navigate through downfall and dense lodgepole forest on the way to the crash site.

traveled double the two miles of direct distance down the ridge. As we went along, Troy tracked the GPS. We finally transitioned into the more open lodgepole, which felt familiar, and I felt guarded optimism. We skirted around what we correctly assumed was the 6,628-foot knob and headed down the beautiful, open-timber final ridge. When Troy announced that we were under a tenth of a mile, we looked ahead on the flattening ridge, and Troy said, "That's looking like a little clearing ahead." We strolled on with easy going in the open lodgepole and pretty sunlight. I held my breath, and I saw Troy walk into the most beautiful, partially regenerated clearing in the world. The GPS location was right on the money. A pair of butterflies flitted around the young trees, and a couple of elk rubs scored the sides of a few larger lodgepole.

Old stumps stood in the green understory; I knew the stumps had been cut by smokejumpers exactly forty-five years ago. I felt relief, and I knew we were there. I wondered if any of the jumpers were still around Missoula, and if they ever thought about what they did here. They would be my age or

On September 1, 2019, Heather and Troy stand in the regenerating clearing cut by smokejumpers on the same date in 1974.

older, so probably in their sixties or seventies. *Maybe,* I thought, *I can track one of them down.*

We walked around in the clearing and took it in. The opening, measuring about forty yards long and about thirty yards wide, perched on top of the ridge. The jumpers also cut about a twenty-yard avenue on the Welcome Creek side to allow the approach of the chopper. We were amazed at the appearance of the stumps and dropped trees; they looked much older than forty-five years. The jumpers felled dozens of trees, most of them lodgepole pine. When I last saw the little clearing in 1998, twenty-four years after it had been cut, little regeneration had taken place. Now, forty-five years after the cut, the regeneration, both lodgepole and fir, had advanced quite a bit.

The understory had also grown. Grouse whortleberry and beargrass clumps glowed gorgeous green in the sunlight. We sat down and contemplated this sunny, remote, and forgotten spot. Then we started searching for the plane.

I remembered that the crash site was located just below the far corner of the clearing. We headed down the Carron-side face of the ridge and walked back and forth, looking for signs in the fairly open lodgepole. As we looked and looked without spotting it, my anxiety grew. We moved back toward the west and kept zigzagging. Finally, Heather spotted the wreckage through the trees, and I again felt relief. All of our preparation and effort had paid off. It turned out that the remains of the plane were actually about 150 yards straight down the Carron face of the ridge from the center of the clearing. Again, so much for my memory.

There's something simple and beautiful about an older lodgepole forest and its intense green understory in the bright sunshine. If the crash had to rest forever somewhere, it might as well be here. Time, gravity, falling trees, and some brush had slowly reduced the visible footprint of the plane, making it less obvious on the landscape. But the crumpled remains of the Champion 7CG still occupied about a thirty-by-thirty-foot patch on the forest floor. The fuselage still extended up about eight feet.

The obvious violence of the impact surprised Troy and Heather. The right wing splayed flat on the ground; trees and brush covered parts of it.

Troy and Heather in a reflective mood at the crash site.

The plane's tail was folded over the fuselage. The fuselage and the cockpit, framed by green, one-inch metal tubing, were still discernible. Tangles of these green steel tubes wrapped over themselves along the length of the bent-over fuselage, in testament to the plane's violent collision with the ground. But the cockpit was still fairly intact. We crouched down and got into the cockpit area. Both Terry's and the pilot's seat frames, formed by the same green metal tubing, were upside down because of the entry angle of the plane. The frames were still attached and held their shape. Most of the synthetic-fabric upholstery was scattered beneath the plane and on the ground, and even after forty-five years, still held a bright red color. Pieces of plastic that formed the windshield were lying inside the cockpit. White and blue artificial fabric, much of it in tatters, covered parts of the plane. A muffler lay in the whortleberry, looking like it could have just been dropped there.

We looked up through the lodgepole canopy to the deep blue sky. We counted three small tree tops that looked like they'd been snapped by the plane when it rocketed almost straight down. No wonder the air searchers had such trouble spotting the wreckage.

Cables used for the controls were still in their places, strung all along the fuselage. They seemed operational, without a speck of rust. They operated easily and smoothly, although they could no longer move flaps that were crushed or jammed.

A nearly pristine Yagi antenna, with much intact black electrical tape wrapped around its side projections, lay in the wreckage. A Yagi, named after its inventor, has multiple cross elements to bolster its directional function. This antenna was missing some of them. Terry probably taped the antenna, adding projections, and strapped and taped it to the strut of the wing. He might have done that the morning of the flight if it was indeed the first time they used this plane in the elk study.

The engine and propeller, which remained when I'd visited the site in the fall of 1974, had since been removed. I'm not sure when it was taken out or why, whether it was part of the investigation or some other reason.

One thing I always wondered about were the seat belts. We took time to examine them more closely. Terry's lap belt looked as if it had been hacked or cut through, perhaps by one of the smokejumpers to free him. This would indicate that he was unable to unhook the belt himself, and that he was unconscious or dead at impact. It is possible that it been chewed through by an animal, but it looked hacked by a knife; maybe it was hard to get to the buckle when the jumpers were trying to free them. The longer chest belt was pristine and hanging down. The pilot's seat in front of Terry's was forced close to the ground; it appeared that he would have sustained a lot of trauma, and it seemed impossible that he would have survived the impact.

After having looked it all over, Troy summed it up in reassuring words I'd heard before from Les: "They didn't suffer."

Before we left the plane, we held a brief tribute for Terry. In a gallon plastic bag that we duct-taped in a protected spot near his seat, we included several large photos of Terry with captions on various treks we had done together in the Bob and the Idaho Primitive Area. I also included a photo of Terry's monument on Grayhorse Point. We left a typed dedication that Heather read out loud (because I couldn't) before we sealed it in the bag:

Terry L McCoy: On August 31, 1974, Terry L. McCoy took his last breath at this spot after going down in this plane operated by a young pilot, who also died in the crash. The plane stalled, rolled, and dove almost straight down into the ground, barely breaking a branch. Terry was locating radio-collared elk using a receiver and a temporarily mounted antenna on this small plane. The plane was found at 7 P.M. the next day, September 1st, after an extensive ground and air search.

Terry was a work study student for the elk/logging study being conducted by the University of Montana. He was born on November 4, 1954, making him only 19 years and 10 months old when he passed.

There is a monument for Terry on the Threemile Game Range on Grayhorse Point.

I'm not sure if anyone will ever visit this remote plane again, but if you are visiting and you are reading this, thank you. This is at least my 5th trip in: three or four times in the 70s, once in 1998, and this day, September 1, 2019, the 45th anniversary of locating the crash. My daughter, Heather, and my son, Troy, are here with me.

I'm 65 now and I've lived a wonderful life in the backcountry. My wife, Dana, and I have three wonderful, grown children. Heather, 26, works for the Rocky Mountain Elk Foundation; Troy, 24, is a police officer in Bozeman; and my oldest, Kevin (29) is an environmental scientist in Alaska. They've all lived wilderness lives.

Terry and I did a lot together in the mountains, including getting a bull elk in the Bob Marshall Wilderness about 10 months before the crash. Terry was not able to experience the joys of parenthood and a long life, but he made his years count. He was one of the first to suggest that this area should be wilderness, and the Welcome Creek Wilderness was designated in 1978.

Terry and I attended the University of Montana together. He was my good friend and his life deserves to be remembered. John Fraley, Kalispell, MT.

We hiked back upslope to the clearing, rested and ate a late lunch before heading back up the ridge. In the sun, the little green clearing and its lush

John readies photographs and the dedication to be placed in a plastic bag and left in the plane's wreckage.

growth looked so beautiful. Heather sat on her upended moose paddle, here in the remote, lost center of nowhere.

We noticed that the bull elk had slashed a pretty good rub on that larger regenerated lodgepole pine. We watched the butterfly pair, whisking around the same lodgepole. These butterflies were *Pieris brassica*, the large, white cabbage butterfly, according to our best guess. We didn't want to disturb them by examining them more closely. They are related to the pine butter-fly, but this high, lonely ridge seemed an unusual site for them. They offered promise and brightened the scene.

Finally, we felt ready to begin the long trek back to Cinnabar Saddle. With a sense of fulfillment, we started moving up the ridge. I wondered at how lucky I've been in my wilderness life, and in the solid support my daughter and sons have given me through the years, and especially in my ongoing search for meaning in this whole endeavor to relocate the plane crash site. I realized I could not have done it without them.

As I turned my back on the homey little clearing, I felt melancholy, but I also knew that I'd paid my respects in every way I knew how, and there wasn't much more I could do. I took in this peaceful site and how the plane had occupied its spot for years and years, as it would for many more. As I walked away, I wondered if it would ever be specifically visited again. I knew that I'd never be back. It isn't easily reached: it took us seven hours of intensive effort and route finding to reach the plane, investigate the site, then trek back out to the truck.

A few days later, I called Les in Missoula. Les wasn't with us that day at the crash site, but he was there in spirit. His first words were, "Was I right?" referring to the rectangular clearing that we could see in the aerial photos he'd given me. I told Les about the seats and the seat belts, and how the plane was sinking a bit more into the ground and leaving even less of a visible footprint in the forest. And I filled him in on the regeneration we'd seen as compared to the 1998 trip. Les' interest was intense. Only a handful of people are still around who are thinking about Terry's story and searching for meaning or closure. The collective memory of this tragedy is nearly gone.

After the trip, Heather said she was haunted when she looked at the photos that we left at the wreck, especially the image of a melancholy Terry leaning against a ponderosa pine high on a ridge with our friend Phil and me deep in the Idaho Primitive Area during the spring of 1974. At that point, he had just a few months to live.

"I felt that I was looking at a ghost," she said. "At nineteen, Terry thought that most of his life was ahead of him; he was oblivious that death was coming for him soon."

I knew exactly what she meant.

I've spent a lifetime enjoying the wilderness that Terry only got to experience for a fleeting few years. Terry was heading for a wonderful career as a wildlife biologist, and his passion for wilderness would have carried him across the Montana backcountry, the Bob, and beyond many times.

His story has shaped my life even more than I realized before closing the loop on this quest. We searched for meaning at the site of the spirit elk in the Bob and the monument on the Threemile Game Range. We ended the quest at this remote and forgotten spot in the Welcome Creek Wilderness where Terry took his last breath and where a trace of his DNA and essence still remains in the wreckage and cycles through the vegetation.

I felt like an enormous burden had been lifted, that I was finally done chasing Terry's spirit, though I could never forget him. But a year later, a wildfire and an unexpected reunion of the smokejumpers brought the story back to life.

Before we hear about that wildfire and what the smokejumpers remembered from that fateful day, join me on a sampling of the wilderness adventures I've enjoyed (and endured) over the course of my life. Terry was part of a few of those trips. He had grown up in western Pennsylvania and, like me, was an avid outdoorsman at heart. When he came to Montana, he was living his dream of immersing himself in wild country brimming with wildlife. Even after he was gone, his passion for all things wild inspired more wilderness dreams of my own. ◄○►

Terry McCoy, John, and Phil in March 1974 on a trip to the Middle Fork of the Salmon River, now in the Frank Church-River of No Return Wilderness. PHOTOGRAPH COURTESY OF ROBERT KRUMM.

CHAPTER 3

Heart of the Scapegoat

It was on an ill-fated, winter attempt to reach Heart Lake that I came face to face with my masochistic side. I discovered that I enjoyed tough or nearly life-threatening situations. If my companions had known this, most of my treks would've been solo affairs.

In the early winter of 1972–1973, as a freshman at the University of Montana, I planned to snowshoe into a lake in the newly designated Scapegoat Wilderness. My friends and I had heard that Heart Lake swarmed with Arctic grayling, a fish none of us had ever seen, let alone caught on a line.

Phil and Terry agreed to join me, and we studied a large-scale map that showed Heart Lake sitting less than a mile from the Landers Fork of the Blackfoot River. Young and inexperienced, we took the map at face value, not realizing that between the river and lake rose a prominent, heavily forested ridge.

Armed with our cheerful ignorance, we headed out from the UM campus in Phil's green station wagon and drove up Highway 200 along the Blackfoot River toward Lincoln. We didn't take much food because we planned on being out only two days, catching plenty of grayling to supplement our few packs of ramen noodles. We'd "live off the land." We had no backup plan if, for any reason, the trip took longer than expected.

The road up the Landers Fork was snowed in, barely passable. We passed a ranch driveway and the going grew worse. Then the snow stopped us, and no formal trailhead, signs, or visible trail greeted us. That should have been a clue.

We strapped on the snowshoes we'd checked out from the campus recreation center and trudged up the drainage, following what looked like an informal trail. Soon, the trace disappeared, but we kept pushing on through the lodgepole, fir, and spruce. We went about four miles and set up camp with a great big fire. It had been a fun slog so far, but we began to doubt our planned route. The snow was just deep enough to require us to use the snowshoes or "webs."

We continued trekking up the drainage for another day, camped overnight, and slogged on another half day, searching for the major river fork that, on the map, was close to where the lake should be. Since we could find no trail, we walked along the stream's edge or through the timber where downed logs blocked our way. When we tired of that, we dropped into the streambed and walked along the rocks. Soon, we saw that the rocks were cutting the snowshoes' leather webs.

Along the way, we found occasional unfrozen pools that held whitefish and trout. We caught a few of the whitefish to supplement our skimpy food supply. At one pool, Phil was crouched down, carefully casting to a few small fish. He cussed me out when I shuffled up behind him, disturbing his stealthy fishing, but his anger was probably just his hungry stomach talking. By the third day, our hunger had grown but our desire for Top Ramen hadn't. We traded each other for our few remaining tasty snacks; a handful of Oreos was worth double their weight in gold. Living off the land lost its appeal when serious hunger kicked in.

Despite the hardship, or maybe because of it, I realized that I loved this misadventure. The challenge and the wilderness felt amazing. There's time enough for basking in comfort in our modern lives. I think Terry and Phil liked it too, but maybe not as much as I did. We were already out nearly a full day longer than planned, and we were missing a day of school. It felt intrepid.

By late afternoon on the third day, we had trekked up the drainage eight miles with no real idea of where we were. It finally dawned on us that we were about as likely to find Heart Lake as we were to stumble upon an all-you-can-eat pizzeria.

With Terry leading the way, we turned around and retraced our route, moving much faster than on the way up. We camped one last night and started early the next morning. By midafternoon on the fourth day we reached Phil's station wagon, much to our relief. "Living off the land" hadn't gone so well. The heater felt wonderful as we drove back to campus.

We were glad to be heading back to civilization, and we agreed that tough trips make the comforts of home more enjoyable.

Back on campus, we washed up a little and headed like hungry bears to the university food service, just in time for dinner. The food was always superb there, but boy it looked and tasted like a royal banquet that evening.

The next morning, we sheepishly returned the snowshoes to the rec center. The clerk's eyes widened when he saw how damaged they were. He pronounced them destroyed and demanded $30 apiece to replace them. He also banned us from checking out any outdoor equipment for the rest of the quarter. We'd see about that—we had friends, that is, accomplices. We planned to find a better map, ask around for advice, and try again the next weekend. We also considered the risks we'd taken. We'd been gone four days instead of two, yet none of our dormmates had worried, let alone sent out a search team. If we hadn't returned, how long would it have been before anyone noticed?

Someone finally explained to us how to reach the Heart Lake Trailhead. We hadn't even been in the right drainage, but now we knew the way. Terry had a rush of wisdom and opted out of our next trip to the elusive lake. Another friend, Bob, signed out snowshoes for himself and me from the rec center. Phil wanted to try a new way to travel over the snow.

A few days before our trip, Phil walked into my dorm room and announced that he was not snowshoeing again. Bob and I looked at each other. I said, "Phil, I know you're tough, a great wrestler and everything, but there's probably six feet of snow and I don't think even you could make it without snowshoes. You'll be sinking in up to your waist."

"I'll make it just fine," Phil replied, "and I'll be pulling grayling out of the lake before you even get there." Seeing our quizzical looks, he announced that he would be skiing in. Bob and I gaped at each other. This was in the days before backcountry skiing became popular. I pointed out that it was uphill all the way in, but Phil said that he'd bought some "fast" cross-country skis. He hadn't tried them out yet, but the salesman had told him the skis would climb hills just fine and were perfect for backcountry travel.

The skis had thin cables and clamps to firmly mount to Phil's hiking boots. We were skeptical, but we figured Phil knew what he was doing.

He'd told us that they were similar to the skis he'd seen racers use in the Olympics. I suggested that he practice a little before Saturday, but he said he didn't need to. I wondered if those Olympic skiers trekked through deep snow with loaded backpacks.

We left campus before dawn on Saturday morning and reached the access road by about 9 A.M. The first leg of the road had been plowed, but we had to park three miles short of the trailhead. Phil unloaded his skis, turned them bottom side up, and started rubbing paste from a little tube onto their bases. Phil informed us that this wax helped the skis glide and also provided a purchase for a kick forward. He ran his hand the length of the skis, saying he was going to absolutely fly over the snow, just like the Norwegian Olympians.

I took my first good look at the skinny little red skis. They were only about two inches wide and looked about as thick and as sturdy as popsicle sticks. I flexed one of the tiny tips. "They seem awfully narrow and flimsy," I said. "They might break if you hit a log." I also wondered how he was going to stay upright on them. To me, they looked more like something you would use in a race on a packed, groomed trail.

Phil didn't say anything, just laid the skis on the snow and started clamping his hiking boots into the bindings. Bob and I strapped into our snowshoes and started up the road to the trailhead, expecting Phil to soon come racing by. After about an hour of plodding, Bob and I reached the trailhead. A sign informed us that it was 4.5 miles to Heart Lake. After our previous boondoggle on the Landers Fork, we were excited to be on a good trail with an official sign announcing that we were on the right track.

We waited for about thirty minutes and still no Phil. We'd even packed a good snowshoe trail for him, so we were starting to worry. Finally, we saw him coming around the bend in the road. When he caught up to us, we could see he was frustrated. He groused about the wax, which was designed for conditions above freezing, but the temperature was hovering around 15 F. Snow was clumped the full length of his ski bases, forming thick, heavy keels. He'd fallen many times, and his heavy pack made it hard to get back up.

Leaving the road, we started uphill on the straight and narrow trail through lodgepole and fir. For Phil, the going quickly got much worse.

We mushed slowly for a while, giving Phil a chance to keep up. Bob and I crossed a small dip in the trail, and then I heard a muffled crash and rustling in the trees behind me. I shouted to ask if he was okay, but the only answer was stony silence.

I caught up with Bob, who was steadily breaking trail. He wasn't tired, but he wasn't happy either. "This is ridiculous," Bob said. "We won't get to the lake before dark at this rate."

We waited for Phil to catch up. When he did, we could see that the skis were just not made for this terrain. Phil's face was red and he was covered with powdery snow and fir needles. Small branches and twigs hung from his backpack. Bob said that he and I would go ahead to the lake, set up camp, and drill holes for ice fishing. Phil would be fine following our packed trail, and he agreed to the plan.

Bob and I mushed the remaining three miles to Heart Lake. The trail followed a gradually sloping bench most of the way, with only a slight elevation gain from the trailhead. We caught glimpses of the Landers Fork far below and could see how misguided our previous route had been.

I was sure glad to arrive at this elusive lake! Heart Lake has two lobes, with a tongue-shaped peninsula dividing it almost in two. The snow sat deep on the ridges above, but winds had scoured much of it from the lake's ice. We set up camp on the peninsula, digging through about four feet of snow to a base where we could start a campfire. We gathered wood from under trees and felt at home. The scene was at once serene and inspiring, a deep silence punctuated by big snowflakes filtering down. Classic Montana wilderness brimming with solitude.

Bob and I drilled holes through two feet of ice with a two-piece auger. We baited hooks and lowered lines down to the bottom, in maybe twenty feet of water. At first, the grayling didn't hit, but as the light faded, we got a few bites. Phil had showed us how to make a "tip up" by forming a cross with two sticks and tying the line on the end of one. When a fish grabbed the bait, the other stick would tip up into the air, signaling us to run over and pull up the line.

Phil finally reached the lake, not in the best mood. Memory is a funny, unreliable phenomenon, and Phil's recollection differs from my own, but as

I remember it, we watched Phil cross the little knoll and stomp down to the lake, sinking up to his knees into the snow. He'd given up on the skis and was just post-holing in our snowshoe trail. He marched directly into camp, next to the fire. We noticed that the tip of one of his skis was missing.

Soon the grayling turned on, and Phil joined us in the fun. Bob pulled in a nice grayling, and we shouted for Phil to come over and check it out. "That's an Arctic grayling all right," said Phil. "See that dorsal fin? It looks like a sail!"

Bob holds an Arctic grayling at Heart Lake, 1973.

Thymallus arcticus, a relative of trout and salmon, is recognized as one of the most beautiful cold-loving, freshwater fish. Arctic grayling are native and numerous in the far north, especially in Alaska. Populations in the Lower 48 went extinct except for a small population in Montana's Big Hole River. The grayling in Heart Lake were introduced but are nonetheless just as showy, sporting iridescent silver and blue sides and a gaily colored, oversized dorsal fin. For Phil and me, as aquatic wildlife biology majors, seeing these fish was a real treat.

We caught about a dozen grayling and cooked them in aluminum foil over hot coals. Deep in the newly crowned Scapegoat Wilderness, the grayling tasted fine to us, but they were a bit mushy and bland compared to cutthroat or other trout.

John with an Arctic grayling pulled from Heart Lake, 1973.

Phil cheered up once we started catching fish. He told us that he'd broken his ski as he tumbled forward, reaching a hand out to break the fall. His hand hit the ski and snapped it like a brittle stick.

The next day, after a long, cool night, we rekindled the fire and gathered around it, hoping to repair Phil's ski. We found a sturdy pine branch and carved it as flat as we could. Wrapping with layers of electrician's tape, we splinted it and the ski tip onto the main ski body. It looked like it might hold long enough to get him back to the trailhead.

We caught more grayling that morning and then packed up and headed back down the trail. As we mushed away from the lake through the fresh snow, all three of us reveled in what we'd accomplished. We had found

Heart Lake and caught plenty of grayling, a first for us. We were steeped in the wilderness and had basked in its isolation and silence. This was just the kind of trip I loved, and I made yet another pact with myself to never leave Montana. On our way out, Phil fell often, but he took it in stride. We reached Phil's station wagon by late afternoon and were soon headed like homing pigeons to UM's food service.

I eventually bought a pair of touring skis, Kongsbergs, just like the ones Terry later acquired. Sure enough, Phil's skis were designed for track racing, too skinny and fragile for backcountry treks. Phil reverted to snowshoes for all our subsequent winter trips.

We revisited Heart Lake several times over the next few winters and always had good luck with the grayling, even ice fishing as early as November. One photo from the November trip shows eighteen grayling lined up on the slushy ice.

Once, on a sunny day in late May, Terry, Phil, and I went bear hunting near Lincoln. Terry and Phil were serious about hunting in the hills south

A nice string of Heart Lake grayling.

of the road, but I planned to hike into Heart Lake, wearing only boots. Phil dropped me off just short of the trailhead, and we agreed to meet up back at the same spot by 6 P.M.

I felt alive and free as I dashed up the trail: who cares about bear hunting when you can enter the Scapegoat and fish for grayling! Besides, this would be the first time I'd seen Heart Lake in the spring. The lower elevations were mostly clear of snow and greening up. Farther up the trail, I ran into snow, in places up to four feet deep. But it was firmly packed, like a sidewalk. As the day warmed, and as I got closer to the lake, I started sinking about four inches into the surface, which didn't slow me down much. I enjoyed the scent of lodgepole and fir, sunshine filtering through the trees, and the Scapegoat's solitude that I'd come to love.

I didn't know what I'd find when I got to the lake: would it be thawed or frozen? I hadn't brought an ice auger, hoping instead to knock a hole in the ice, if need be, with a stout lodgepole branch. Sure enough, ice covered the lake, but it was honeycombed with holes and dark areas. I remembered reading about carrying a long stick when walking on thin ice to hold you up if you fell through. I found a dead lodgepole about twelve feet long and four inches around and carried it, walking gingerly onto the slushy surface. Taking short steps and testing the ice with the lodgepole as I went, I approached one of the holes and looked down into the water column. It was deep enough to hold fish.

I dropped my line through the star-shaped hole and watched the hook spiral down into the dark greenish-blue water. Soon enough, I had a strike and hauled a shoe-sized grayling up and onto the slush. Heart Lake never seemed to disappoint. I caught a few more grayling and set them in the slush on the ice. I wanted to pack them out and cook them for dinner in an actual frying pan with oil and spices.

After fishing awhile and basking in the sun, I figured it was time to head back so Terry and Phil wouldn't have to wait for me at the trailhead.

I looked forward to the mostly downhill trek, until I started hiking. My hours at Heart Lake had given the sun and warm air time to soften the snowpack. I knew I was in trouble as soon as I topped the little ridge above the lake and started wallowing through the snow, which had lost its firmness. I had no broken trail, because I had walked on top of the crust on the way up.

What had been a pleasant stroll on a snow-sidewalk coming in turned into an exhausting death slog on the way out. I learned why post-holing in deep, crusty snow exhausted you more than just about anything. The surface held as I put my weight on it, then I plunged deeply in as I shifted to my other foot. The footing was better in the shade, but that never lasted long, and I'd be breaking through again, up to my thighs or worse. In places, I'd splash into water running beneath the snow.

Each step seemed like torture. I hurried as much as possible because I didn't want Phil and Terry waiting for me at the trailhead. Before long, I was exhausted and anxious. I'll confess now that this was the only time before or since that I've shed a few tears over an endurance test in the backcountry. After an eternity, I reached the last mile or so where the snowpack lessened. When I finally staggered out to the trailhead sign, an hour or two late, Phil and Terry were waiting and beginning to think about coming to search for me.

They hadn't seen any bears on their hunt, but they enjoyed the sunny day. I learned a good lesson about over-the-snow travel, and that I wasn't as tough as I thought. But I didn't mention that to my friends. We headed back to Missoula to cook up the grayling.

Over the next few years, we pushed into the Scapegoat Wilderness many times during winter, sometimes for an extended trip. On one such trip, we entered by way of the North Fork of the Blackfoot River. We drove as far as we could on the access road across Kleinschmidt Flats and had to park about five miles short of the trailhead. We left Phil's station wagon and started mushing up the snowed-in road.

The trip started out in comfortable weather above freezing. At our first camp, a site locally known as 40-Below Camp, it felt more like a late spring trip. We walked the snowbanks along the river in the narrow canyon and fished for mountain whitefish with wet flies and wooly worms; we even caught and released some nice cutthroat.

But the nice weather didn't hold; the next day greeted us with blowing snow as we followed the trail up the steep-sided canyon. We passed the dramatic sweep of Big Slide and crossed over to the east side of the drainage on a pack bridge. The trail snaked along the river through the heavily wooded landscape and then through Sourdough Flats. The drainage was gorgeous, heavily timbered and mysterious. That would all change after the devastating 1988 fire that could be seen from space.

A few miles farther, we reached the North Fork guard station, where we planned to camp. The temperature plummeted and we were wet and soggy, so we decided to see if we could get inside the cabin and fire up the woodstove. We knew we were taking a chance, but figured if we got caught, we could claim that hypothermia gripped us, and that wasn't far from the truth.

Terry McCoy and Phil snowshoeing near the divide between the North and Dry Forks of the Blackfoot River.

The next day, we explored the North Fork Gorge up to the falls and above. Then we trekked up to the junction with the East Fork, on to the Dry Fork area, and camped a night in our tent. I wished we could have spent a week exploring that country and crossed into the Danaher in the South

Fork of the Flathead. I took photos of the crew near the Dry Fork; Phil and Terry looked tough and intrepid. Even though we were far from it, we felt like Lewis and Clark. It was all new country to us and so remote. But we had to turn back, retracing our route to the trailhead. What a great adventure, but it only whetted our appetites for more wilderness.

During early June 1973, just before spring quarter finals, we headed into the Scapegoat again. This time we trekked through the big canyon of Arrastra Creek Gorge. "Arrastra" refers to a primitive mill for crushing gold and silver ore, but we never saw any sign of mining.

I studied for finals on the drive to the trailhead and back. Just going into the Scapegoat again had me fired up. This would be a long-distance and strenuous hike that we hoped to accomplish in just four days.

We headed up the Arrastra Creek Trail and in three miles reached an unnamed pothole lake, crossed a gentle, 6,600-foot pass that still held snow, and dropped into the East Fork of Meadow Creek. A small stream led us to a larger tributary, forming the East Fork proper, then on through scenic Alpine Park, arriving finally at Meadow Lake and its clear, meandering stream. This part of the Scapegoat is easy to love. Rising above the lake to the west stands bare-shouldered, 8,171-foot Bugle Mountain. To the east, a four-mile, 8,000-foot ridge runs north to south, stretched taut above the valley. We quickly set up a camp and fished the stream and lake.

Oddly, we had little luck. Perhaps the fish were deeper in the lake or maybe had moved down to the East Fork of the North Fork of the Blackfoot. We finally caught fish when we hiked downstream, through timber and lingering snow, to the East Fork.

I was only a freshman in wildlife biology, but I longed to study the fisheries of remote waters like these. I wondered if someday I could get a graduate study in this drainage. I caught some small cutthroats in the East Fork, and I wondered if they interbred with the fish we'd seen in March above the North Fork Falls. Holding one of these cutts in the stream, I had the idea of marking as many as I could, then see if I could recapture any later that summer or fall. I realized that my sample size would be a drop in the bucket, but I wanted to try anyway. So on about a half dozen trout, I removed a small tip of anal fin, a typical way to mark salmonids. I didn't have a clipper handy, so I bit off that portion of the fin with my teeth. I don't think I told Terry or Phil. They already thought I was a little off; I didn't need to give them more evidence.

My life as a UM freshman had inspired me. I watched the East Fork flow by and counted my blessings. I loved Montana and felt so fortunate to be studying biology and nature. And I had discovered that I actually loved academia. That spring quarter, I was enrolled in some challenging classes: Organic Chemistry and lab, Ecosystem Biology Lab, Introduction to Geology, Zoology, and Math for the Biological Sciences. I was lucky to be learning from some stand-out professors: Dr. Forrest Thomas, Dave Alt, and Bob Bohac. Reflecting the spirit of the 1970s, Bohac taught classes wearing a colorful *serape*, a peasant blanket.

On the drive back to Missoula, I studied hard for my finals. I nailed the exams and received straight "As" for the quarter. If I kept up my grades over the next three years, I'd have a decent chance to get into grad school and study my passion, aquatic science. In our Survey of Wildlife Careers class of several hundred students, renowned wildlife expert Dr. Les Pengelly told us that because the wildlife field was so competitive, only a few of us would stay in Montana or ever get a permanent job in wildlife. I'm not sure I believed him, but I vowed that I would be one of the few. Terry and Phil likely had the same ambition. ⟴

CHAPTER 4

Skiing the 'Roots
The Funnel, snowslides, and frostbite

The 1.3-million-acre Selway-Bitterroot Wilderness is one of the largest wilderness areas in the Lower 48. Established January 1, 1964, the Selway-Bitterroot straddles the Idaho-Montana border along the spine of the Bitterroot Range. The Bitterroots look spectacular from the valley on the Montana side. According to Norman Maclean in *A River Runs Through It*, one of the big, glaciated canyons looked like a "Hole in the Sky." I can see what he meant.

As a Missoula college student in the early 1970s, I drove south and looked at those gaping U-shaped drainages like Big and Blodgett, Bass and Kootenai, and felt such a draw. I couldn't wait to explore them all, especially in winter.

To me and my friends, these canyons offered nearby, challenging ski or snowshoe trips in a beautiful, recently designated wilderness. I don't remember seeing any other travelers on our trips; backcountry winter travel was much less common than it is today. We trekked up Bass and out Kootenai, then did it in reverse; skied in the South Fork of Lolo Creek drainage and out Bass, and reverse; trekked into Big Creek Canyon to Packbox Pass; and so on. When I look back at my snapshots of so many trips during my undergrad years, I wonder how I found the time. My energy and enthusiasm then were limitless.

By the winter of 1973–1974, I was using waxable Kongsberg wooden skis, made in Norway. When conditions warranted it, I still used snowshoes. I skied and snowshoed a few hundred miles in the Bitterroots during a three-year period, but two trips stand out in my memory as epic, not for the best of reasons: the snowslide funnel trip and the frostbite trip.

The Funnel
In January 1974, Terry, Bob, and I tried something that almost never works: we split up and started in adjacent canyons—Kootenai and Bass Creeks—

planning to meet on the pass between them. We'd all camp there for the night, then head back down Bass Creek to the waiting car. In my VW Bug, we drove to the Kootenai Canyon Trailhead and dropped off Terry on his Kongsberg skis. Then Bob and I drove to Bass Creek and headed for Bass Lake and the pass.

Terry would ski ten miles up Kootenai Canyon, while Bob and I had nine miles to reach Bass Lake. From either canyon, it was a little over a mile to our meeting spot on the pass. It looked simple enough on the map. But in reality, the plan was foolish from the start given all the variables in the mountains during winter. We should have known better.

It wasn't long before the plan started unravelling. As Bob (snowshoe-ing) and I (skiing) headed up Bass Canyon, Bob announced he wasn't feel-ing well and didn't think he could go the distance. I convinced him to continue as far as Bass Lake and camp there. A few miles below the lake, we had to detour around a huge avalanche. The chunks of hardpacked snow were as big as my VW.

We reached Bass Lake in the late afternoon and set up a camp in the shelter of a stand of large conifers. Then I continued on to the pass, keeping to the plan of meeting Terry there. I left Bob with the tent and carried a snowmobile suit in my pack in case I had to spend the night out. I zigzagged up the 400 feet in elevation to the pass, a snow-filled flat below 8,855-foot Bass Peak. By this time, it was getting dusky and a snowstorm moved in.

I yelled for Terry (oh yeah, that's going to work) as I peered over the other side into a steep, bad-ass drop into the Kootenai drainage. Engulfed in a blizzard, seeing that Terry's route was steeper than we anticipated, I was getting worried. I had one skier (Terry) who hadn't shown up as planned and a sick companion (Bob) camped at Bass Lake 400 feet below. The bliz-zard's intensity seemed to increase. (I later wrote a "poem" about standing in the blizzard at dusk on the Bitterroot crest. When I read it years later, I real-ized that there's nothing worse than bad poetry.) There wasn't much more I could do right then, so I dug a little snow cave, pulled on my snowmobile suit, and climbed in. Surely, Terry would show up in the morning.

The temperature moderated and my night wasn't too uncomfortable. I crawled out of the cave just after dawn and yelled down into the Kootenai

John in the Bitterroots as a blizzard moves in.

side. Then, worried about Terry, I dropped partway down that side. He was a better skier than me, and he should have crested the pass by then. I side-stepped down the steepest part and descended maybe 500 feet in a half mile, shouting off and on for my friend. Seeing no sign and hearing nothing, I began to think Terry might have run into some difficulty and decided to turn back. I decided to turn around, re-crest the pass, and ski back down to Bass Lake to collect Bob and head out.

I side-hilled up the last pitch and neared the top of the pass, but then my stomach lurched in fear. A crooked crack in the snow suddenly zippered across the slope in front of me. Time paused, then the snowpack broke and slid into the little bowl of the pass, taking me with it. Almost immediately, though, I saw that I could ride it out—the slab was soft and only about two feet thick. I never lost my footing, but I did bend a pole. When the world came to a stop, I gathered myself and looked at the terrain with fresh eyes. I could see that the slopes on either side formed a funnel, and I was standing smack in the outlet at the narrow end. From then on, we called this back pass "the Funnel." I made my way across the

John on the saddle, near "the Funnel" between Bass Creek and Kootenai Creek.

flat and on down the relatively gentle slopes to Bass Lake. Bob was hanging around the tent, feeling no better.

We were worried about leaving before Terry caught us, but we figured he must've turned around. We convinced ourselves that, knowing Terry, he'd ski from the mouth of Kootenai to the Bass Creek Trailhead and be waiting at the car. So we headed down Bass Creek. Bob was moving slow on snowshoes in his weakened condition. We reached the trailhead in late afternoon and decided to wait for Terry until about an hour after dark. If he was still a no-show, we'd drive the forty minutes back to Missoula and drop off sickly Bob so he could go to bed. Then I'd drive back and check both trailheads, waiting, hoping Terry would show up.

When I returned to the Bass Creek Trailhead that night, I was relieved to find Terry's ski tracks right at the trailhead. But no Terry. I knew he was out of the mountains but had no clue where he'd gone. All I could do was drive back to Missoula.

It turned out that Terry had reached the trailhead probably not long after Bob and I left for Missoula. He walked out to the highway and hitched a ride back to town. When we reunited early the next morning, he told his side of the story.

Terry had skied up the Kootenai drainage nearly to Kootenai Lakes, missing the side drainage that would have taken him over the pass to Bass Creek. He backtracked, looking for the right drainage, but ran out of light. The next morning, his route up to the pass turned out to be super steep and difficult. He started up the steeper part of the climb and was swept down in a much more serious snowslide than I had been. He lost a pole and got a serious scratch on his right cornea, which was really painful and made it difficult to see out of that eye.

With one pole and one good eye, Terry tried the pass again, avoiding the steepest grade. This time he made it, but the going was slow. He was probably only two hours behind us when he finally found signs of our camp at Bass Lake. He followed our tracks down to the trailhead, but Bob and I hadn't waited there quite long enough.

That should've been the end of the story. But it wasn't. Terry was disappointed and felt like I'd abandoned him.

From my standpoint, I'd made a big effort to find him in the high country, then waited at the trailhead until after dark, and then returned to the trailhead later that night after I'd gotten Bob back to Missoula. I felt torn. On one hand, I had a sick friend. On the other, I had no idea where Terry was and actually thought we might have to call in search and rescue. Terry eventually forgave me, even though he strongly disagreed with how I'd handled it. I felt bad and would've felt even worse if I'd known that Terry had only seven months to live.

I've never felt right about this trip, and in hindsight I can see why Terry felt the way he did. He was cold, his vision compromised, and when he'd reached the trailhead we weren't there to meet him. In retrospect, Bob and I should've waited until dawn if we had to. The thought that Terry felt abandoned has nagged at me ever since.

Frostbite and Search Plane

The other Bitterroot ski trip that gnaws at my conscience ended much worse. In January 1975, looking for a big challenge, I made a plan to ski up Bass Creek, cross over a pass, and come out the South Fork of Lolo Creek, a distance of about twenty-four miles. As usual, I didn't know anyone who had done this route. I also didn't bother to find out the nature of the trail over the pass and especially down the long South Fork Lolo Creek drainage.

All that would have been okay except that I agreed to take along Clark, who would snowshoe. I don't think Clark had ever snowshoed, but I figured everything would work out. I didn't know Clark well. I'd met him through Jack, one of my housemates in East Missoula. Jack and Clark had come from Iowa, and Clark had worked on a ranch in eastern Montana the previous summer. He was fired up to get into the mountains during winter.

To save money, I lived in a lot of odd dives during my college days, but the East Missoula place may have been the most unusual. The owners had recently converted it from a "cathouse" to a rental unit. I guess "business" had been slow. My room had no actual heat, so I used a space heater. The windows were stained red, the carpet was red, and the ceiling was covered in red plastic tiles.

There were about eight or ten of us living there, a very eclectic bunch. Hal was a biker who worked at the Bonner Mill and ran around with a semi-intense motorcycle gang. Another guy ate anything that wasn't tied down. A few of us got tired of this, so we melted chocolate Ex-Lax and spread it on some vanilla wafers. We put them on a plate on the kitchen table. Sure enough, the next morning they were gone. Apparently, the culprit missed a test that day because he couldn't leave the bathroom. Today, a stunt like this would probably get you arrested, but back then it was just innocent fun.

On a Saturday morning, Bob drove Clark and me to the Bass Creek Trailhead in my VW Bug. He would pick us up at the South Fork Lolo Trailhead on Sunday evening. We figured two days, twenty-four miles, no problem.

I don't remember where we got Clark's snowshoes, but they weren't the best. The leather bindings weren't snug, so he had to retighten them often. With my Kongsbergs—cable bindings and hiking boots—I was set.

We slogged up Bass Canyon about eight miles, climbing 3,000 feet, and made it to the lake by late afternoon. We worked our way around the north side of the frozen lake and aimed for the obvious notch leading to the pass and the headwaters of the South Fork of Lolo Creek. Clark struggled to keep a decent pace, and it was dawning on me that he wasn't ready for such a major trek. Being oblivious to safety and common sense, however, we kept going. As we zigzagged up the slope, we stopped often so he could take a breather. I carried as much of his load as possible, moving weight to my pack, including his sleeping bag.

Clark in deep snow on the ill-fated trip down the South Fork of Lolo Creek, January 1975.

Not long before dark, we reached the narrow 7,400-foot pass. The snowpack supported our weight well enough, but snow was falling and the temperature plummeted. We set up our tube tent and dug a pit to have a base for a fire. Dry wood for fuel was scarce. We warmed up a bit but mostly got smoked out.

Overnight, conditions worsened. Any prudent person would've retreated rather than press on. We woke to three feet of fresh snow. Sure, it was four miles shorter if we retraced our tracks down Bass Creek, but we figured the snowpack would dwindle as we dropped into the South Fork of Lolo Creek.

So we packed up and headed down. The fresh powder and gravity's help made the descent easy and fun, at first. Of course, after dropping 2,000 feet in two miles through deep snow, there was no turning back. As we hit the flatter part of the South Fork Lolo drainage, the snow didn't decrease as we'd hoped. Instead, with every step, we sank in knee deep, even on skis and snowshoes. I broke trail and realized that at our pace, we wouldn't reach the South Fork Lolo Creek Trailhead that day.

Whether through lack of use or the sheer amount of snow, the trail was nonexistent. Worse yet, we had to climb over a lot of downed timber. Sometimes it seemed that downed trees blocked any path forward. We kept slogging till late afternoon and then set up our tent. Despite my

John breaks trail through deep snow near the bottom of the South Fork of Lolo Creek, January 1975.

nagging, Clark wouldn't eat much other than nibbling from a jar of Koogle, a banana-flavored peanut butter. Clark and I slept back to back, trying to keep warm, and shivered anyway. Anything we didn't want to freeze solid went with us into our sleeping bags. I slept with my boots in my bag, but Clark left his out, a mistake he'd pay for. I wondered what Bob would think when we didn't show up at the trailhead that night as planned.

The next day, we started the long slog again, deep snow, downfall, and fatigue slowing our pace. I figured that we had about eight grueling miles to go. I broke trail, weaving around and over downed trees from some long-ago blowdown, adding miles to our route. At Lantern Creek, about two miles from the trailhead, the trail climbed out of the creek bottom and along Lantern Ridge. By late afternoon, we broke into a little clearing and heard a small airplane approaching. Being overdue, we knew what that meant.

I was surprised by what the pilot did next. He cut the engine so his passenger could yell down to us, using a megaphone, "Make a cross if you're in trouble, a circle if you're okay to make it."

I've thought of this many times since. The two men in the plane risked their safety by cutting the engine (that's what it sounded like; maybe the pilot throttled back to idle) so we could hear their instructions. We quickly mushed a big circle into the snow.

An hour or so later, near dark, we finally reached the trailhead. Bob, a search official or two, and a few other friends were waiting. We were embarrassed. We'd caused a lot of people a long day of worry and effort. We thanked the search official profusely and apologized for our recklessness. They seemed to understand that the unexpected snow had caused our delay, and we had done our best under the circumstances.

The next day, the headline "Missing men sighted" ran in the January 28, 1975, *Missoulian*. "Two men, believed to be lost during a weekend cross-country trek, were spotted by a search plane Monday afternoon on the south fork of Lolo Creek," the story read. It mentioned our names and ages (I was twenty) and said that we had to "hole up during the winter storm that passed through western Montana Saturday and Sunday" as we attempted to cross the Bitterroot Range and come out the other side. We never "holed up" but had pushed along as fast as Clark could go. It went on to note,

"Officials who spotted the pair said they looked in good health." Well, not quite, as we soon found out.

We were so happy to have made it. We'd learned that the South Fork of Lolo Creek is a monster drainage with no good trail and a tangle of downfall. Add three feet of fresh snow, and you have real trouble. We had been lucky. It may seem that this story had a happy ending, but it didn't.

Back in Missoula, I dropped off Bob and Clark at their places and went to my room in the cathouse. A few hours later, Clark called. He told me that his feet were "solid" and alabaster white. The next morning, they turned black and blue, and Clark headed for the doctor with an obvious case of serious frostbite. Over the next few months, he had to really baby his feet, coating them with Vaseline and plastic bags, then socks. He wore soft booties for a while. He lost some toenails, and the skin blistered and sloughed off, but in the end he fully recovered.

I don't remember Clark mentioning that his feet were numb during the trip, but maybe I "forgot" this detail to assuage my guilt. I should've checked his condition every couple of hours, but I was used to trekking partners who took care of themselves. It was a harsh learning experience for both of us.

I had done a number of misguided backcountry treks in my young life, but this was by far the worst—it left my companion with a serious injury. Clark and Jack tried to assure me that it wasn't my fault, and that Clark had asked to go. Looking back, I can't imagine how I hatched such a reckless plan, almost a death march.

I lost touch with Clark, but he seemed to recover amazingly well. Do I still feel guilty all these years later? Recently, I searched for the cathouse, but it must've been razed. Its demolition didn't erase my guilt for my poor friend whose feet may still suffer in cold weather. I'll take that guilt to my grave.

In an act of penance, or maybe madness, I vowed to reverse the trip later that spring. I made the twenty-four miles in one day, in late May. I skied the middle ten miles but hiked the rest. When I reached the Bass Creek Trailhead, people in shorts were basking in the sun. The next day, I stopped by the Forestry Building to tell Dr. Bob Ream that I'd done it in one day. He laughed, but I said I was serious. To this day, I'm not sure he believed me.

Looking back, I'm astonished at how many ski trips I did in the Bitterroots during those few years at UM. Was I escaping the conformity of university life, or proving something to myself, or simply savoring the joys of being engulfed by the snowy silence of wilderness? Maybe all three. To me, the winter wilderness felt comfortable and safe, as if the arms of the backcountry welcomed me in and held me. And I kept going out, regardless of the weather or risks. It's remarkable that my friends tagged along.

One late-winter morning, Phil and I headed for the Big Creek Trailhead in his big green station wagon, planning to spend a night at Big Creek Lakes. We hoped to explore the Bitterroot crest around Packbox Pass and look into the headwaters of the Lochsa River.

We parked short of the trailhead and walked up the icy access road. Phil slipped and fell sideways, breaking his fall with an outstretched hand. He got a nasty gash that looked like it needed stitches. Reluctantly, Phil decided to return to town. I accompanied my friend to the UM health service so he could get treatment. Nearly a half century later, Phil still has the scar. I decided to do the trip alone and returned to the trailhead that same day. I got a late start, but I kicked into a higher gear to ski to the lakes, ten miles and 2,000 feet in elevation up the trail.

I reached Big Creek Lakes and skied a mile and a half around and across to its south end, then climbed a fairly gentle mile toward Packbox Pass. I considered dropping my backpack at the lake but decided to keep it on for safety. As I neared the pass, it began to snow heavily and daylight faded, so I stopped short of the top. The snow and wind would've obscured any view down the headwaters of the Lochsa anyway.

I pointed back toward Big Creek Lakes and fought for control using my limited downhill skills, relying on the heavy snow to slow me. In all my years of skiing, I never became confident swooshing downhill. But I made it to a sheltered spot, set up camp, and crawled into my tent that night, excited to be at the lake and already making plans to return so I could ice fish, which I did a few times over the next few years.

Looking back, my relentless draw to wilderness was likely a substitute for socializing, my lack of which bordered on extreme. Being a loner might've been awkward on campus, but it was an asset in the backcountry.

And maybe my wilderness experiences helped develop my confidence. I completed my Bachelor of Science degree in March 1976, a quarter early. Later that spring, I finally went on my first date. I met her on the "M" Trail on Mount Sentinel and we hit it off. She was a cross-country and track runner from eastern Montana, and seemed nice. I summoned the courage to ask her out: would she like to climb Lolo Peak that weekend? (It had to be the Bitterroots, of course.) She stunned me by saying yes, and at age twenty-two I had my first date. That Saturday, I picked her up in my Bug and we drove up the access road as close to the trailhead as we could get. We trekked up the trail in our boots, scooting across the supporting snowpack. I noticed that she could really move up the trail. We had a nice time. We traversed a long, gorgeous ridge, but I don't remember if we made it to the peak's summit. That evening, I dropped her off at her dorm and we shared one awkward kiss, my first. For one reason or another, I never saw her again.

In April, I began a temporary job with the U.S. Bureau of Land Management in Missoula, conducting stream surveys in the Garnet Range. I had my own truck and a dream job. Fortunately, I'd graduated early and was available to take it.

Andy Sheldon, my aquatic ecology professor at UM, had recommended me for the job. After three months, I would head to graduate school at Montana State University to do research on the famous Madison River. Suddenly, I was on my way; life was progressing in a direction that was at once exciting and humbling. I owe Dr. Sheldon a big thank you. In spite of the odds, I would be one of the few UM wildlife biology grads who would stay in Montana and work on its second-to-none aquatic resources. Take that, Dr. Pengelly. ◄○►

CHAPTER 5

The Impassable Canyon

Adventuring in the Middle Fork of the Salmon

The deep, steep-walled canyon of the Middle Fork of the Salmon River.

The Middle Fork of the Salmon River in central Idaho cuts through a complicated geological formation known as the Idaho Batholith, forming one of the deepest, most remote canyons in the Lower 48. It's deeper than the Grand Canyon and almost as deep as Hell's Canyon of the Snake River. The river itself drops more than 3,000 feet from its headwaters at Marsh Creek through many wild, Class IV rapids down its 100-plus-mile course; an astonishing drop of nearly thirty feet per mile. Canyon walls rise to dizzying heights along much of the river's length. An early explorer christened the lower seventeen miles of the Middle Fork "The Impassable Canyon," and it's easy to see why.

Compared to the surrounding mountains, the canyon bottomlands are warmer and drier, home to sagebrush, ponderosa pine, grasses, and lots of rock. Here and there along the river, sandy beaches tucked among the cliffs offer beautiful campsites. It was the Middle Fork's promise of "early spring"—a wilderness that was snow free and relatively warm—that lured me, Terry, Bob, and Phil to the area during spring break and Easter break from one year to the next. The Middle Fork's long, storied history was also a draw.

For thousands of years, the region was home to the Tukudika, a band of Shoshone known among early explorers and pioneers as the Sheepeaters for their reliance on bighorn sheep. Other Shoshone, the Nez Perce, and other tribes also used the Middle Fork, as evidenced by ancient petroglyphs, elegant stone projectile points and tools, and other relics scattered along its length. These people must have enjoyed a bounty of food resources. Bighorn sheep, mule deer, elk, bull trout, cutthroat trout, and whitefish abounded. And a big bonus swam up the river spring through fall: anadromous chinook salmon and steelhead trout, arriving every year after a marathon trip from the Pacific Ocean. My friends and I imagined what it must have been like to be the masters of this drainage for thousands of years as the tribes once were.

Sheepeaters and others thrived here until the late 1800s. They clashed with Euro-Americans in the "Sheepeater Wars" in 1879. Then prospectors found gold and fanned out across the drainage. As the years went by, more prospectors followed. Earl Parrott, the "Hermit of the Impassable Canyon," returned from the Yukon gold rush in 1897 and prospected along the Middle Fork. He had a cabin and gardens amid the cliffs hundreds of feet above the Middle Fork. Parrott once claimed that he went decades without seeing another person, entirely plausible given his remote homesite. In fact, it's hard to imagine a riverscape more remote and with a more interesting history. We were captivated by it and wanted to explore it all.

The 104-mile Middle Fork of the Salmon was one of the first rivers to receive Wild and Scenic designation in 1968, championed by Idaho senator and conservationist, Frank Church. The river rises in the Sawtooth Range at the junction of Bear Valley and Marsh Creeks, then flows north over a boulder-filled channel to join the Salmon River about forty miles downstream from North Fork. Along the way, the river cuts through the 2.5-million-acre Frank Church–River of No Return Wilderness, the largest contiguous wilderness area in the Lower 48. It nearly joins with the 1.3-million-acre Selway-Bitterroot Wilderness, separated only by an unimproved dirt road.

From left to right, John, Terry McCoy, and Phil on the Stoddard Pack Bridge, heading up the Middle Fork, 1974.

In the 1970s, my hiking friends and I knew it as "The Idaho Primitive Area," which was its official name until Congress knighted it as wilderness. In 1980, Frank Church carried the Central Idaho Wilderness Act, which incorporated several areas, including the Salmon River country.

The act, signed by President Carter, created the River of No Return Wilderness and added more than 100 miles of Wild and Scenic designation to the Salmon River system. In 1984, in honor of Frank Church, who had fallen ill, Congress renamed it the Frank Church–River of No Return Wilderness. President Reagan signed the bill in April, less than a month before Church's death.

My friends and I learned that Dr. Bob Ream and his wife Cathy, drawn to all things wilderness, often headed for the Salmon River in spring for its typically milder climate. In fact, Terry had accompanied Bob, Cathy, and their two children on a trip to Corn Creek Campground on the main Salmon River about eight miles below the Middle Fork. Terry told us that the Salmon country, especially the Middle Fork, was wild and remote, and it might be snow free. So, during our March 1974 spring break, after mushing around in the Scapegoat's deep snow for five days, Terry, Phil, Bob, and I drove south on U.S. Highway 93 to the little wayside of North Fork, Idaho. There we picked up Idaho fishing licenses, brochures, and Middle Fork maps.

Then we drove almost forty miles west on the gravel Salmon River Road to the Stoddard Pack Bridge, which spans the main Salmon just below the confluence with the Middle Fork. The landscape was wonderful—a gorgeous, clear river flowing over boulders, cutting a path between high mountains rimmed with cliffs, and no snow. We shared an excitement of exploration, reveling in a new place so different from what we were used to.

John, center, with friends, in the 1970s at a trailhead in the Idaho Primitive Area, soon to become designated wilderness.

We hefted our backpacks and walked out on the pack bridge, snapping a few photos of our group. We didn't know the area but we had the power of youth and enthusiasm on our side. Our goal was to reach Stoddard Creek, five miles up the canyon. But we'd heard the lower end of the Middle Fork Canyon was "impassable" because of steep cliffs and a narrow gorge. So, after crossing the bridge, we started up the switchbacked trail and climbed four miles and nearly 3,000 feet in elevation, roughly paralleling the river. This trail runs about twenty miles, all the way to Big Creek, where it descends to the Middle Fork. We didn't have enough time for that, and snow would block our way. So instead, after studying the topo map, we planned to bushwhack down about 2,500 feet into the Middle Fork gorge. We would camp a few nights and make our way upriver if we could. The canyon was so deep and rugged, we really didn't know what to expect. Thousands of feet below, the Middle Fork whispered in its canyon. Looking over the steep sides of the canyon we'd have to descend gave us all the willies.

Art, Mike, and John high above the Middle Fork, plotting a route to drop into the canyon.

As we rounded one bend in the trail, two mountain lions, long tails extended, dashed across a gully ahead of us. None of us had ever seen one of the big cats before, and we all felt a rush of excitement. We'd heard that a professor from the University of Idaho, Dr. Maurice Hornocker, was conducting a study of the pumas near Big Creek.

Near the head of Color Creek, we began dropping into the canyon, picking our way between coulees, cliffs, and hillsides. Several bands of bighorn sheep let us get fairly close before trotting away, another reminder of the country's wildness.

We climbed down for several hours and bottomed out somewhere between Color Creek on the west bank of the river and Roaring Creek on the east. On this first trip to the Middle Fork, we savored our time at the river, exploring upstream to Stoddard Creek. We saw sheep galore, and caught and released whitefish, Dolly Varden (*Salvelinus malma*), and cutthroat. We saw several steelhead that had traveled more than 700 miles from the ocean. There was no snow, and the sagebrush, buttercups, and other wildflowers awakened around us. Scattered ponderosa pines brightened the landscape with their green needles and cinnamon-colored trunks.

After a few days immersed in the canyon, it was time to head home. We scrambled back up the steep canyon slope, not wanting to risk following the river in the canyon bottom. It was too cliffy, we thought. We regained the trail and descended to the Stoddard Pack Bridge. On the drive back to Missoula, we talked nonstop about the wildlife we'd seen and the fish we'd caught. Best of all, we never saw another person. We all agreed that this had been a great spring break adventure and planned to return, which we did, many times. (Sadly, this was Terry's only Middle Fork trip; five months later, he would die in the plane crash in the Sapphire Mountains.)

Over the next few years, we did about eight more trips into the Middle Fork. One trip really sticks in my mind. The year after Terry's death, Phil, Bob, two other friends, and I decided to go straight up the bottom of the "impassable canyon" in an attempt to reach Big Creek. This large tributary joins the Middle Fork seventeen miles upstream from the main Salmon. We left Missoula on March 20, 1975. We stopped at the Angler's Roost, a quaint combination of RV park and fly shop, in Hamilton to buy Idaho fishing licenses, then drove to the Stoddard Pack Bridge, hiked a few miles in, and camped.

Our plan was innovative but risky. Based on what we had seen and heard on previous trips, we knew the canyon was likely impassable on foot. So we hit on the idea of using a small, light raft to get around the cliffs and maybe even cross the Middle Fork when the other bank offered easier going.

The next day we dropped into the canyon to the banks of the Middle Fork of the Salmon. We headed upstream, hopping over boulders until an impassable cliff blocked our way, forcing us to inflate our postage stamp raft to skirt the edge of the towering rock. The inadequate raft and the nasty cliff so spooked two members of our party, now sopping wet, that they set up camp and would go no farther. They planned to retrace their steps in a day or two and return to Missoula. Bob stayed to shepherd them out, while Phil and I continued on. We figured that we could hitchhike back to town after we came out from our longer trip, an inconvenience but not insurmountable.

John getting into the lightweight raft on the Middle Fork of the Salmon River.

This raft strategy worked surprisingly well. It helped that the water level was very low; at higher flows we never would've made it. We tied a fly line to the stern of the raft, and then one of us paddled upstream along the cliffs, with our backpack balanced in the raft, while the other waited. The person waiting—with the other end of the fly line—then pulled the empty raft back downstream, got in, and paddled up to reunite.

Thinking back on it, this was a foolhardy endeavor. First of all, our little K-Mart raft was flimsy, and we didn't have life jackets. And if anything had gone wrong, such as the line breaking, we might have lost a pack or been stranded on either side of a cliff. Also, the leapfrogging was slow going; we covered about five miles upstream per day, so it took us three days to reach Big Creek. But somehow, rock-hopping and cliff climbing, we made it— we'd traversed the Middle Fork's "impassable canyon."

John paddling around a cliff on the Middle Fork of the Salmon River, 1970s.

At Big Creek, Phil and I saw a trail on the river's east bank, coming out of Waterfall Creek from the rugged mountains to the east, the Bighorn Crags. The Crags rise to over 9,000 feet, making the canyon nearly 6,000 feet deep at that point. To our delight, a footbridge spanned the Middle Fork just upstream from the confluence with Big Creek. Trails and bridges: we'd reached "civilization." After seventeen miles of uneven footing on boulders, the tension built up in our muscles finally eased.

At the mouth of Big Creek, the Middle Fork's largest tributary, the canyon gentled out a little. We camped there for a day or so. We followed a trail up Big Creek, through a narrow gorge with an overhang decorated with petroglyphs. According to an archaeological survey in the mid-1970s, Big Creek was a hotspot for native culture. The local geology was rich in argillites and quartzites, good raw materials for stone tools. I took a photo of Phil standing in the narrows near the petroglyphs, with a mountain whitefish he'd caught, strung on a stick. We were living the wild life.

Phil fishing at Big Creek near the petroglyphs.

The next day, we continued up the Big Creek Trail, heading for a research cabin we'd heard about from Dr. Ream. His colleague, Dr. Maurice Hornocker, used the station as a base for his mountain lion studies. Nearing Cougar Creek, flashes of brown hair, the drum of hooves, and mews of cows surrounded us as we walked right into a nice herd of elk. After seven miles of trekking up the trail, we reached the University of Idaho's Taylor Wilderness Research Station, a complex of about five cabins and an airstrip. Here, the landscape was more timbered and gentler. The half-mile-long airstrip was grass-covered, and patches of snow dotted the landscape. We were amazed at the size of the station.

We'd eaten much of our food, and we fantasized about all the tasty unattended canned food we might find at the research station. "Well," I said to Phil, "if we did go in and borrow some canned food, we wouldn't take much." In the middle of my statement, a door opened and out walked an older man; we hoped he hadn't heard me. We met face to face with the caretaker for Dr. Hornocker's mountain lion study grounds, an old-timer who lived at the Taylor Wilderness Research Station. Boy, was he surprised to see us. He told us he'd never heard of anyone walking up the Middle Fork canyon from the main Salmon River. Phil and I were surprised, too; we hadn't known that someone would be here this early in the spring.

The research station is probably the most remote biological outpost in the Lower 48. Dr. Hornocker later told me that the caretaker was Arlow Lewis, "a colorful character who stayed in all winter and came out twice a year, staying drunk for two weeks." Hornocker said that after Arlow left for the last time, it took two planeloads to transport the years of beer cans piled up behind the station.

Arlow invited us in to the cabin and we sat down on benches. We stared hungrily at the shelves lined with canned food; the corned beef looked especially good. But he didn't offer any food and we didn't ask. He quizzed us on how we'd made it there on foot. We explained that we used our little raft to shuttle us around cliffs or even across the river if needed. He still seemed surprised that we were able to negotiate the seventeen-mile canyon. I have to admit that the route was touch and go at times. The first mile of the Middle Fork is narrow and straight as an arrow, then it bends back and forth between the canyon walls. Sometimes we had to climb to get around cliffs. In one photo, I'm standing on top of a cliff about 1,000 feet above the river. The terrain and depth of the canyon almost defies normal topographical lines to portray it.

We didn't linger long with Arlow, though he did tell us that the east bank of the Middle Fork was generally more passable. He asked us to assure "the brass" that he was taking good care of the place. Phil and I headed back down Big Creek to our camp on the Middle Fork. I complained, noting that "he could have at least given us one can of corned beef." It had been a cold, lean trip. We would leave the next day for our seventeen-mile return trek downriver on the east side.

Much to our pleasure, we were able to walk down the east side without using our raft, which greatly reduced our trekking time. Along with that though, we had to climb up and around some pretty high cliffs. That suited us much better than unpacking the raft and worrying about hauling ourselves and our packs around cliffs on the river. And we would need the raft to cross the Middle Fork near the mouth.

After a while, Phil announced that he'd had enough of the climbing and cold weather, saying, "I'm going to bust my butt out of here." I told him I wanted to linger. So we drew straws to see who would keep the raft. We figured the other person could go downriver at the mouth and take his chances crossing on a USGS cable, an extremely foolhardy idea. I won the straws contest and retained the raft. Phil took off.

It wasn't long before I started feeling bad about leaving Phil without the raft. I sped up and caught my partner, who had been climbing higher to look for a shortcut. I saw him ahead among the boulders. "Hello stranger," I said.

After another day of intense hiking and climbing, we made it to the mouth of the Middle Fork. We pulled out our raft, and I crossed the river along with my pack. Phil pulled the raft back across with the fly line and followed. Phil admitted that he was spooked when he looked down and could see the bottom in the deep pool. Because of the unusual cold snap, pieces of ice were floating in the river.

Glad to be out, we walked up to the Stoddard Bridge and crossed over the main Salmon. We stuck out our thumbs and got picked up by an older

Phil, left, and John hiking back down the Middle Fork of the Salmon, 1974.

guy who was going as far as North Fork. He told us it had been the coldest spring he'd ever seen. From there, we hitched a ride on U.S. Highway 93 over Lost Trail Pass, into the Bitterroot, and back to Missoula on March 28.

We'd passed the "impassable canyon," and survived to tell about it without a single injury. I still haven't run into anyone who has repeated our feat, but I'd like to. Dr. Hornocker hadn't heard of anyone else doing it. Were we the first? It seems unlikely, but who knows? As King Solomon said, "There's nothing new under the sun." But we enjoyed thinking we might have been the first.

Over the years, each spring we returned to the Middle Fork to savor its solitude and snow-free landscape. On one trip, we made it about eight or nine miles upstream on the east side of the river to Parrott Placer Camp, named for the eccentric prospector, Earl Parrott. We brought along maps and a pamphlet on the history of the Middle Fork, and we fly-fished and relaxed on the sandy beach.

About a year later, I got the wild idea to try to negotiate the entire 104-mile Middle Fork by ski, snowshoe, and foot from the headwaters near

Bear Valley Creek to the mouth on the main Salmon. This would require more than twenty miles of skiing just to reach the trailhead, then on to Sheepeater Hot Springs. After we eventually dropped below the snow level, maybe another twenty miles, we would burn our skis and snowshoes and continue hiking down the trail to Big Creek. From there, we'd scramble down the last seventeen miles of the "impassable canyon" (like Phil and I did) to the Stoddard Pack Bridge. From there, we'd hitchhike back to town. It was the perfect plan. Unfortunately, I found a person who was as reckless as I was.

I've tried, but I honestly can't remember his name. This guy was big and strong, and a phenomenal hiker. He told me that he could "keep up with anyone forever on dry land." He wasn't very experienced on snowshoes, however, and had no winter experience in the backcountry. Regardless, we planned the trip and set aside a week in late March to complete it. Of course, we weren't familiar with the upper Middle Fork country and had no idea how rugged it was, or how much snow to expect, or even how many river crossings were before us.

He and his girlfriend were both from New England. She volunteered to drop us off at the head of the drainage near Stanley, Idaho, in the Sawtooth Range. The day we arrived, deep snow covered the area, but we followed the plowed Bear Valley access road to a snowmobile trailhead. My friend and I unloaded our gear, eager to begin our trek. His girlfriend drove away, and the two of us mushed down the unplowed road toward the Boundary Creek Trailhead.

It didn't take long for our plan to unravel.

We made maybe ten miles along the deeply snowed-in access road that first day and camped. The temperature dove well below zero. The next morning, already spooked by the cold, we continued but began to have problems. I was using Phil's racing skis (see Chapter 3) because they were disposable. But I needed them to work at least until we dropped out of the snowpack. Those skis were just plain bad luck. After all the trouble they'd given Phil, you'd think I'd have known better. One of the skis, which Phil had broken going into Heart Lake, already sported a plastic replacement tip. As I trudged through the deep snow, it broke again. I pulled the plastic tip off the broken piece and put it on what was left of the ski. Between the

John (sitting on snowbank) and companion marvel at the deep snowpack on the Bear Valley access road.

deep snow and the bitter cold, my friend wasn't feeling so good about the trip, and it worried him to see my ski break. I assured him it didn't matter, I was doing fine, and if everything worked out, we'd be burning our skis and snowshoes in three or four days anyway.

We reached Boundary Creek Campground near dusk the second day and noted that we had fifteen miles to go to reach Sheepeater Hot Springs. But the temperature had plunged well below zero again, and that really unnerved my companion. We dug down through the snow and squeezed into an outhouse and shivered through the night. It provided shelter but no warmth. This was supposed to be a "spring" trip. I kept thinking that, after we dropped 1,000 feet in the Middle Fork Canyon, the weather would break and it would be spring-like, like it was on my previous trips.

By the time morning came, my friend had developed a serious case of "cold feet." I convinced him to at least go for a few more miles, since we weren't far from the trail junction that led us down the Middle Fork. We

John's companion pauses at a sign indicating that Sheepeater Hot Springs is thirteen miles distant.

followed the snowed-in trail through spruce and fir. We reached a sign that read, "Sheepeater Hot Springs 13 Miles," which was encouraging—a hot soak sounded good. We mushed another mile or two.

Finally, my friend decided he'd had enough. He said he could keep up with anyone forever on dry ground, but this kind of trekking just wasn't for him. He was a very proud and accomplished guy, and I know it bothered him to be the one to pull the plug.

He later told me that watching the ski snap was part of the reason he wanted to turn around. Between that, the cold, and the 100-plus-mile length of the trip, he was just plain spooked and worried that we couldn't make it safely.

Of course, I didn't want to give up. But I will always be thankful my friend called it off. A lot of things needed to go right for us to make the entire trip, and things were already off to an inauspicious start.

We turned around and headed back toward Boundary Creek in our packed trail. Luckily for us, some snowmobilers had ridden into the campground. We flagged down the zooming riders and asked for a ride when they headed back out the access road. We plodded up the road, and when they caught up to us, they picked us up. In fact, we rode on the sleds most of the way back to the plowed parking lot. From that day on, I've always had a soft spot in my heart for snowmobilers.

From the parking lot, we hitched a ride to the highway near Stanley and then on back to town. This aborted trip turned out to be my last foray to the Middle Fork of the Salmon. I loved the place, but I guess I finally got it out of my system. And for once, the "impassable canyon" had lived up to its name. ❧

CHAPTER 6

Second Chance in the Scapegoat
I finally get my wilderness bull

I've always been a casual hunter. My dad bought me a 6mm Remington in 1971 and I've hunted with it ever since. Never did much shooting, just enough to sight the rifle in each fall. I should have been more responsible; that is, practiced more and taken better care of the rifle. Had I done that, I'd have been much more successful.

But I am a dedicated "nature-hunter." I thought of it like this: I'm not that much of a marksman or hunter and I have cheap gear, but if I hike in far enough the people would be few and the animals would be less wary.

In the mid-1970s, each fall I hiked into the Scapegoat Wilderness to hunt for deer and elk. The early rifle season opened in mid-September, nearly two weeks before classes started at the University of Montana. I felt free and a bit daring because I rarely saw anyone else.

It was a seven-mile hike into my spot, past Heart Lake and nearly to Webb Lake, about fourteen miles due north of Lincoln as the raven flies. That time of year, the weather was usually gorgeous, what we quaintly called "Indian summer."

I got the idea to hunt in this spot one late spring as my friends and I skied across the Scapegoat in a big traverse. I saw the slopes of nice pine and fir parklands, and it just looked like great elk country. The terrain was gentle, and for a fit person and former wrestler, it wasn't too far from the trailhead. With a lot of oomph, you could pack out pieces of elk on your back if you were lucky enough to get one. It seemed the perfect place— remote enough to discourage others from hunting on foot, but too close to civilization for outfitters headed deeper into the wilderness.

I didn't know much about hunting elk in the backcountry. Terry and I had bagged one bull in the fall of 1973 in the Bob, and I bagged a cow elk later that same year in the general season. Terry was gone now, so I hunted the Scapegoat by myself. I loved to be alone in the wilderness, especially doing something as exciting as hunting elk. My friends thought it was too far in, and the pack-out would be excruciating. As I discovered, they were right about the packing out. In part, that's the price you pay to hunt in wilderness. By definition, it's beyond road's end. One particular hunt levied that price and more.

I left town one fine September day and pointed my VW Bug past Lincoln to the Heart Lake Trailhead. Following the gentle, wide trail through the lodgepole, past Heart Lake, I reached Ringeye Creek, which drains the Bob's highest peak. Red Mountain rises to 9,411 feet, and it is one huge mountain, a fat, rust-colored hump trending north to south. I set up my camp at about 6,000 feet in the shadow of the mountain. In the wild solitude, I felt a kinship with Lewis and Clark; I was in ecstasy.

The mornings were cold, but the afternoons were sunny and cool on most of the three days I hunted. I'd killed a mule deer in this area before but hadn't yet harvested an elk. On this trip, though, it all came together.

On about the second evening hunt, I stalked up the parkland ridge, going from tree to tree, looking for elk. I'd seen tracks the day before and got a glimpse of the tail end of an elk. The semi-open country up the ridge featured flatter benches that looked like great habitat. Each time I reached a bench, I peeked into another nice, grassy flat. Thick lodgepole covered the back side of the ridge. It was classic edge habitat that wildlife favor—cover and forage close together. Aldo Leopold, who coined the "edge effect" in wildlife ecology, would have approved.

As I walked, I scanned ahead but also watched my step, trying to move quietly. Suddenly, looking up, there they were—a nice spike bull elk (legal then) and a cow. The pair stood broadside to me at about thirty yards. My thoughts raced: I'm going to get this bull; he will be packable because he's a yearling; the meat will be incredible; I can piece him up right here and hang the quarters in the big branches of a tree, come back after them and get them down to camp, then start the several-day pack out.

The two elk stood rock-still, staring at me. I raised my rifle, put the scope on the bull, and pulled the trigger. Boom! I expected him to fall, but the two elk bolted over the ridge into the timber. How I missed him,

I had no idea, and still don't. There was no trace of blood. To blow such an awesome opportunity on a wilderness bull after all the work to have this chance was completely deflating. I was sure I'd never get a chance like that again.

I didn't see any more elk as I hunted back to camp, getting there about dark. I felt crushed. I slept little that night, beating myself up about the lost opportunity. I wondered if I'd ever take a wilderness bull.

The next morning, I woke just before dawn. As I readied my pack, I heard a bugle. Then another bugle, and another. It sounded like two bulls bugling at each other, not far from camp, not up on the ridge but up a little valley right above my camp. This seemed uncannily similar to my hunt with Terry, where those early morning bugles drew him up the ridge. This time, though, I could hear them.

I stalked toward the bugling, which came from a willow wetland and meadow. Two bulls, both branch-antlered, held forth at opposite ends of the meadow, surrounded by brush, bugling at each other. I could see that the bull on the far end of the meadow was "huge," in my mind at least. But there was no opportunity for a shot.

The larger elk must've caught my scent—he bolted and ran. The smaller bull, a five-point "raghorn," also ran from the meadow, but he came obliquely toward me into the open lodgepole where he caught up with a small herd of cows and turned broadside, about sixty yards from me.

I held the crosshairs on the young bull and fired. This time, the bull stumbled and lurched into the lodgepole to my right. He didn't travel far though, because my little 100-grain 6mm bullet had pierced his lungs.

I had gone from the depths of despair to the pinnacle of joy and excitement. I had missed a spike but bagged a beautiful five-point bull elk in the Scapegoat Wilderness. It was one of the happiest moments of my young life. It was also a good life lesson: don't feel bad about missing an opportunity because a better one may soon present itself. There was a reason I missed the spike bull the previous evening. It was just meant to be.

My bull lay in the beargrass under the lodgepole, a gorgeous sight. But soon reality began to set in. *Wow, this is a huge animal,* I thought. *And I'm about seven miles from the trailhead. And I have a cheap backpack with marginal straps to pack it out.* Some people would call me crazy right then, and they'd be right. But at that moment I was glad to be crazy.

I field-dressed the bull and started quartering him. I did my best to pack the fewest bones out as possible. But I'd found in my limited experience that the meat maintained its quality much better if you left the hams on the bone and allowed them to cool before carving them off later.

John's bull elk in the Scapegoat Wilderness.

I left the meat and hide on the two rear legs. This made up the majority of the best meat. I boned out everything else: the front quarters, neck meat, backstrap, and so on. It was early afternoon before I finished the job. I decided to head out with a load that afternoon, then hike back in empty and stay at my camp that night. That meant I had fourteen miles to cover before dark.

I hung most of the elk and started for the trailhead with one rear leg and the rack, at least eighty pounds. That was about 60 percent of my own body weight. It was punishing. After a few miles, my back and shoulders were burning, so I shifted the weight to my lower torso by tightening the hip belt. I cinched it progressively tighter to bear more weight, which relieved my shoulders but pulled on my waist and hips.

An elk quarter and the rack, ready to be packed out.

Each mile or two, I sat down on the slope above the trail, balanced the backpack, and took the weight off my body. I didn't remove the pack because it was so hard to get it up on my shoulders again. The trail seemed like a torture tunnel through the lodgepole.

The hip belt was like a tourniquet, and oddly, my groin went numb. But soon everything hurt equally, and I pushed on to the trailhead, stopping occasionally to ease the load. Never had I been so happy to see my VW, and I felt I was floating after easing the meat and rack down under the hood (where the trunk is located on a Bug). Then I turned and headed back to my camp, making it just before dark, thoroughly exhausted. The next day, I awoke aching all over but packed out another load, once again cinching my hip belt to the point that my groin went numb. Then again I returned to camp.

Packing out yet another load, I ran into a game warden who was riding in to check outfitter camps farther into the wilderness. He quizzed me about where I got the elk. I described the area, and he seemed satisfied that I'd in fact killed the bull well within the early rifle season hunting boundary. He rode on without asking me to show him to the kill site. He must've believed me and probably felt it was a bit irresponsible to shoot a bull that far in without horses or friends to pack it out. By then I too was having my doubts. Later, an outfitter rode past me, heading out with pack stock. He didn't offer to help pack the elk, and I didn't ask.

On the third and last day, I headed out from camp with the final load of boned meat and my camping gear. By then, I'd had enough of meat packing for a while. It was definitely one of the toughest things I've ever done, especially the mental aspect. But it felt amazing to drive my Bug loaded with elk meat away from the trailhead. I'd done it; I'd killed a bull elk in the Scapegoat Wilderness and packed it out on my back.

I couldn't help thinking about the hunt Terry and I had shared in the Bob when he killed his beautiful wilderness bull elk. Now, I was lucky enough to have taken my own.

Back home, my whole body ached for several days—not surprising considering I'd packed more than 200 pounds of meat and gear a total of thirty-five miles over the course of three days. I was motivated. Definitely motivated. But also crazy. Definitely crazy.

A few days of rest and some aspirin took care of most of my aches, and the soreness from the shoulder straps and hip belt gradually subsided. But one problem remained: the swelling of blood vessels in my groin—specifically my scrotum. It seemed different than any hernia, and was worrisome enough that I finally went over to the health service to get it checked.

"What can we do for you?" asked the young woman at the reception desk. I told her I needed to see a doctor. She asked what was wrong, and I said that I'd rather keep that between me and the doctor. She said that was fine. I was relieved because it would have been embarrassing to explain my problem to a woman. A nurse led me into an exam room. I didn't share my problem with her either. After about ten minutes, the doctor walked in.

She greeted me and asked what my issue was.

I was immediately anxious and embarrassed, not just because of the location of my problem but because I'd never taken off my clothes in front of a woman doctor. I didn't know what to do, so I blurted, "I guess I should've told the receptionist that I'd like to see a male doctor."

She seemed a little hurt. No doubt she worked hard to get through medical school and had faced sexism constantly. In a slightly defensive voice, she said, "I'm perfectly capable of handling whatever problem you might have." She mistakenly thought that I preferred a male doctor because I was sexist, which was definitely not the case. Competency was not the issue. She added, "I can ask that a male doctor see you if you insist." Right then and there I decided that I wanted to support this young woman, and I regretted that she felt I didn't value her because of her gender.

"No," I said, "You'll be fine." She asked me what my problem was and I told her: my scrotum had some swelling and maybe some enlarged blood vessels. She asked me to drop my pants so she could take a look, which I did. The young doctor examined me carefully and seemed mystified. As I remember it, she said, "I've never seen anything like this." Not exactly what a young man wants to hear. Then she said, "I'll have to get another doctor to take a look."

She left the room and soon returned with an older male doctor. He examined me and said I had a varicocele—a swelling and distension of veins in the scrotum, sometimes caused by injury or trauma. It's hard to say just why hauling those loads had impacted me like that, but there was definitely trauma involved in packing out that elk.

The doctor said in serious cases, surgery was called for, but didn't feel it was warranted. I'd just have to live with it He told me that sometimes the condition can limit fertility, but only time would tell.

So I'd killed a beautiful wilderness bull elk, but, indirectly, that elk got revenge. Thankfully, the fertility issue never developed, although I had to wait years to find out. I have two brilliant sons, both over six feet tall, and a genius daughter. They are all great athletes.

I think I got the best of that bull after all. →

CHAPTER 7

White River Interlude

Great fun on the first survey of South Fork Flathead River tributaries

Some backcountry trips start with an omen of things to come.
In late August 1981, I led a crew of fisheries workers into the Bob Marshall Wilderness to conduct the first biological surveys on the tributaries of the South Fork of the Flathead River. It didn't start out well. My crew included administrators from Helena (Pat) and Bozeman (Fred), and our solid Flathead fisheries crew: Rick, Tom, Jay (who we called Mario), and Mark.

Our packers were a nice couple from Nyack, Cork and Linda (Robertson) Hill. They knew horses and stock and turned out to be great packers and charming companions. From the beginning, they thought we were a little off. In fact, by the end of the eighty-mile trip, Linda said that we were so strange that she planned to write a book about us. I don't think she meant that as a compliment. But she never wrote the book.

The trip required a big shuttle. We unloaded the horses and all the gear at Owl Creek Packer Camp near Holland Lake. Then Jay, Tom, and I moved the horse trailers and a few other vehicles to Meadow Creek Gorge, upstream from Spotted Bear, the trailhead where we would exit the Bob. On the return trip, we stopped around midnight for hamburgers in Columbia Falls. It was 2 A.M. when the three of us arrived back at Owl Creek after driving more than 300 miles to complete the shuttle. While we did the shuttle, the rest of the crew headed up to Upper Holland Lake to camp for the night.

The three of us laid our sleeping bags out on the ground at Owl Creek and planned on getting a 6 A.M. start to cover the six miles to Upper Holland Lake and join the rest of the crew before they moved out for Gordon Pass. Already, Jay and Tom felt queasy.

The rumbling in Tom's and Jay's stomachs was a bad sign when they woke up at 5:30 A.M. We hoisted our packs and started up the steep, dusty trail to Upper Holland Lake, but Jay and Tom were so sick that they got down on their knees and just tried to survive their nausea. Each time Jay expelled some of the previous night's hamburger, a cloud of dust would rise around his head. We had no choice but to keep going because most of our gear was with the pack train up ahead. I'd avoided the food poisoning.

Somehow Tom and Jay kept going, counting on catching the crew before they broke camp and headed over Gordon Pass. Jay hoped some coffee or tea might help his stomach. I think more than anything he was looking for some sympathy. We humped up the switchbacks through subalpine fir and open meadows and reached our crew's campsite at the upper end of the lake just as they were saddled up and pulling out. We felt for Jay, but all we could do was fall in behind them and keep moving to our next campsite nine miles distant. Our surveys would begin that afternoon.

We trudged over Gordon Pass and descended to Shaw Cabin on Gordon Creek, a major tributary of the South Fork of the Flathead River. We set up camp below the ranger station in the beautiful little meadow known as Shirttail Park. The drainage was timbered with lodgepole, spruce, and fir, plus some scattered larch. At that time, before a big fire swept the area, it was a deep, dark, basin.

Gordon Creek flowed gently through conifer-rimmed Shirttail Park, and it held surprisingly large westslope cutthroat. Seven years earlier, I had caught some sixteen-inch cutts here, and mountain whitefish as well.

That afternoon of August 25, we divided into crews and started conducting our stream measurements on several sections of the creek. We also began the snorkel surveys. Snorkeling these clear, fish-filled streams is an experience no biologist should miss. After squeezing into a wetsuit, you start snorkeling at the downstream end of the section and pull yourself upstream. The sample sections are usually 150 meters long and take in different stream features such as pools, runs, and riffles. When you stick your head in the water, the submerged world opens before you with stunning clarity. Since fish orient themselves to face upstream (to feed on whatever the current delivers to them), you see the river from a trout's perspective.

John in a wetsuit, snorkeling to count fish.

Amazingly, the fish, when approached from behind, stay in their positions and can be easily counted and classified by approximate year class (young-of-the-year, yearlings, three-year-olds, and older). In a productive stream, more than 100 cutthroat can be counted in a single section. Where woody debris rests in the stream, the fish use it for cover but can still be seen by the snorkeler.

A person walks along the bank with the snorkeler and records the data at stopping points. Sometimes, the snorkeler records the fish counts on a slate, but that's more difficult. Cutthroat are easy to count because they hover suspended in the water above the substrate (streambed). Bull trout juveniles are much harder to count because they hug the rocks and substrate.

John looking for fish in a log jam.

We counted big numbers of fish while snorkeling in

95

the two reaches of upper Gordon Creek. In the 150-meter uppermost reach (Reach 4), I served as snorkeler and Rick recorded the data. We began at 2:30 P.M. with an air temperature of 81 F. and a water temp of 56 F.

After about ninety minutes, we'd completed the count. In Reach 4, I counted a stunning 224 westslope cutthroat trout, 8 juvenile bull trout, and 21 adult mountain whitefish. This count was a bit inflated because it included a pool at the foot of the waterfall where about 60 cutts were pooled up. I even saw one mature bull trout spawner. This upper reach measured 27 to 46 feet wide and only 8 to 20 inches deep.

In Reach 3 downstream, the count added up to 116 cutthroat, 45 juvenile bull trout, and 17 mountain whitefish. These counts in upper Gordon Creek showed amazing numbers of fish in such a modest-sized stream.

As part of our stream surveys, we also measured all the physical characteristics: flow, width, average substrate size, and amount of instream cover. For each reach, we completed two different stream habitat rating forms.

In Reach 4, there is a cascade and waterfall where George Creek enters Gordon Creek, and in the falls pool we easily caught about 30 westslope cutthroat trout via fly-fishing. We measured the fish and collected a few scales from each one and placed them in a scale envelope. This was a good sample for analyzing the growth rings or "annuli" on the scales, which would be counted later in the lab.

After our surveys, as we sat around the campfire, Pat announced that he had re-injured his bad ankle and would have to hike back out. Luckily, we had driven his little Ford pickup as one of our shuttle return vehicles, so it awaited him at the Owl Creek Packer Camp. Pat, the fisheries chief, was our first "casualty."

The next morning, we said goodbye to Pat and headed down the Gordon Creek Trail. My crew would travel twelve miles down to the confluence with the South Fork of the Flathead, then four more miles down the South Fork to a campsite at Cayuse Prairie near Big Prairie.

Since we wouldn't be retracing our steps, I planned to collect scales from cutthroat in Gordon Creek near Cardinal Creek and the Cardinal Peak Trail. As I walked down the drainage, I felt the excitement of surveying these streams as I had hoped to for years. Gordon Creek flows strong, even in late summer, and the cutthroat trout were plentiful. The ridges and peaks of Una and Bullet Nose framed the drainage to the north, and through the heavy timber I caught occasional views of Cardinal, Kid, Gordon, Fossil, and Pilot Mountains to the south.

At the Cardinal Peak Trail, I cut off from the crew and dropped down to Gordon Creek and began fishing. The cutthroat cooperated really well; it was one of those mornings that somehow signaled to the fish that it was time to feed. Maybe they could feel autumn coming on and were instinctively loading up on calories to prepare for winter.

It took me a few hours to catch, take scale samples, and release 43 westslope cutthroat trout in about a half mile of Gordon Creek. I carefully tucked the scale envelopes in my pack and continued down the trail to rejoin my crew, who by then had probably reached the South Fork of the Flathead River.

As I headed down the trail, I walked into a small surprise that gave me a big thrill. I heard the growl of a plane overhead, and I soon broke out of the timber into a little meadow where I could see the events unfolding above. A small fire had broken out on Kid Mountain to the south. As I looked across the canyon, toward the smoke, I enjoyed the rare opportunity to watch several smokejumpers, chutes deployed, float down to the upper ridge. What amazing skills and courage these airborne firefighters have! I didn't know it then, but soon my crew and I would also be in the middle of a wildfire.

As a base for our surveys of Youngs, Danaher, and lower Gordon Creeks, we used the Big Prairie camp near Brownstone Creek known as Cayuse Prairie, sometimes called Smoke's Camp. We'd be staying there a few days. We divided into three two-person crews to get our work done. The surveys went smoothly in these clear, productive tributaries that support native cutthroat, mountain whitefish, and juvenile bull trout.

We also sampled the South Fork of the Flathead River in the Brownstone Creek area. We caught cutthroat at a good rate and collected scales to get an idea of fish growth and numbers, and snorkeled the river and counted fish. The crew completed snorkel surveys on Danaher and Youngs and found moderate cutthroat densities. We also measured streamflow in cubic feet per second (cfs) for each tributary. (To visualize a single cubic foot, picture

The South Fork of the Flathead River near the camp upstream from Big Prairie Ranger Station.

a basketball. Then you can imagine a streamflow of, say, 20 cfs as twenty basketballs going by every second.)

It had been a dry August. The Kid Mountain Fire, small and in the rocks, had kicked up after an evening or two of lightning. So far, we had been lucky, and we hoped that we could get our surveys done and head down the South Fork before a big blaze started. Then a low-intensity blaze broke out not far from our camp, in the flats upstream from Big Prairie. It had burned slowly for a day or two and remained mostly a ground fire.

I was upriver when a Forest Service employee walked into our camp that evening and cautioned the crew about the fire. Mark, always helpful and enthusiastic, announced: "We work for the state, we'd be happy to help fight the fire!" Happy or not, we were now committed. My crew informed me of the situation when I arrived at camp a little later, and I realized that it would be an adventure. This trip was full of surprises.

The Forest Service gave us tools, mainly Pulaskis and shovels, and protective shirts. I don't think any of us had ever fought fire, but it actually turned out to be fun. We worked all night putting out hotspots in the lodgepole and meadows. It turned out to be not much of a fire, and the feds cut us loose the next morning. (About a month later, we all received small federal checks for our efforts.)

We finished the upper drainage surveys over the next few days. I lingered at the gorgeous junction of Youngs and Danaher Creeks, where they become the South Fork of the Flathead. In that very dry year, the flow measured just 100 cfs.

We then completed our measurements on Youngs, Danaher, and the lower section of Gordon Creek. These stream reaches supported limited numbers, but larger cutthroat. We grabbed samples from 23 cutthroat in the river at the Big Prairie area and eventually delivered them to the University of Montana genetics lab. Fortunately, to our delight, they proved to be pure westslope cutthroat.

On August 27, Tom and I snorkeled the South Fork of the Flathead from Butcher Creek upstream to the mouth of Gordon Creek. It was a sunny day, with perfect light conditions for counting fish underwater. When we started, it was already 60 F., and the water was 56 F.; that's not bad for the South Fork headwaters. We snorkeled a 3,000-meter stretch of stream that had a reputation for holding lots of fish. That reputation proved to be exactly right.

I stuck my head in the stream, and the view was calming and beautiful. Over the next four hours, we counted 148 cutthroat of various ages, mostly age-two and age-three-plus, hefty numbers for the headwaters area. And with only two snorkelers in the river, we weren't seeing all the fish. We also saw 766 whitefish, mostly adults. We even saw 2 juvenile bulls.

We saw so many fish that when we were done, I saw whitefish and cutthroat when I closed my eyes. The upper South Fork is a salmonid paradise. The biggest treat of all was 3 lunker bulls I saw that had migrated upstream from Hungry Horse Reservoir and were no doubt ready to enter their natal tributary to spawn. One 30-inch fish rocketed downstream right past me. I'll admit he scared me a little. It was great to be in this secret, underwater world.

We had completed the upper portion of the drainage, and on about our sixth day out, under a beautiful summery sky, we began moving our operation downstream along the South Fork. Our next major camp was seven miles downstream at the confluence of the White River in a beautiful series of ponderosa pine meadows known as Murphy Flat. The spot is named for wilderness pioneer Joe Murphy, who, with a rare special permit, operated a guest lodge here in the heart of the Bob for many years, starting before 1920.

We pulled into the White River campsite in early afternoon. So far, Cork and Linda Hill had done a great job with the stock, packing our equipment and camp. We hadn't had a single problem with the horses, a great testament to Cork and Linda's skill.

But Fred was suffering from a digestive disorder, probably giardiasis. He struggled to walk from Big Prairie to the White River camp. When we arrived, we put Fred in a separate tent for obvious reasons. He crawled in and we didn't see him much for a couple of days.

We planned to stay about four days in the White River area, using the beautiful campsite as a base to survey Little Salmon and Big Salmon Creeks and a couple sections of the White River. We also hoped to collect scales from the river-dwelling westslope cutthroat in the South Fork of the Flathead, and do another snorkel fish count.

A beautiful hole stretches across the South Fork of the Flathead where the White River comes in. Incredibly clear, the hole teems with fish. Mountain whitefish nearly pave the bottom of the hole's tail, and westslope cutthroat crowd throughout the water column near the middle reach and upstream end. We saw a few large bull trout migrants that had come upstream from Hungry Horse Reservoir and were preparing to spawn in South Fork tributaries over the next month. I couldn't wait to snorkel here.

We caught many cutthroat in the Flathead at the confluence, and collected a good sample of scales. Fred, an expert fly-angler, felt a little better, and he showed us how to use an additional dropper fly on the leader. He sometimes caught two fish at a time. We were impressed.

We collected scales from caught-and-released cutthroat in each stretch of the river. All told, we caught 151 cutthroat in 40.5 "angler hours" (one angler fishing one hour), for a catch rate of 3.7 fish per hour in the river from Gordon Creek downstream to Little Salmon Creek. These westslope cutthroat averaged 9.1 inches, almost exactly the same size found in a 1961 quick sample of 80 fish. (In 1983, two years after our survey, regulations were changed to protect cutthroat over 12 inches, and the average size has since increased.)

We surveyed the targeted tributaries with two crews of two people each. Most of the crew headed downstream the next morning to begin surveying sections of Big Salmon and Little Salmon Creeks for habitat measurements and fish numbers. These are both large streams and would be physically demanding to complete. Cork and Linda packed their wetsuits and equipment and went along to help. Fred, still a bit queasy, stayed at the river camp and collected scale samples from river cutthroat. He also tossed the pants he'd been wearing on the campfire.

On August 31, a partly cloudy, 60 F. day, Jay and I snorkeled the Flathead from the White River downstream 3,000 meters, beginning with the wide and beautiful run right where the White dumped in.

The river temperature was a "balmy" 56 F. The clear, underwater world opened up before us as we carefully snorkeled downstream in this larger reach. We began our count at 1:30 p.m. and snorkeled 2,131 meters of run features and 868 meters of riffle features. The water was as clear as pure air, so beautiful.

The stream averaged 22 meters wide in the fourteen runs surveyed, and 35 meters wide in the eleven riffles. We counted and classified by age 45 westslope cutthroat, 57 mountain whitefish less than 6 inches in length, and 368 whitefish greater than 6 inches.

With only two snorkelers, we knew that we were seeing only a portion of the fish in such a large stream, but it would serve as a good baseline, and gave us a sense of the ratio of cutthroat to whitefish. Interestingly, all the cutthroat we observed were larger (three years and older).

By the time Jay and I finished the section, we were shivering a little, but it was worth it. For three hours, we'd had an osprey's-eye view of the secret, underwater world in this remote, pristine river. The cutthroat and whitefish seemed to live in total harmony. They divided up the stream, with the whitefish mostly on the bottom and the cutthroat up in the water column. And the whitefish seemed to hang in the lower part of each run, with some even in the riffles.

We went back to camp to warm up, but I knew we were running out of time to survey both sections of the White River. The crew had already measured the physical characteristics and estimated streamflow of the White's lower section, so I pulled myself away from the campfire and pulled my wetsuit on again. It was after 5 p.m., but the afternoon was bright, and the sun glinted into the stream's water column. I planned to snorkel the section just upstream from camp, a low-gradient channel typical of the habitat of the entire five-mile reach upstream to the forks of the White River.

The White River is unlike any other stream I've seen. The water appears bleached, chalky white, as it flows over bright, white, cobbles that have eroded from the limestone escarpment of the Chinese Wall about six miles upstream along the Continental Divide. But in reality, these waters are clear as glass. When you slip beneath the surface and view it from the fish's perspective, the river comes alive.

The White River takes its name from the predominance of pale cobblestones lining its bed.

I began pulling myself up carefully along the bottom of the stream, noting the species of fish and their approximate size class and age. Cutthroat are a little like chameleons, taking on the hues of their surrounding substrate and water. These fish were the classic "green backs" with silvery sides typical of pure westslope cutthroat, but these definitely had a paler cast to them compared to fish in any other stream I'd snorkeled. Whenever I looked ahead to some sort of cover—a log or rock outcrop—I'd see a few fish congregated there. In this stream filled with loose cobbles, cover was at a premium. Every so often, a mountain whitefish came into view.

Even on this mild, last day of August, the water's chill penetrated me and made me shiver. I've always been "body-fat challenged," so that doesn't help. The chill does make you feel closer to the fish. It's easy to understand that when fish are lifted out of the water, going from 40 or 50 degrees to 70 degrees, they suffer extreme temperature stress. I was experiencing the same effect, but in reverse.

I continued pulling myself slowly upstream, stopping briefly to emerge from the water at intervals to record the results. It took ninety minutes to snorkel the 150-meter section. Despite the cold, I was in the groove and completely in the moment. The fish count piled up. You would never know that these shallow, choppy waters could support such a diversity of ages of cutthroat; I even saw some tiny, young-of-the-year fish. Even the stream edge and undercut banks held a few fish. I counted as many whitefish as cutthroat. In the final run, I saw 2 small whitefish and 15 lunkers.

I reached the upstream end of the snorkel section, climbed out of the stream, and recorded the last few fish. When it was all said and done, I'd counted 23 westslope cutthroat in three different age classes and 22 whitefish.

I noticed an outfitter camped just above the section. One of his wranglers, a young woman, had watched me snorkel part of the section. After changing into clothes, I walked into their camp to say hello and explain what I was doing. The folks at the camp seemed interested. They invited me to stand near the fire and warm up. That felt great.

Then another young wrangler walked up to the fire. I was surprised to see that it was Kevin, a brother to one of my fellow graduate students when I'd been at Montana State University. With this connection, I got an invitation for dinner, which would be ready soon. How could I refuse?

And what a dinner it was. The jovial young crew was preparing zucchini spaghetti and a big salad, too. After about ten days in the wilderness, this dinner was stupefyingly good. I felt a little guilty to be treated to this homey repast when my crew would not have anything close. But I enjoyed the fun interlude with these happy folks, including a trail-blazing young woman who was obviously seen by the others as an equal. Since then, I've always loved spaghetti with zucchini.

The next morning, my crew packed up and prepared to head downstream to the Black Bear Ranger Station where they would picket the horses and spend a last night in the wilderness. I wanted to snorkel the upper White River toward Needle Falls to round out our sampling on this unique stream.

Understandably, after eleven long days of effort, the crew could smell the barn and wanted to head downriver so that we could exit the wilderness the next day. But I just couldn't let the White River go. I was already in there, I had my wetsuit, and the thought of snorkeling this unique stream was irresistible. I knew the river pretty well. I'd spent a few days along it in the 1970s, and I'd surveyed the stream by helicopter to break it into reaches just a few months before this trip. I was already attached to it.

Mark and I had done the physical inventory of the upper reach of the White River (Reach 2) on August 30, but even he declined to go with me. So I decided to hike the five miles to the White River forks and snorkel Reach 2 of the stream alone. Then I would hustle back fourteen miles down the South Fork to catch up with my crew at Black Bear Cabin that evening. If all went well, I could complete the White River survey and still reach the cabin by dark. I said goodbye to the crew and headed up the White River. Traveling light, with just my wetsuit and fish gear, I didn't take much food.

At five miles, I reached the forks of the White River. The South Fork of the White drains the south end of the Chinese Wall and the range known as the Flathead Alps. I swung up the North Fork of the White toward Needle Falls, between Rampart Mountain and the backside of the Chinese Wall. I used a measuring tape to mark a 150-meter section.

The water was 51 F., which doesn't sound bad, but that's a little chilly, especially given that the air temperature was only 54 F., with intermittent clouds. I pulled on my bright yellow wetsuit and neoprene booties and stuck my head in the water. The water clarity yielded a stunning underwater view. Cutthroat trout held themselves facing upstream in the water column,

The White River near the confluence of the North and South Forks.

darting here and there to grab aquatic insects that the current delivered to them. I knew it would be nip-and-tuck to get the survey done and reach my crew by nightfall, but I was so captivated that I didn't care.

The crystal-clear water, occasional beams of sunlight, and submerged cobbles with scattered boulders combined for an almost mystical view, a swirling contrast of light and shadow. Fish came in and out of sharp focus as they hovered in the water column, moving in and out of the underwater sunbeams. We call this type of feature "pocket water" because of the way it flows around and over boulders, creating little mini-pools.

The thought hit me that I was probably the first hominid over the millennia to ever explore the underwater side of this remote stretch of stream with a good wetsuit, mask, and snorkel. This upper reach was deeper and less bleached looking than the lower five miles. Up here, the stream bottom looked more stable, and trout cover was more abundant. I could tell right away as I began the count that the fish density would be higher here than in the lower reach. I was so glad that I didn't miss documenting it.

It's so quiet when you are submerged in a mountain stream; you become a part of it. I counted cutthroat clustered behind rocks, some in the shadows, some illuminated by intermittent sunbeams from the sides and above. These fish had a slightly deeper background color because of the darker substrate.

It was fun to think about where I was and what I was doing. I was dragging myself, submerged, up a stream that drains the most remote backcountry in Montana, counting native cutthroat and whitefish that have resided here virtually unaltered for thousands of generations. How do you beat that?

The cutthroat in this stretch were nearly all age-three and above. I noted a few that probably measured 16 inches; they looked like whales through my mask, which makes everything look bigger. I saw whitefish hovering just above the stream bottom throughout the section.

As I rounded a bend, I saw, in a run above me, something different. Westslope cutthroat are in a subgroup of true trout. They sport dark spots against a light or silvery background. But ahead of me I saw an olive-colored trout with generally light spots and white-edged pelvic fins. This "char" had to be a bull trout. As I closed in on the fish, I could confirm it. This trout was maybe 10 inches long, which would be considered a pretty large juvenile bull trout. It was not mature and would not reproduce for a few years. It was either resident in the stream, a migrant from the river, or had followed a large mature bull upstream from Hungry Horse Reservoir. I'm sure there were many more juvenile bulls in the section, but because they associate with the rocks, you rarely see them while snorkeling.

I continued snorkeling upstream toward the top of the section, adding more cutthroat to my total. Most were age-three, 8 inches and longer. It had been time consuming to classify each fish and record everything at intervals on my slate. By the time I made the upstream end of the section, I'd counted a total of 43 age three-plus cutts, 3 two-year-old cutts, and a young bull trout. For whitefish, I had a total of 29, all of them adults. What a show these native fish had put on for me. I carefully transferred the data from the slate to a Write-in-the-Rain fish inventory form. Now, more than forty years later, I'm holding that very card in my hand. The card reads: "9/1/81. Snorkeler, J. Fraley, recorder, J. Fraley."

The White River flows toward the South Fork of the Flathead, in the heart of the Bob Marshall Wilderness, as seen from Tillson Peak.

I completed the snorkel survey in about two hours. Even though it was a fairly warm day, maybe 60 degrees when I crawled out of the water, I was shivering and my teeth chattered as I sat warming up in the late afternoon sun. Wetsuits are designed to keep you "warm" by holding a water layer near your skin that's warmed by your body. But warming the water sucks away your body heat, especially for a skinny guy like me. And new cold water continually finds its way in.

By about 5 P.M., I had completed the fish count on this never-before-surveyed stream. I got out of my wetsuit and spread it on the rocks to drain. For my last task, I needed to catch 15 or 20 cutthroat to collect scale samples. This proved to be easy. I caught 15 on dry flies and wet flies in 1.3 angler hours. They ranged from 8 to 11 inches in length. I'd seen lots of larger cutts while I was snorkeling, but these were the ones that took the flies. I had my sample.

I felt really fulfilled. The unique White River deserved a thorough survey; this upper stretch was so different from the lower reaches. I relaxed on a rock along the stream and reveled in the remoteness of it all. As I got dressed, I felt so lucky.

I had eaten my last granola bar a few hours before and started feeling intensely hungry. Then it hit me—I was sitting on a rock above the forks of the White River in late afternoon, I had no food, and I had five or six miles to go down the White, then fourteen miles to Black Bear Cabin, where my crew was probably already relaxing and turning out the horses. I needed fuel to warm back up and to cover those twenty miles. I stuffed the wetsuit in my pack and headed down the trail. Just below the forks, I was surprised to see the outfitter's pack string, led by Kevin and the gal wrangler, in the distance ahead. They must have been visiting the forks area so their guests could fish the big pool at the confluence.

They seemed to be in a hurry. I didn't try to catch them to say good-bye, but at a bend in the trail the gal wrangler looked back my way and tossed something over her shoulder, kind of like throwing a treat to a dog. I thought, "Did I just see what I thought I saw?"

I hiked along and reached the spot where I thought I saw her toss the object. There in the middle of the trail lay a Snickers candy bar. That wonderful, strong, confident young woman must have suspected that I was hungry and wanted to cut me a little break, but not too much of a break. Gosh, I wished I could have thanked her.

I moved quickly and made it back to the junction of the White River and the South Fork of the Flathead by about 7:30 P.M., where I'd left my crew eight hours earlier. I could picture them at Black Bear eating dinner on the east side of the river across from the ranger station. I figured I'd be joining them by about 11 P.M. and hoped they'd save me some leftovers.

I sped down the river trail. After about five miles, I passed Salmon Forks at the mouth of Big Salmon Creek, across the river on the west side. I continued down the trail into the heavy timber of Mud Lake Flat (it's since been cleared out by a fire). In the trees, dusk was turning to full darkness, and I stopped to dig out my flashlight. No luck—either the batteries were dead or the bulb was gone, or it got wet from my wetsuit.

It was now too dark to follow the trail, and it hit me that I wouldn't be joining my crew that night. I found a flat spot under a fir tree and curled up to spend the night. I decided not to build a fire because it had been so dry, and a fire in the duff would be hard to extinguish. I used my wetsuit bag for a pillow. It was a cool night and I didn't get much sleep, maybe two or three hours.

As soon as dawn was breaking, I sped on down the trail toward Black Bear, about five miles away. I passed Damnation Creek and then Helen Creek, then dropped into the flat across from the Black Bear Ranger Station. I reached the crew at about 7:30 A.M., just as they were packing up to head out. They hadn't been worried. In fact, I believe they secretly enjoyed knowing that I'd had to rough it. I thought I saw a trace of a smile, or maybe a smirk, on Jay's face.

Cork got me some food out of a panier, and wow it tasted good. I fell right into line with the string, and we headed for the Meadow Creek Trailhead and our vehicles that we'd dropped off a dozen days earlier. We had about eleven miles to go, and I think we were all ready to go home. -◦-

CHAPTER 8

Cutthroat in the Wild
Tracking westslope cutthroat in the heart of the Bob

As a fisheries biologist for the state, part of my job entailed monitoring and documenting the population density, health, and genetic diversity of native trout, including westslope cutthroat. Their range spans parts of Idaho, Montana, British Columbia, and Alberta, with the Bob Marshall Wilderness Complex at its heart. Early in my career, I realized that the pristine, remote headwaters of the South Fork of the Flathead River, deep in the Bob, likely held genetically pure westslope cutts. But to confirm that and learn more about their ages and growth, I had to survey them. That would require epic treks into the wilderness, carrying a pack heavy with camping gear and research tools such as a fly rod and reel, vials, envelopes to hold fish scales, and data books. It would mean selfless days away from my desk, standing in cold mountain streams endlessly casting a fly over sparkling pools and dark eddies.

It was a tough assignment, and I couldn't help but nominate myself for it.

It's important to look at many years of data to really measure the growth rate and movements of trout under differing conditions. I figured twelve years would do it. Every summer, from 1985 to 1996, I made the four- or five-day trip, twelve years in a row, kicking in lots of volunteer time. I loved it. One biologist called it "excessive monitoring." I think he was just jealous.

There's more than one route into the confluence of Youngs and Danaher Creeks—the headwaters of the South Fork—but none is shorter than about twenty-four miles. I often covered the distance in a single day, spent several days in the backcountry surveying cutts, and then hiked back out.

Most years, after collecting scales and data, I hiked out the same route I'd followed in, over Pyramid Pass or Youngs Pass. Once, I floated out the

110

South Fork; Jack Rich packed in an inflatable kayak and left it at my camp-site where Youngs and Danaher Creeks meet. Another time, I trekked up Danaher and came out near Ovando.

The clear waters of Youngs and Danaher Creeks tumble for many miles over riffles with colorful cobbles and join together to form the finest wilder-ness river in Montana. If Lewis and Clark had passed by here, they probably would have described this gorgeous, trout-filled confluence as "a singular point of geography." You can't find a "fishier"-looking confluence pool anywhere. During late-summer low water, we measured the flow of this source-pool of the South Fork at about 100 cubic feet per second. It averages a modest forty yards wide. But this gently flowing stream brims with westslope cut-throat trout, along with some mountain whitefish, sculpin, and bull trout that migrate upstream in the summer and fall.

In fact, these streams hold the largest, oldest, and most genetically pure stream-dwelling westslope cutthroat that we know of in the country. Over the twelve years of my "study," I handled 1,349 of these piscine gems, their silvery sides speckled with black spots and their chins marked by red-orange slashes on the underside. I clipped tiny bits of tissue from the fins of some of these fish for analysis at the University of Montana genetics lab. They all tested as pure westslope cutthroat. Later samples from 2010 and 2015 gave the same result.

You'd think after all the time I've spent with westslope cutthroat trout I'd have them figured out. But as I stared into those thousands of expression-less eyes over the years, they never seemed to care or even notice what I was doing. I saw them as mysterious, but they knew what they were up to. After all, they'd thrived here in the same form for thousands of years.

All of my annual trips were memorable, but a few stand out.

1991 - Cutthroat Should Be Easy to Catch,
But Sometimes They Fool You

On July 25, 1991, I left my office in Kalispell around 5 A.M., excited to hike into the South Fork headwaters again. After six consecutive annual trips, this magical area had come to feel like home. I left the Pyramid Pass Trailhead out of Seeley Lake just before 8 A.M., hiked over the pass, and continued downhill twelve miles to the confluence of Jenny and Youngs Creeks.

After a short break, I headed down the Youngs Creek Trail, and by 4 P.M. I was at Hole in the Wall, visiting with some fly-fishermen who seemed a little skeptical that I'd left the trailhead that morning and covered twenty-three miles in about eight hours. After a brief visit, I strode down the last four miles to the headwaters of the South Fork, arriving at 5:30 P.M. Sure, I was sore, and I felt the pack in my shoulders and hips. But as a so-so triathlete, I was in decent shape and the day's distance wasn't that bad. A mental challenge, really, more than anything.

That evening, however, I wrote in my data book, "Too much with a full pack in one day. Never again!" It was just a weak moment; I wasn't close to being done with these annual trips, and I knew that a little pain wouldn't keep me from challenging myself. If anything, it was a small price to pay to learn more about my "spirit fish," the indigenous westslope cutthroat trout that lived in these incredible headwaters in the center of the Bob.

As usual, I set up my camp along the South Fork a few hundred yards below the junction of Youngs and Danaher Creeks. Then I started fishing. With the late start, I managed only 1.75 angler hours in the junction area but caught 17 fish. Ten of those were large enough to tag.

The next morning, the first 6 fish I brought to my net were all under 10 inches. With my first good-sized fish I said hello to IR9278, a nice 13.2-inch trout that I'd tagged the year before. He'd grown 2.5 inches in a year, a terrific growth rate, and I was excited to see him again. I went on to catch 18 nice cutthroat as I fished down the first mile or so of the South Fork. It's a funny thing with these fish: sometimes, you catch only smaller cutthroat; other times, it's the larger ones.

After several hours of fishing the South Fork, I waded back up to fish the lower ends of Youngs and Danaher Creeks. I spent 1.33 angler hours on Danaher and sampled 15 cutts of a variety of sizes. After that, I swung over to Youngs and fished a little over an hour, catching 11 cutthroat, including one 16-inch lunker. As always, the fish favored the Adams Irresistible, Royal Wulff, and Joe's Hopper dry-fly patterns, in that order.

As it turned out, I had to work for the fish that day and I didn't catch many large ones. I'm not sure why, but I suppose the cutts had their reasons. It's almost as if they all communicate and decide what to do, but likely

John with a westslope cutthroat at the South Fork headwaters.

they're all triggered by something—a slight change in water temperature or turbidity, perhaps, or some other environmental factor. All told, I caught and worked 49 fish in just under 7 angler hours.

The next day, July 27, I had to work to catch 34 fish to complete my sample minimum of 100. While I was at it, I re-caught 4 cutthroat that I'd tagged the previous two days. No one ever said that westslope cutthroat weren't gullible. But it's not their fault.

Think of how they evolved. Westslope cutthroat live in a very unproductive environment that affords a short growing season. They've found success by grabbing every item that floats by and testing it to see if it's edible. That worked really well for them before hominids showed up. The same trait that helps them survive under limited food conditions becomes a liability when anglers dangle artificial flies in front of them. Being "easy to catch" earns them a reputation that they're "dumb." But actually, they're simply following their DNA sequencing. Over millennia, the least discerning cutts secured the most food and so survived to pass on their genes.

So the fishing in 1991 was not what it could be but was adequate and I got my sample. In three days, I put in 11.75 angler hours and caught 100 fish. They didn't come easy. In contrast, the year before, I had caught and processed 133 cutts with about the same effort.

As always, I visited with any anglers I met, reminding them of the regulations and asking them how they were doing. The morning of July 28, I packed up camp and headed for the trailhead. I was excited to see my son, Kevin, who had recently turned one year old, and I was eager to take him camping and fishing along the South Fork near Spotted Bear. Never too young to introduce him to this very fine fish.

1992 - Hyper-Fishing and Greeting Previously Tagged Cutthroat

I returned in 1992, going in on July 21 from the Lodgepole Creek Trailhead. I hiked the ten miles to Jenny Creek, spent the night, and the next morning continued to the South Fork headwaters.

By 12:15 P.M., an hour after my arrival, I was in nirvana, wading down the clear river and casting a dry fly. I covered the river from the junction of Youngs and Danaher Creeks downstream about 1.5 miles. By now, I recognized every landmark and bend in the river, every undercut bank and run. To this day, I can see the first stretch of the South Fork in my sleep and I love it. I caught fish after fish in the runs, using almost exclusively Adams Irresistible dry flies along with a few hoppers. Fishing to collect a sample is a little tense for me, because what would happen if I didn't catch enough? I stopped at 7:30 P.M. after 5.5 angler hours. It was one of those magical afternoons of outstanding fishing.

Many people say the best stream fishing happens in early morning and late evening. But on the South Fork headwaters, you can't predict when the cutthroat will turn on. If I had to name a time window, I'd say the hottest action happens from 10 A.M. to 2 P.M., although the weather is a factor. This day, for the first hours, I caught smaller fish, watching them flash back and forth in resistance as they came to the net, and feeling thankful for each of them. Then it seemed like the switch flipped to larger cutts. Go figure.

The South Fork's water temperature, usually in the 50s F., is ideal for the trouts' metabolism and verve. They fight insanely hard and hyper-quick. It's always a challenge to bring these fish to the net with the least possible disruption to their lives. Their mortality would soar if I played them to exhaustion, so I do the best I can. The small mortality risk is worth it to gather such crucial data on this cutthroat population.

Think of how short of a season these fish have to grow—really just a few months. Like bears, they probably have bouts of hyperphagia, piling on the calories before the water temperature drops in late September. By October, stream temperatures dip into the lower 40s F. and the trouts' metabolism fades into near-dormancy.

What an afternoon I had, landing and processing 64 westslope cutts. One old-timer measured 17.4 inches and weighed nearly 2 pounds, one heckuva fish. Bringing in these lunkers made me tense but also excited. I thought of how much work and luck it took to hook such a large and valuable native fish, and for the sake of the sample, I didn't want to lose it. I also thought of the razor's edge chance of landing the wildly struggling fish at the height of its energy and prowess. I might've lost a few, but somehow I made my sample quota.

That day, I hit the jackpot on recaptures. Four of the cutthroat I caught that day sported numbered tags from previous years. Given the modest number of fish tagged and the life challenges these fish face, this was an amazing number of recaptures. It was also evidence that the survival rate for the fish I processed and released was decent. And each "recap" supplied key information on growth.

The first recap, IR9425, measured 13.6 inches long. I had first tagged him in 1990 at only 10 inches, so he'd grown an average of 1.8 inches each year since I saw him last, about double the normal growth rate. But it makes sense, because the data show that smaller fish have a greater growth increment each year. The larger ones don't grow in length as fast, but they pile on the weight and girth. This cutthroat must have been chowing down on everything that moved. When I see a fish grow that fast, it makes me think that he's more "piscivorous" and less "insectivorous" than average, perhaps acquiring an appetite for bigger food items such as young fry of whitefish, sculpin, or his own species.

Recap number two measured a chunky 15.0 inches. I had tagged IR8159 on July 27, 1991, at 14.6 inches. His scales revealed an age of six, so as I handled him a year later, he was now a healthy seven-year-old, and he'd grown nearly a half inch, which is about average. It was nice to see him again, and I was glad he'd made it another year.

My third recap, IR8124, was 12.1 inches when I tagged him in 1991, almost exactly a year before. In those 361 days since, he'd grown to 14.7 inches. The tale of his scales when analyzed showed him to be seven years old—a very unusual, middle-aged, fast-growing cutthroat, demonstrating how much variation you find in a population and why it's important to collect a wide sample over time.

Finally, about 7 P.M., at the end of the river section, I caught IR9282, a nice 14.6-inch cutthroat. I'd tagged him two years before at 12.5 inches and five years of age. He was now seven years old, and he'd had a nice growth of 2 inches in those two years.

At that point, a little over a mile downstream from camp, the lunkers had turned on and I caught a few nice fish, including a beautiful and impressive 17.4-inch, hook-jawed male. What a day of fishing: 64 fish at the rate of 11.6 fish per angler hour. Any anxiety I had about catching my sample quota drained away.

Curiously, it was proving to be busy at the headwaters on this 1992 trip. Two people had been camping near my usual spot for ten days. They had actually built a "raft" out of lodgepole pine logs and cast off to float down the river not long after I reached the headwaters. With the log jams and some shallow riffles in the first miles of the river, I wondered how far they would make it with that heavy, unstable craft. Ten other anglers launched on five inflatable rafts to float the South Fork all the way to the pullout above the gorge at Mid Creek, about thirty river miles downstream.

Given all this activity and angling pressure, I was doubly amazed at how good the fishing was for me that day. It was a gift from the cutthroat gods.

After returning to camp, I made a quick dinner and crawled into my little tent. It rained most of the night and into the morning. The next morning, I fished my way up Youngs Creek. This gorgeous stream averages about twenty yards wide and has a moderate flow with a few short stretches of cliffs and deep holes in the lower half mile. I caught 23 robust cutts in 2.5 angler hours and carefully processed each one using a submerged net bag. About half of them exceeded 10 inches, ranging up to 14 inches. Unfortunately,

I lost the two biggest ones that I tied into. When a big fish you've been carefully playing ditches your hook and your line goes slack, it's an empty feeling, especially when you are working under self-imposed pressure to get a sample in a limited time in the middle of the wilderness.

By 2:30 P.M. I'd waded back down Youngs Creek and swung upstream into the Danaher Creek drainage. This stream flows gently over red, green, and gray cobbles in the last reach before it joins Youngs to form the South Fork. Danaher is not large, requiring probably six or eight long strides to wade across it. The channel was timbered back then, before the big fires, and on each major bend the stream flowed against a cliff or bank, forming a nice run or pool. The cutts were beautifully colored, visible in the clear water, and seem supercharged when hooked. In 2.5 angler hours, I caught 33 cutthroat, and most of them exceeded 10 inches. I caught 2 lunkers that exceeded 16 inches, each probably seven or maybe eight years old and weighing about 1.5 pounds. Each one gave me a touchy battle. Those are big native cutthroat trout in a small, remote stream, carrying on a heritable tradition extending back for millennia. And to be on the Danaher with them was special because, to me, it's the most beautiful of streams.

By 6 P.M. I had waded back down to the confluence and began fishing down the river. In another 1.5 angler hours, I landed another dozen mostly small fish except for one nice 15.7-incher. By 8 P.M. I finished up and headed back to camp.

All told, July 23, 1992, was a long, intense, spectacular day. I'd put in 6.5 angler hours and processed 68 cutthroat trout, spread out through the study section. That's 10.5 westslope cutthroat per hour, pretty stellar for any stream. My feet were numb; I finally took a breath. It doesn't get any better. I felt like I knew these cutts like family, but they still seemed to eye me with disregard. They just wanted to get back into the stream, back to what they were doing, what they've done forever.

Totaling up the July 22–23 sampling, I'd caught and released 132 cutthroat at an angling rate of 11 fish per hour. Better than half—59 percent—exceeded 10 inches, and 23 percent were longer than 12 inches. Two intense days with cooperative cutthroat and I had my sample.

The next morning, I packed up camp and headed out. On the way, I met outfitter Jack Rich, who was packing in eleven anglers to the headwaters. I also met two backpackers heading for the confluence. In all, I counted thirty-two anglers fishing the area. That the streams can take that much pressure and still be world class is a tribute to those "dumb" indigenous cutthroat who have learned to survive over thousands of years. The regulation requiring anglers to release fish greater than 12 inches, in effect since 1984, is crucial. Research shows that, for female cutts, fecundity (reproductive capacity) is correlated to length—the older, bigger trout lay more eggs. These special regulations also help to reduce the risk of overfishing.

1993 - I Catch One Buddy Cutthroat for the Third Year in a Row, and Four Bull Trout Grab My Cutts

The next year, Dana and my kids dropped me off at the Lodgepole Trailhead on July 20 to begin the annual trip. My son, Kevin, was three and Heather was only seven months old. At thirty-nine, I was a relatively old parent, and I always missed the kids when I was in the backcountry. But it wouldn't be long before I'd be dragging them all over the wilderness. It was great of Dana to watch the kids in their younger years while I headed into the wild. Our kids benefited greatly; there's a special place in heaven for such nurturing moms.

I headed up the trail in the rain, over Youngs Pass, down Jenny and Youngs Creeks, and arrived at my usual headwaters camp eight and a half hours later. The whole way was muddy, but in the wilderness you have to accept whatever the weather throws your way. I learned to pretend that I loved the mud. In my notes, I wrote, "The hike felt great—good route and used my internal frame pack."

At dusk when I arrived at the junction of Youngs and Danaher Creeks, I saw right away that the river was flowing higher than usual, and I knew that might present a challenge for getting my sample.

The next morning, I found out that the swift water made it harder to present the fly and harder to reach the holes. I had to really work at it. In 6.0 angler hours I caught 47 westslope cutthroat, spread throughout lower Youngs and Danaher and the first mile or so of the South Fork. More than usual, bull trout were chasing the cutthroat I was bringing in. It almost became a nuisance. In a large hole in Youngs Creek, adult bull trout grabbed three cuts in a row as I drew them in. One of the bulls, probably about a six pounder, had the cutthroat nearly all the way down his gullet and finally spit the poor fish out right as I brought him to shore. It isn't uncommon for these big predators to nail cutthroat as you play them, but three in a row was definitely a record for me.

One cutthroat wore a tag and had a special story. I originally caught and tagged IR8124 on July 26, 1991, at 12.1 inches and six years of age. I recaptured him on July 22, 1992, at 14.7 inches, a nice growth of 2.6 inches. This year, on July 21, I measured him at 15.8 inches; he'd grown 1.1 inches over the last year. To catch an individual westslope cutthroat three years in a row in a remote wilderness river is unspeakably lucky, probably a once-in-a-lifetime experience. It also provided critical data. I released the beautiful eight-year-old cutt and watched him swim back into the current. I don't think our years together meant as much to him as they did to me.

The next morning, July 22, I started out fishing lower Youngs. I was bringing in a 9.4-inch cutthroat when a big bull trout grabbed it, stretching the limits of my pack rod and the 4-pound-test leader. The bull was stubborn and kept hold of the cutthroat until he was right at my feet, then spit it out. Luckily the cutthroat wasn't killed, but he bore a few teeth marks and seemed in shock. He was able, however, to swim away after I measured him.

These adult bulls were migrating upstream about sixty stream miles from Hungry Horse Reservoir a little earlier than usual, maybe having something to do with the higher flows and cooler water temperatures. I usually had maybe one bull grab a cutt each year, but this made it four times in just two days.

In Youngs that morning, I caught a total of 13 fish, including 7 that would be considered big. One fat fish was 16.2 inches and was everything you could want in an indigenous cutthroat.

I fished the South Fork next; I caught 9 nice cutthroat but no big ones. The velocity of the current really limited the presentation of my fly and my catch rate. The cooler water also may have shut down the cutthroat.

To finish off the afternoon and evening, I headed up the reliable Danaher, where I caught 25 more cutts ranging in size from 7.9 to 16.7 inches.

The next morning, July 23, I fished the South Fork near camp for about an hour and caught 7 cutthroat. Not far downstream, I was floating a size 12 Adams Irresistible along a log jam and a monster cutt came out of the water and grabbed my fly. After a tense fight to keep him out of the jam, I slid the fish into my net and the fish-working net bag. My gosh, what a fish, 17.3 inches, hook-jawed, chunky, and probably 2 pounds. He vibrated with verve, and it was a challenge to even measure him. A perfect fish to end my 1993 trip.

In total, I sampled 101 fish in 13.0 angler hours for a catch rate of 7.8 fish per hour, just a bit lower than average. I was happy to have scored a nice sample number and distribution of sizes; 24 of the cutthroat measured larger than 12 inches, also about average.

I prepared to leave the headwaters but in a different way than usual. Outfitter Jack Rich had packed in and dropped my Sevylor inflatable kayak, pump, life jacket, and paddle near my camp. I was excited to try it. It seemed narrow as I inflated it, but once I loaded my pack and gear and settled into it, the boat proved to be stable and really fast. The high streamflows helped.

In late morning, I packed up and shoved into the current. I passed Big Prairie, Salmon Forks, and Independence Park, and stopped for the night just above Black Bear Cabin near Snow Creek. On the way downriver, I had contacted twenty-three anglers, most of whom were outfitted. Many of the anglers had fish on, so I was careful not to interfere with their experience. They were aware of the cutthroat size restrictions and enthusiastic about the great fishing they were having, in part because of those regulations.

The next morning, it didn't take long to paddle the eight or so miles down the choppy waters of the South Fork to the takeout at Mid Creek, just above the tumultuous Meadow Creek Gorge. I deflated my boat and rolled it into a duffle bag along with the pump and two-piece paddle. I packed everything else into my backpack. I hoisted the backpack and held the duffle in a bear hug in front of me, and began the four-mile hike to the trailhead at the Meadow Creek Gorge footbridge.

After a couple miles, I noticed a horse and mule pack train coming up behind me. I said hello to Cameron Lee, an outfitter I'd known through my work with FWP. I'd seen him and his son, Jason, when my family and I fished and camped around Spotted Bear. As always, this generous, eccentric, and jovial man brightened my day. He insisted that one of his fishing guides load my kayak onto one of his mules. At the trailhead, I hopped in their truck and rode to Cameron's dude ranch lodge. Late that afternoon, one of Cameron's guides drove me to the Spotted Bear Ranger Station, and there I ran into a Forest Service crew headed down the fifty-five-mile gravel road around Hungry Horse Reservoir and into Kalispell. I've always been lucky when finding rides and hitchhiking, but this chain of events left me feeling humbly charmed.

1994 - Lunker #5677, the Elder,
Comes to My Net for the Third Time Since 1988

In 1994, a friend, Les, and I left a car at the North Fork of the Blackfoot Trailhead near Ovando on the afternoon of July 15. Then Les drove me to the Lodgepole Creek Trailhead. I would cross Youngs Pass, hike downstream to the head of the South Fork to conduct my survey, then hike up Danaher Creek to come out at the North Fork Blackfoot Trailhead. On the way out, I would be able to check out some weirs I'd heard about near the pass between Danaher Creek and the Dry Fork of the Blackfoot. Like killing two fool hens with one stone (which you are not allowed to do).

I said goodbye to Les at 4:30 P.M. and headed up the Lodgepole Creek Trail. I topped the gentle pass into the South Fork basin and reached the Jenny Creek junction at 8 P.M., crossed Youngs Creek, and reached Big Slide along Youngs Creek an hour later. I hadn't seen another soul but didn't feel lonely. I made camp in some timber along the creek. The weather was cold and wet for July. A couple of Franklin's spruce grouse chicks followed their mom in the brush and timber. They were drenched, and I wondered whether the little birds would make it.

The next morning dawned clear. I left Big Slide at 7:45 A.M. and strode along the good trail that parallels Youngs Creek, past the falls and on to Hahn Creek. I continued for miles down the drainage on the muddy trail and finally arrived at the gentle junction of Youngs and Danaher Creeks at 11:30 A.M. I was anxious to start fly-fishing. I set up camp in my usual spot, in a grove of lodgepole and fir along the west side of the river not far downstream from the confluence. I ate a quick lunch. By 1 P.M. I was fishing.

Conditions were perfect: the streams were low, the sky cloudless. I fished the first mile of the South Fork and put in 6.0 angler hours, using dry flies exclusively. As usual, Adams Irresistible, Royal Wulff, and Joe's Hopper patterns worked well and did the trick that day.

The fishing was terrific, better than average. I caught, processed, and released 56 westslope cutthroat. That's a great catch rate of 9.0 fish per angler hour. And I hit the jackpot: the two biggest cutthroat I caught sported numbered tags from previous years, a very valuable and highly unlikely result. I couldn't wait to check my notes to see when I'd tagged them and how much they had grown. This was a fantastic start to the trip.

Tag number IR8159 measured 16.1 inches and weighed just under 1.5 pounds. The lunker, IR05677, was 17.3 inches long and weighed in at 2 pounds. I checked the notes. If fish could talk, both of these older cutthroat would have had great stories to tell since the last time I had handled them. In fact, I handled them each three times over the years. Given the small sample size, it doesn't seem possible that I'd caught each of these fish multiple times over the years. But I did.

Take the lunker, IR05677, for example. Years before, on July 12, 1988, I'd caught this 15.1-inch native cutthroat out of a headwater run and carefully netted him. After taking a scale sample, I'd affixed the numbered tag just behind the dorsal (top) fin. At that point, the fish had been lucky: based on his size, he'd survived to be at least five years old, much more likely six.

Most tagged cutthroat never show up again, especially a year or more later. Their lifespans are short due to the many mortality threats they face: hungry bull trout, ice in the winter, and so on. Overall, I recaptured only 2.7 percent of all the fish I'd tagged over the course of the study. The first time I caught IR05677 in 1988, it didn't occur to me that I might see him again. And since regulations prohibited keeping any fish over 12 inches in length, I figured anglers probably wouldn't turn in the tag.

But a couple years later, on August 9, 1990, at the headwaters, I looked into the eyes of IR05677 again. In the two years since I'd first seen him, he'd grown 1 inch, to 16.1 inches. How lucky I was to catch him again and document the average growth rate of about 0.5 inch per year typical of older fish. It was great to see IR05677 again, and I bade him farewell as I released him into the stream. At that time, I had no idea that I'd see him yet again years later.

In 1994, he was the first fish I caught that afternoon. I'd now handled this eleven-year-old fish (maybe the oldest ever documented), three times over a span of six years. So unlikely, so mind-blowing. His eyes gave no hint of recognition or even concern. Maybe he was used to it by then.

Another cutthroat, IR8159, also had an interesting story. On July 27, 1991, I caught and tagged the 14.6-inch fish near the headwaters pool. According to the scale growth rings examined later, the fish was six years old at the time, almost an old-timer already. On July 22, 1992, I caught her again. She had grown to 15.0 inches, or just a little under 0.5 inch, in the past year. Amazingly, on July 14, 1994, I caught the now nine-year-old cutthroat again. I looked for some sign from her eyes, maybe a flash of recognition or a smugness for living so long, secrets to success, but saw nothing. This cutthroat looked healthy and robust. Beginning as a 1-inch fry and for years after that, she avoided getting grabbed by a bull trout or scoured in the spring ice flow. This tough fish had reached 16.1 inches and 1.4 pounds. She was a genetic superstar, graced with luck to survive the many close calls she must have had.

Another cutthroat, IR8124, showed up three years in a row. I caught him in 1991 at 12.1 inches, then again in 1992 at 15.0 inches, a huge growth spurt in the course of a year. What was he eating? In 1993, I caught him again at 15.8 inches and seven or eight years old. Another exceptional life for a stream-dwelling westslope cutthroat.

All told, from 1985 through 1991, I tagged a sub-sample of 513 westslope cutthroat. I tagged only fish greater than 10 inches in length. I used slim, numbered "floy" tags, which are attached by a plastic "gun" similar to clothing tags at a department store. I recaptured 14 of these fish at least one year after tagging for a recapture rate of 2.7 percent. I recaptured 3 cutthroat more than once.

During my study period, no cutthroat from downstream in the drainage in other sections of the South Fork or Hungry Horse Reservoir ever showed up in the headwaters, despite the fact that more than 1,500 were tagged during the period. The headwaters section looks to be a population that centers on that area. We call this a "fluvial population"—the fish likely are born, grow to maturity, and spawn all in the reaches of Youngs and Danaher Creeks and the first few miles of the South Fork.

The 1994 sampling was going swimmingly well. Such great data. Excessive monitoring? I don't think so.

All in all, that first day I sampled 23 fish less than 10 inches in length, 15 fish between 10 and 12 inches, and 18 fish that were longer than 12 inches, including a 17.5-incher. That's a pretty solid size range for wilderness cutthroat. It had been an eventful, wonderful day in the wild.

Most people think fishing is relaxing, but it becomes really intense when you're striving for a good sample size. You have to carefully bring in the cutthroat, net them into a mesh bag in the water, collect scales, measure and weigh each one, and then release them, and do it all as quickly as possible to avoid stress on the fish.

The next day, July 17, 1994, my angling luck continued. I caught, worked, and released 15 cutthroat in lower Danaher Creek, 18 in the South Fork, and 11 in lower Youngs Creek, for a total of 44 in 5.75 angler hours. Four of these were in the lunker category, greater than 16 inches in length.

Between the two days, I'd processed 100 fish, right at my hoped-for sample size.

I fished the junction of Youngs and Danaher for 0.75 angler hours the next morning and added 4 nice cutthroat to my sample. Totaling up, I'd caught and processed 104 westslope cutthroat in 12.5 angler hours for an average of 8.5 fish per angler hour. Not bad. I was always careful not to oversample the cutts; once I had a sample in the range of 100 fish, I usually called it good.

I left the headwaters about 11 A.M., heading up the Danaher on my way to exit the wilderness near Ovando. On the way, I passed century-old remnants of Thomas Danaher's failed homestead in the open meadows. About dark, I arrived at the divide between Danaher and the Dry Fork of the Blackfoot. The next morning, I spent a few hours exploring stream channels on the Dry Fork Divide. This unusual pass is mostly flat and serves as a source of both streams. I found an old dam or weir at a bend of the Dry Fork about 200 meters up the Dry Fork Trail blocking a dry channel of the Danaher headwaters. Why build a weir there? I'm not sure—maybe to prevent the one stream from capturing the other where their headwaters almost meet. Maybe the weir helped maintain flows to Danaher's homestead.

I left the pass a little after noon and trekked down through the huge 1988 burn, following the North Fork of the Blackfoot River past the falls and out through the lower canyon. The drainage looked far different than it had before the fire. Most of the timber on the steep canyon sides was gone, right up to the ridgetops.

At the North Fork Trailhead, I loaded my pack into the truck we'd left there five days earlier and drove to Trixie's Saloon, an old-west place in Ovando. Yep, those fish-and-chips and a cold Coke sure tasted good, maybe the best ever, after those five days in the wilderness. I reflected on how lucky I was to investigate and learn about these cutthroat in one of our finest and most pristine rivers. I'll always treasure that opportunity.

1996 - Slow Fishing, But I Finally Catch the Behemoth

I decided to do one more year in my series of sampling to see if I could get any more tag returns and fill in a few sampling holes (maybe try for a bigger maximum-sized fish). On July 18, 1996, I left the Pyramid Pass Trailhead at 12:15 P.M. and headed up the trail. I crossed Pyramid Pass, marched down Jenny and Youngs Creeks, and dropped my pack at my usual headwaters campsite at 9:30 P.M. Not bad, just over nine hours to cover abut twenty-four miles.

When I woke up the next morning and looked at the river, my heart sank. It was murky and high. The water temperature was in the 40s F. It didn't look good. I fished the swift South Fork for 3.0 angler hours and landed only 4 fish, although they were nice ones. I was worried; it would be just about impossible to get a full sample.

I fished up Danaher Creek and had decent luck, sampling 29 fish in 3.0 angler hours. Many of these cutthroat were small, but I caught a few larger ones up to 16 inches.

I fished up Youngs Creek in the evening and caught 8 fish in 1.5 angler hours. That was encouraging, and all of them were 12 inches and larger. In fact, one behemoth measured 18.5 inches, the biggest cutthroat I'd seen in my twelve years of sampling. He probably weighed 2.5 pounds. So, if nothing else, I finished off this last year by extending the maximum size of my sample. It was beyond lucky to catch the biggest fish in the entire sample in all those years on the last few hours of fishing. The cutthroat gods gave me a little win.

Over the twelve years, I now had a sample of 1,349 cutthroat ranging from a puny 4.7-inch two-year-old to the 18.5-inch show-fish, which was probably ten to twelve years old. I felt that I'd captured the range of sizes and ages that typified this remote, indigenous, wilderness population of Montana's state fish.

The years went by and I finally analyzed (with a lot of help) and published the mounds of data from my little South Fork Flathead River study in *Northwest Science* (Vol. 79, No. 1, 2005). I was happy to make the information public so others could compare their cutthroat populations to the South Fork fish.

2010 - Checking on the Cutthroat Crew and Floating Out on Kids' Rafts

By 2010, I found some time to retrace my steps into the headwaters and check on the cutthroat. All the tagged fish were long gone by then, but their great-grand-fish would be the new piscine crew holding positions in the runs and pools of the upper South Fork, Danaher, and Youngs. It would be good to track the genetic purity of the fish and take a look at their size and growth. And, to be honest, I missed those headwaters cutthroat.

A lot of the landscape had burned in the decades since 1996. I wondered if that would affect the fishes' growth rates.

For the trip, I enlisted my daughter, Heather, seventeen, and son, Troy, fifteen, who by then had been my trusted backcountry companions for years. Dana dropped us off on July 22, 2010, at the Lodgepole Trailhead. We loaded up our backpacks and set out for the trek over Youngs Pass. Our load included two small, cheap, inflatable rafts to float us and our gear out the thirty-plus miles of river after our sampling work at the junction of Youngs and Danaher Creeks. The Sevylor Super Caravelle we had with us sported pretty good-sized tubes; we had used it in a lake before. We had bought a second raft for this trip, and the saleslady at the sporting goods store told us that the Solstice was similar in size and sturdiness to the Sevylor. The box pictured a person in the raft, making it look like the craft was big enough. So based on her recommendation, we didn't take the raft out of the box to look it over. Troy liked the looks of the photo, and the raft was brand new, so he said, "I've got dibs on the Solstice." We knew it was likely that these cheap rafts would spring leaks, so we brought along lots of duct tape just in case.

We crossed Youngs Pass and strode down to Jenny, then on to the Hahn Creek junction. The landscape along the route had burned intensely right down to the Youngs Creek channel since I was last there.

All three of us suffered some on the trek in, weighted down with our fifty-plus-pound packs. Even the youngsters complained. We rested a few times to ease the weight on our shoulders and hips. During a rest stop at Hole in the Wall, I lounged on the grass, but Troy and Heather went for a half-hour run back up the trail (they were both competitive runners in the middle of their training). Finally, after twenty-four miles and eleven hours, we arrived at the headwaters. I hadn't seen the area since the last big wildfire and was dismayed by the scorched landscape and acres of dead standing timber.

Just then a big windstorm blew in, and the dead standing trees creaked and clattered. My usual campsite was occupied, probably because it still harbored a few green trees. We had to camp in the burned area, worrying about the possibility of a dead tree falling onto our tent. The night was windy and spooky.

We were deep in the heart of the "Burnt Marshall Wilderness." The late Bud Moore, one of my top mentors, was chief of fire and air operations for District 1 of the Forest Service, and he advocated for the benefits of wildfires. But I'm not sure even Bud would have liked this scene; from the trailhead to the headwaters and all the way out to Spotted Bear, years of fires had charred much of the forest.

The next morning dawned clear and calm. The people in my old camp-site pushed off in their raft to head downstream, so we moved our camp. By 9 A.M., we began our two-day sampling regime.

The first fish, a gorgeous, 13.2-inch cutthroat, came to Heather's net at the pool right at the junction of Youngs and Danaher. I was reminded of how stunning these fish really are: electric energy, silvery sides with dark, well-defined spots, deep red slashes under the throat, chunky form. We mea-sured, weighed, and took a fin clip from her fish while we gently held it in a net bag in the water. The sample was underway.

Over the two days, our goal was to weigh and measure 60 cutthroat and remove a small sample of scales from each fish. From 30 of the fish captured one kilometer downstream from the junction, we snipped a tiny piece of anal fin to send to the University of Montana genetics lab. This actually was our primary purpose: were my beloved fish still genetically pure? We had plenty to keep us busy.

Troy provided one of the big highlights of the trip when he hooked into a massive cutt in a large pool on Danaher Creek, just upstream of the

Troy's 20.1-inch westslope cutthroat trout on Danaher Creek.

junction. It was nip and tuck, but he landed it without any harm. We worked the fish as quickly as possible, keeping it in the water.

The tape stretched 510 mm from nose to tip of tail, a solid, honest 20.1-incher. In all my years, I'd handled thousands of cutthroat, but this fish was the largest any of us had ever measured throughout the South Fork. Lots of guides tell me they and their clients catch 20-inchers, but this is the first one we'd ever measured. We were probably looking at a twelve-plus-year-old fish. The lunker weighed in at 1,077 grams, or a hefty 2.4 pounds. It was our privilege to meet a superstar cutthroat at the far, far edge of the norm.

Troy, my youngest, my charmed overachiever, had done it again. This fish was an incredible old-timer, and likely was related closely to the eleven-year-old I had caught in 1994. After all, the genetic results showed all these fish were part of one population.

The old-timer hid his age though. Maybe the population was tired of being analyzed and the word had spread through the cutthroat grapevine that I was back. I thought I finally sensed a look in his eyes, almost a subtle smirk. Later, when we tried aging his scales in the lab, they were too eroded to see beyond his seventh annuli (year mark). Hmm….

Soon after we landed the monster, Heather hooked into another big cutthroat in the same pool. She played it carefully and brought it close to the net; Troy tried to scoop it up, but the powerful fish made a flip and threw the hook. My daughter broke into a rare fit and implied that Troy did a poor job trying to net the big cutt, while Troy put the blame on her. Either way, it did briefly cast a pall over our mood. Heather and Troy were as passionate about the sample as I was.

By the time we were done sampling on our second day, July 23, it was obvious that the cutthroat were thriving in the South Fork headwaters. The average of the 60 fish in our sample measured 12.2 inches, as compared to the average from 1985 to 1996 of 10.4 inches. The size of cutthroat in our sample was statistically greater than the previous twelve-year sample or any single year in the previous period.

Why? Much of the drainage burned in the interim between 1996 and 2010. These fires torched much of the timber from the drainage and returned a lot of nutrients into the water. Even though we measured only 60 fish, our data seemed to indicate that the fish might be benefiting from the nutrients, or maybe from warmer water temperatures because of less shading. If we think of cutthroat growth in these headwaters as being limited by available nutrients and water temperature, it makes sense. Also bolstering this view, longtime outfitter Jack Rich believed that the cutthroat were getting bigger in the headwaters area, and you can take Jack's observations to the bank.

I'll admit that our sample size in 2010 was limited. But the stats suggest the increased growth was real.

We ended our second day with the good feeling of having caught and released a great sample, including many large cutthroat. We carefully protected the thirty fin clips in their vials, and wondered what the genetics results from the UM lab would show. I hoped against hope that the old-timer would test clean.

He did. I thought I'd finally seen a knowing and smug look in his eye, almost as if he was saying: "Dang straight I'm clean, and I'm the biggest there's ever been in these parts. Where have you been?"

When we got the results back from the lab, we celebrated. The folks at the UM lab concluded that there was zero genetic material in any of the 30 samples from anything other than pure, indigenous westslope cutthroat, all from a single population (meaning that individuals are highly related, including to my earlier sample of fish). UM's test is high-tech and thorough.

The analysis looks at fourteen "loci," or locations, on chromosomes. At each of these, sequences of genetic entities called "nucleotides" reveal any hybridization from rainbow or Yellowstone cutthroat trout. The conclusion was these were all westslope cutthroat, as pure as the clear waters of the South Fork. It's impossible to estimate the value of these fish, a population that hasn't changed or been altered for thousands of years. So, a couple hundred years ago, when Meriwether Lewis saw the westslope cutthroat that Silas Goodrich caught east of the divide at the Great Falls of the Missouri, these fish were already ancient. I'll bet those cutthroat looked upon the explorers with that same indifferent expression: We've been here for millennia, where were you?

The next morning, we made ready to push off downriver in our rafts. We pumped up the Super Caravelle, feeling reassured by its sixteen-inch-diameter side tubes. We expected the Solstice to be equally stout. Troy carried the box over to a flat spot and began pumping up the Solstice. I looked over after a while and said, "Why don't you pump it all the way up, Troy?" He was bent over at the waist, looking glum, and said, "This is its full size; it's tiny." I looked it over and my mood crashed. The tubes on the Solstice were less than a foot in diameter, and it was maybe five feet long. There was no way these two rafts could carry the three of us and our three packs thirty-five miles, through the rapids and rock fields, all the way down the South Fork. I felt embarrassed by the folly of not examining the raft before we packed it in.

Troy squeezed into the Solstice raft on the South Fork of the Flathead River.

I'd gotten our crew into a tough spot. If we had to, we could pack up the rafts and just hike down the drainage all the way to the trailhead, where Dana was scheduled to pick us up in a few days. But that sounded punishing. We decided to jam our packs and gear into the two rafts and hope for the best. Heather and I squeezed into the Caravelle with the packs, and Troy manned his Solstice. A few bends downstream, two big, buckskin-colored whitetail bucks stood in the middle of the river, and we had to stop to let them cross. I considered that a good sign.

The South Fork is pretty gentle those first six or so miles to Big Prairie, and the floating wasn't bad at all. But space was at a premium; we sat on top of our packs and draped our legs over the side tubes.

When we reached Big Prairie, we pulled over and left our rafts on the riverbank at the footbridge across the South Fork. We walked across the prairie to talk with Guy Zoellner at the ranger station. Guy and his wife, Keagan, were spending summers at the Bob's biggest ranger station, thirty-two miles from the nearest trailhead, and would later raise a family there (see my book, *Heroes of the Bob Marshall Wilderness*).

Troy navigates the South Fork of the Flathead River by the Big Prairie pack bridge.

They chuckled about our "rafts" (we showed them a digital photo I'd just taken), but they were impressed that we had packed in life jackets so we were legal. We shared a few cups of Kool-Aid, which tasted like nectar way back in the Bob.

While floating the ten miles to Bartlett, we'd had to line the rafts down any significant rapids to avoid swamping. Also, the raft material was not puncture resistant. We camped that night on the east side of the river in a beautiful ponderosa grove. We laid out the rafts on the cobble beach and used about half of a roll of duct tape to patch holes, but the leaks on the Caravelle's floor tubes couldn't be fixed. Troy and Heather went for a run along the river and were surprised by a black bear.

The next morning, we made our way downriver. At each rapid we had to line the rafts close to the shoreline to avoid swamping or more punctures. Luckily, we had decent wading footwear.

Late that afternoon we reached Salmon Forks where a large raft party had a fancy camp, packed in on horses, complete with tables, awnings, tarps, portable showers, barbeques, and wall tents. The party was being serviced by a guiding outfit known for its opulent trips.

As we floated by their camp, jammed into our toy rafts, some of their group gathered to watch us. One lady chuckled and pointed; she yelled out to us: "My God, I can't believe you are floating THIS river on THOSE tiny boats." Some of her companions laughed along with her.

We thought that she was a bit smug; she seemed to be mocking us. But I felt pretty good about it. We hadn't spent thousands of dollars each for the trip, and I think she secretly envied our minimalist approach. We waved enthusiastically, and paddled on by with our heads held high, heading for Damnation Creek and Independence Park.

The next day, we continued our float down the choppy, clear South Fork. Soon we passed Black Bear Cabin, and after another five miles we reached the mouth of Black Bear Creek. There, on the rock shelves, we unloaded the rafts and packs and spread everything to dry in the gorgeous sunshine. With the sketchy rafts we had, we didn't want to float to the usual takeout point at Mid Creek, above the gorge, about three more miles downriver through the canyon. We were done with the Caravelle, and we were especially done with the Solstice.

We crammed our gear into our packs and hung the paddles and rafts on the outside. The packs were heavy because all our gear was still wet. We headed up to the trail, crossed Black Bear Creek, and swung toward the trailhead. We hit a few great huckleberry patches, which slowed us down. A few hours later we met Dana, coming up the trail on her own little fishing trip. We all headed for the Meadow Creek Gorge footbridge and the trailhead.

On our five-day trip, Heather, Troy and I had covered sixty-five miles by raft and on foot. We did it on the cheap, but we felt good about getting a heckuva sample of those pure, indigenous fish.

2015 - Over the Continental Divide and into the South Fork Headwaters: Were the Cutts Still Pure?

We let our headwater cutts rest for five years before testing them again. Montana Fish, Wildlife & Parks had an ongoing project to remove all the hybrids from mountain lakes draining into the South Fork. I'd played an information and outreach role on this project for decades. So there were still some rainbow and Yellowstone cutthroat genes that could possibly dribble in to the river and work their way into the pure westslope cutthroat we'd been testing.

In August 2015, our management team headed into the Bob via the Benchmark Trailhead to chase a number of objectives, among them to spend one day sampling cutthroat in my headwaters section for size and genetics. At sixty-one, I would be retiring in a few years, and the younger guys wanted to see me in my native habitat before I left. They were curious to see firsthand why this cutthroat population had been a passion of mine since 1980. I humored them and tagged along.

Our warden captain, Lee, and the South Fork backcountry warden, Perry, rode in on horses and packed in our gear on three mules. We planned to stay at Basin Cabin near Danaher Creek, and the wardens would do their patrols from there. We could also access the headwaters from that point, and we were to meet the Big Prairie ranger there. Wildfires were brewing all around the Bob that summer and were about to get worse.

We headed across the South Fork of the Sun River on the suspension footbridge. The clop-clop of the stock's hooves kept beautiful time as the sun rose in the sky and began to bathe us in optimism. We headed up the South Fork of the Sun for about three miles and then hung a right up the Hoadley Creek drainage.

The clear day offered great conditions for our planned survey of elk habitat around the base of Scarlet Mountain by the foot soldiers: Mark, the fish manager; Neil, the wildlife manager; Jim, the regional supervisor; and me, the outreach coordinator.

Left to right, Jim, Neil, and Mark were the crew for the August 2015 cutthroat (and elk habitat) surveys.

We crossed the Continental Divide at about 7,000 feet into the South Fork of the Flathead drainage at the headwaters of Stadler Creek. Soon after, we hung our packs and headed up the ridge toward the Scarlet Mountain escarpment. Mark volunteered to stay with the packs while the rest of us went up the mountain. The wardens rode by on the trail; we'd reunite at the Basin Cabin on the Danaher that evening.

We foot soldiers had agreed that we wouldn't climb to the top of Scarlet, stopping short to look at elk habitat in some sweeping benches to the south. But Jim couldn't be satisfied with that. He got summit fever.

I was sitting with Neil on a rock and thinking that this would turn out to be a relaxing exploration across seldom-visited, high-elevation elk and bear habitat. The next thing I knew, Jim came climbing by and announced that he was headed for the top of Scarlet. Clearly, this had been his plan all along. We couldn't let him scale the cliffs alone, so I called him an A**H*** and fell into line. So much for a relaxing day.

From where we left the trail, the top of Scarlet "towered" about 1,500 feet above us. The trek turned steep and rocky. A series of cliffs slowed us down, but after some consternation, we made it to the top. The last 100 feet involved a little exposure but was worth it. Spread before us, extensive benchlands with scattered high-elevation grasses and conifers swept to the east into the Scapegoat Wilderness and the Sun River Game Range. Such a gorgeous plateau, so remote.

We knew we enjoyed a view shared by few others. We knew that none of us would ever stand here again. We took plenty of photos of these rarely visited benchlands for our habitat files. Then we trekked back down and rejoined Mark. We loaded up and headed down the trail.

After about five miles, Stadler Creek joins Basin Creek about a mile or two shy of Basin Creek Cabin. A few Franklin's grouse or "fool hens" walked along on the trail ahead of us for fifty yards; I think they believed that they were part of our group. Finally, the grouse scooted off the trail. I love those trusting birds. They just seem to put everything at ease and in perspective.

A mile or so later, we wandered into the grounds of Basin Cabin, right along the creek. The trip from Benchmark to Basin Cabin covered about seventeen miles. About a quarter mile across the meadows, Danaher Creek flows by on its way to join Youngs Creek, six miles downstream. The wardens had opened up the cabin and turned the pack stock into the corral to eat and rest.

But Perry looked like he'd been attacked by a mountain lion. His shirt and even his gloves were torn, and bloodstains showed here and there. I blurted, "Gee Perry, what the heck happened?"

He described a major wreck: the stock got tangled up in their lead ropes and bucked in circles at a creek crossing, tangling with Lee's horse. Perry was thrown, but no one was seriously hurt. Later, someone told me that Lee rarely completed a backcountry trip without at least one wreck.

I pumped water from Basin Creek for everyone with my filter. We ate dinner and settled in for the evening. I was excited for tomorrow, when we would head downstream to the junction of Youngs and Danaher to collect our size and genetics sample of westslope cutthroat. Thirty years after my first sampling in 1985, would my buddies still be as large, robust, and genetically pure?

Perry waters some of the stock at the headwaters of the South Fork of the Flathead River, August 2015.

That night, the Basin Cabin lived up to its reputation for varmints. Packrats, mice, you name it. But I faced a threat that I hadn't expected: the place was crawling with bats. Now I know that bats are part of the ecosystem, eat a lot of bugs, blah, blah, blah. But I still don't like them. In fact, I can't stand them.

I set up a cot on the cabin porch, and the bats immediately didn't like it and acted like I'd moved into their territory, which I guess I had. I'd never seen bats hang around in lodgepole pine trees and scold, but that's what they did to me. As the evening light faded, they dive-bombed the porch to intimidate me. Mice are one thing, and we trapped a bunch, but there's not much you can do about bats. I just covered up and hoped that they wouldn't join me in my sleeping bag.

After a nice breakfast at Basin Cabin, we all headed down the Danaher Trail six miles to the junction with Youngs Creek and the South Fork headwaters. After a five-year hiatus, I looked forward to seeing the cutthroat again. How would the population look, given the additional wildfires and the fishing pressure from increased floating use?

I needn't have worried. When we reached the junction pool, Mark made one cast and caught a 16-incher. Yep, that was a great sign. We split into two groups of three and divided up the first 1.5 kilometers of river into two sampling zones. It was late in the year, August 19, and the water was low. We could see the big cutts in the pools and runs, and we saw a number of bull trout, too.

Jim, Neil, and I walked downstream and covered the lower part of the section, while Mark, Lee, and Perry covered the upper section from the junction down 750 meters. Given the low water, the fishing wasn't fast. But the fish size was stunning. After a few hours, we'd collected our 32-fish sample of fin clips for genetics, and scales, and carefully measured the fish. One-third of the fish measured 16 inches or greater, blasting previous length samples out of the water. Something was happening with these fish. A small sample size, yes, but that's a lot of large fish. They are living long lives and growing big and robust. And it just might be related to all those wildfires that I don't like.

Jim with a nice cutthroat at the South Fork headwaters.

We were psyched to see the cutts doing so well. I'd been watching them for exactly thirty years and had seen their size and condition progress, kind of like watching your kids grow up and succeed in life. I wonder what that smug eleven-year-old I had handled three times a few decades ago would think of his offspring thriving to this degree. No doubt about it, these are the good old days for westslope cutthroat trout in the upper South Fork.

The science of genetics keeps hurtling along, adding new twists each year. To test for hybridization, the geneticists at the University of Montana genetics lab used to analyze fourteen loci, or locations, on their chromosomes. Now they peered into the genes of these fish at about sixty loci. Twenty of the markers test for Yellowstone cutthroat hybridization, nineteen test for rainbow trout markers, and twenty for westslope cutthroat. We later learned that all our sample fish contained only westslope cutthroat markers; no rainbow or Yellowstone alleles or genes were present. And when thirty westslope loci were tested, they showed that these westslope cutthroat came from a single, random mating population. So, that's the way it's been for thousands of years at the headwaters. You can't get any cleaner than that.

As we wrapped up our fishing, Guy Zoellner, the Big Prairie ranger, arrived to confer with Perry on fires and trails, and it was nice to catch up with this dedicated, highly respected backcountry ranger. But smoke clouded the skies, and Guy wasn't sure whether he'd be asked to gather things up and head out for safety along with his family and crew members at Big Prairie and around the upper South Fork. We bid him luck and headed up the Danaher Trail and back to Basin Cabin.

After a great meal at homey Basin Cabin, we turned in. The bats were a pain again, and one or two of them hung upside down on the eaves of the cabin, but they weren't quite as aggressive as the night before. Just to show them what we could do, we hung four mice we'd trapped under one of the lodgepole where the bats hung out. If I'd had some way to kill the bats, I'd have jumped on it.

We started the race back to Benchmark early the next morning, after a breakfast of sausage and eggs. I noticed that the sausage on the plate Lee gave me seemed cool to the touch, but I didn't think much of it.

I padded the precious cargo of fin clips of the 32 cutthroat we'd collected and preserved in vials of ethanol, and stowed them in my pack. After the wreck the wardens had on the way in, I didn't want to take any chances with these invaluable samples that would tell us if the cutthroat stock was still pure westslope.

We agreed to race the seventeen miles out to Benchmark. We figured that we could beat the wardens and their pack string to the trailhead. We made a bet on it, but I can't remember what the winnings would be. Lee seemed supremely confident that they would win. Hmm, I wonder why.

We foot soldiers lined up wearing our day packs and were off. Lee and Perry loaded the stock and gave us a small head start. Jim, Mark, Neil, and I jogged through the big meadows past the Basin-Danaher trail junction, then headed through smaller meadows and timber up the Basin Creek Trail. After a few miles, we hung a right on the Stadler Creek Trail and climbed it to the divide below Scarlet Peak. We strode through the open timber and scattered rocks at the 7,000-foot pass; so far we'd covered about seven miles and climbed 2,000 feet.

We remained comfortably in the lead. Via radio contact, we figured we had about forty-five minutes before they crossed over the divide. We needed the head start, because once they started downhill, they would quickly gain on us. We had ten miles to go to the Benchmark footbridge, the agreed-upon finish line for our race.

After a quick break, we sped down the other side as fast as we could go. Based on our communications, we were now about a half hour ahead of the string. Lee asked on the radio how we were feeling; we wondered why. We later found out that he thought the undercooked sausage he gave me would be the ticket to slowing us down.

We jogged down the trail along the South Fork of the Sun, but after a few miles, we just had to stop. We could see these beautiful holes in the stream. In the late-summer low water, the cutthroat splashed around, feeding on caddis and grasshoppers that blew into the water. Finally, I dug out my fly rod, and the crew gathered around to watch while I climbed down the cliffs and flipped a few Adams Irresistibles into the current. They could easily see the cutts rise to the flies and nail them. Jim, who is not really an angler, gave me constant advice as I fished. In spite of his advice, I was still able to catch a few big ones and we marveled at them. Their compatriots, just over the west side of the divide, were pure cutthroat. I wondered about the status of these cutts in the South Fork of the Sun (descendants of the westslope cutts Lewis saw at the Great Falls of the Missouri). Rainbows thrived downstream in the drainage, so I feared these cutts were compromised. We knew that we should test them. We all agreed to come back again someday and fish this awesome stream. We haven't and probably won't. There's only so much time in one life.

As I started climbing back up the cliffs, we heard Perry shout, "There they are, and one is carrying a fishing pole." It was the wardens; they had caught up. They were referring to us almost as animals, just intent on beating us to the Benchmark suspension bridge, about a half mile farther down the trail. We didn't like it, and we were not about to let them win now.

We began sprinting down the trail, Mark leading the way. Now we were moving probably five or six miles per hour. This caught the wardens by surprise, then one of their lead ropes caught on a branch, causing one of Lee's trademark rodeos.

That gave the foot soldiers the win. Lee was mystified; he later admitted trying to lightly poison me with the undercooked sausage. He was confident, noting to Perry that "all we have to do is catch one of them."

Well, it didn't work.

Wrapping It Up with a Cutthroat Mystery

After all my years of interacting with the westslope cutthroat in the South Fork, a final unanswered question nags at me: What flips that feeding switch for cutthroat? It's a great question. After all the cutts I've fished for and all the thousands of cutts I've caught, I still don't know the answer.

One great example has always stood out to me. It happened late one afternoon in the late 1980s, below the Youngs-Danaher junction. I was accompanied by an angler volunteer, the Mattress Man, whom I'd met along the South Fork the previous year. He owned a huge mattress business in the Midwest and had timed his trip this year just to help out on the cutthroat project before he and his party headed down the river on rafts. We were fishing the lower end of the headwaters section when, very quickly, thunderheads built, the sky darkened, the clouds opened, and the rain thrashed down. We sheltered under some big pines while the big wind-driven raindrops pelted the South Fork.

Just as suddenly, the clouds receded, and the warm sun emerged. We resumed fishing. I made one cast, and the fly began floating into the gentle chop water—the sweet spot at the head of the run. Our eyes bugged as about a half-dozen cutts of various sizes, small to hog-sized, launched themselves into the air and came down fighting over my Adams Irresistible. I raised my rod and set the hook on one of them. Mattress Man looked at me wide-eyed and said, with great emotion, "I love this!" For the next ten minutes we caught cutt after cutt as they came with gusto to our flies. It seemed that our joy and enthusiasm was one with the trout, and I'll never forget it. When I think of my passion for catching these cutts, this is one of the moments I remember.

I've seen this kind of bite spree a number of times on the section, but it's really not predictable. I remember fishing a special hole one morning on the Danaher where the same kind of frenzied biting spree took me by surprise. It was as if every cutt of every age and size went crazy at once.

I wonder why. A five-minute talk with a cutt would tell us all we need to know. But it will never happen, so we'll always have to wonder. ◄○►

CHAPTER 9

Travelin' Trout

Bull trout in the Flathead swim one of the longest migrations of any freshwater trout

One of the biggest mysteries in nature is how animals navigate long distances and return to a particular birth spot. Bull trout that grow to adulthood in Flathead Lake can swim 100 miles or more to reach their natal areas and spawn in small streams in the upper Flathead drainage. You hear theories of fish navigating by sensing water chemistry, physical cues in streamflow, even based on the stars. But only one thing is for sure: nobody really knows, and that makes it fascinating.

I love bull trout, and for more than forty years, I've monitored them each fall by counting their nests in small tributaries. Now retired, I still volunteer to count these nests or "redds"; it's an inseparable part of my being.

For millennia, bulls have traveled one of the longest migration routes of any freshwater trout in North America. Averaging 25 inches and about 6 pounds, these hefty fish look amazingly out of place in the small streams of the upper Middle Fork and South Fork of the Flathead. As I found out when I first snorkeled Granite Creek in the Great Bear Wilderness

A mature bull trout encountered while snorkeling in the Middle Fork near Clack Creek.

in 1980, in a stream you can almost jump across, a mature bull trout looks like Moby Dick.

These lunkers leave Flathead Lake in the summer, migrate upstream through the forks, and reach the tributary of their birth in August. It's thought that most bull trout are faithful to their natal tributary. They spawn in September and early October, once water temperatures drop below 50 F. After spawning, these big chars swing around and head back downstream through the river system and eventually return to the lake, probably by late October. The males hang around the redd for a short time before heading downstream, but the females tend to depart right away.

Unlike Pacific salmon, bull trout do not die after spawning and can spawn several times during their lives. Most of them first spawn at about age five and six (mostly six), and then spawn one or two more times before they expire. (Bulls as old as nine have been documented.) Their eggs hatch in January, then "fry" emerge from the gravel by spring. The young bulls eat mostly aquatic insects and grow in the tributary for their first two or three years, then they migrate downstream to Flathead Lake. If they survive the predator gauntlet through all this travel, they might make it back to their natal stream to spawn for the first time as six-year-old adults.

Bull trout are actually "chars," one of the two main divisions of the trout group. Chars (including brook trout and lake trout) sport light spots on a dark background, and spawn in the fall. Their coastal cousin is referred to as Dolly Varden. Bulls and Dollies were considered the same species until 1978, when they were officially split by a busybody fisheries scientist named Ted Cavender who couldn't leave well enough alone.

Once common throughout the Pacific Northwest, bull trout originally ranged from southern California to the Bering Sea. Over the eons, they've developed three different lifeways, including this migratory lake style, river residents, and tributary residents. In the Flathead, we believe most bulls follow the lake-migratory path in the forks of the Flathead and in the Swan River system. Bulls in the South Fork of the Flathead drainage mature in Hungry Horse Reservoir and then spawn mostly in wilderness tributaries like the White River and Little Salmon Creek. Many other lakes throughout the drainage host bull trout, including Big

Salmon Lake and lakes in Glacier National Park that feed the North Fork of the Flathead River.

When big bulls build their redds in these tributaries, they pull out all the stops. The female lies sideways, fans, and moves hundreds of pounds of gravel and cobbles in the stream bottom. She deposits eggs, while the male fertilizes them. The gravel that the female churns up as she moves upstream covers each egg pocket. When done, the nest is shaped like a big teardrop, with a final, wider pit, and a "tail" of sorted gravel extending downstream. These excavations are easy to see as you walk down the stream, and they can range from a few feet to fifteen feet long. From past studies, we know that on average, about three bull trout work on each completed redd.

A bull trout on a redd in Granite Creek.

A good-sized female bull can deposit 5,000 or more eggs buried about six inches in a large redd. This is a shotgun strategy, where the female spews out thousands of eggs but gives no parental care. These fish rely on sheer numbers for survival of young in a high-mortality environment. It must work because these big piscivores have been around for thousands of years.

We monitor bulls by counting their redds in late September and October in various tributary streams. One advantage to this method is that we don't have to handle the fish. That's important because these big adults have been away from the lake for months and are in a somewhat weakened condition.

Years ago, we operated traps in a few streams to count the number of big bulls entering tributaries to spawn. We ended this practice, though, because these big fish suffered some mortality in the traps. One of our technicians, Jay, had a theory: Bulls have a special psyche, and when they are briefly pulled out of the water and as much as see a human, they are compromised. I don't know about that, but it's interesting to think about. I do know they are sensitive. Jay urged me to halt the trapping of bull trout spawners, and we did.

Jay was an interesting guy, full of verve and humor. We affectionately called him "Mario," because he shared his last name with a famous opera singer. Jay had lots of theories about the motivations of different fish species, and they were always fascinating. Who knows, some of his theories may have been right. He was a fun person to be around.

Jay loved fish, and he also loved the Rolling Stones. The band and their music were very important to him. In fact, with his big eyes and hair, Mario bore a striking resemblance to Mick Jagger, and it was probably deliberate. When he smiled, which was almost all the time, his face seemed to expand and glow.

One August, Jay had a ticket to attend a Stones concert in Seattle. This had been a lifetime dream of his. The day before the concert, Jay and another crew member were surveying a Middle Fork tributary that was accessed via a gated road and then a three-mile trail. The gate was open and unlocked, and they drove right through. After finishing the work late that afternoon, they hiked back out to the pickup and drove back down the road. Jay had been excitedly talking about the concert all day and was eager to leave on his 600-mile drive to get there.

They drove around the bend in the access road and came up to the gate. Someone had closed the gate, and on top of that, chained and padlocked it. Jay's face, always expressive anyway, expanded and reddened, and his bug-eyes got even bigger. He exploded and vowed that the gate wouldn't stop him from attending the concert.

He pulled slowly ahead, pushing against the gate with the pickup's front bumper, trying to force it open. The gate bent a little, but it was obvious that there would be a lot of damage to the truck and gate if he kept pulling forward.

Finally, Jay decided to drive through the timber and over the rocks to skirt around the gate. It wasn't pretty, but they made it, chopping down a few trees and suffering just minor damage to the truck. Mario left for Seattle that night and he made the concert the following day.

I was sure glad it worked out for Jay, because he was not to live much longer. In April 1981, he and I went on a raft trip down the Middle Fork to electro-fish tributary mouths. On that trip, he confided in me that because of a freak disease, he had lost his spleen and had other internal problems, including a poorly functioning liver. He drank orange juice because he had to avoid alcohol. He knew he had a limited life, and maybe his sense of mortality led him to look at "fish psyches" in a different way.

A few years went by. Jay was a valued and popular part of our fish crews, but he eventually headed to Alaska to work in construction. He always wanted to go farther north. He once told me, "I didn't come west to Montana to live in Evergreen." After Mario left Montana, I lost track of him.

One day in the mid-1980s, we had finished a redd count on the "gated stream," and it made me think of Mario. I got back to the office the next Monday and was stunned to hear that Jay, only in his early thirties, had dropped dead that weekend at a construction site in Alaska.

I'd spent a lot of time in the backcountry with Jay and always enjoyed his fish wisdom, sense of humor, infectious personality, and brilliant smile. We counted bull trout redds and trapped juvenile and mature bull trout together. It's tough to think of someone dying so young who just exuded such over-the-top life. Rest in peace, Mario.

Bull trout redds are easy to see and count. As long as you survey the same stream reaches each year, it's a great way to measure the annual size of the spawning run of Flathead Lake bull trout. And it's hard to beat redd counts for pure enjoyment. The weather that time of year is often sunny and crisp. You travel light—your only equipment a data book, GPS, waders, bear spray, and a measuring tape.

The lighter hue inside the circle is a bull trout redd, easily seen when you know what to look for.

There's a certain easy familiarity and repeatability in counting bull trout redds. The adults migrate to the same stream sections each year, with a stunning site loyalty. I began surveying Granite Creek in 1980, and I'm still counting it. The big bulls build their redds in nearly the exact locations in the stream each year. There's a reason for this. When a big female bull arrives at the general spawning area, she senses the stream bottom for upwelling springs. She can feel the cold water bubbling up through the gravel, or at least that's what we think. Somehow, she "knows" in an evolutionary sense that this is the spot to bury her eggs. Success of incubation and emergence of fry in the spring yields success in passing along her genes.

In Granite Creek over the past forty-plus years, we can just about predict where the redds will be at each bend in the creek. Not only do I know every inch of this Great Bear Wilderness stream, I feel like I know where the redds will be before they are even built. My count in 2020 was within a handful of redds of my count in 1980. The redd locations varied a little, but most were still concentrated in the "high-use" upwelling reach of the creek.

John with his data book in Granite Creek.

Bull trout migration and spawning show incredibly tight timing and predictability. The big chars finally enter the tributaries just before the larch needles turn golden, and usually complete spawning when most of the needles have dropped.

On the first of October 1980, my crew and I rode a small Cessna into Schafer Meadows in the heart of the Middle Fork and Great Bear Wilderness. It took two trips to transport our crew and gear. We planned to count bull trout redds in tributaries around the wilderness, and we looked forward to spending nearly two weeks in this backcountry during the beautiful sunny weather of an Indian summer.

All summer, we had been surveying tributaries, snorkeling to count fish and measuring physical characteristics. We used packhorses on these trips to carry our wetsuits and other gear, covering the entire drainage from Bear Creek to the head of Strawberry Creek. But owing to the small amount of equipment needed for fall redd counts, we decided to fly in to the central portion and backpack around the drainage.

Game warden captain Lee Anderson helps count bull trout redds in the Great Bear Wilderness.

We landed at the tricky Schafer airstrip in midafternoon and stayed in the Schafer Meadows Ranger Station bunkhouse the first night. The next morning, we broke into two crews and headed up the trail along the Middle Fork of the Flathead River. We crossed the river at the Schafer ford and reached the junction of the Dolly Varden and Schafer Trails. One crew continued up Schafer Creek, the other up Dolly Varden Creek.

I was on the Dolly Varden crew. This incredible stream flows placidly through willow meadows and lodgepole forests, with some spruce, fir, and larch. The gentle gradient, upwelling springs, and clean stream bottom gravel offer perfect spawning conditions for the big bulls. And the bulls' large excavations show up like beacons through the transparent water.

As we counted redd after redd, wading upstream, we noticed that each redd seemed huge. I didn't know if particularly athletic bulls had entered this stream, or what was going on, but it was exciting. By the time we were done counting that evening, we had catalogued 21 redds. At the rate of 5,000 or more eggs deposited per redd, we'd documented the deposition of more than 100,000 potential indigenous bull trout fry to emerge the following spring. Dolly Varden Creek was "fully seeded," which made us overjoyed.

At the upper end of the section, we found one dead lunker, a male bull trout, probably about 28 inches long, lying in the shallows on the stream margin. He may have hung around the redd a little too long and got smacked by a raptor from above, or maybe he was just trapped in too shallow a spot for him. Thinking of this fish, we mused about how he was a sacrifice in a long lineage of indigenous bulls that kept the genetic line pure over the millennia.

We turned around at Argosy Falls, hopped out of the creek, and angled over through the timber to the trail for the six-mile stroll back to Schafer Meadows. Back at the ranger station, the other crew said they'd counted 10 redds in Schafer Creek. That seemed low, but we were thankful that we had 31 redds between the two tributaries.

We moved our camp fifteen miles up the drainage to the upper Middle Fork spawning tributaries and staged out of the Gooseberry Ranger Station cabin. This upper section of the Middle Fork is a long, low-gradient reach with lots of available spawning gravel. We even found a few bull trout redds in the river itself.

We spent the next day surveying Clack and Bowl Creeks. Clack Creek winds through a broad, gentle valley, dropping from Trilobite Ridge on the Continental Divide. It's full of clean spawning gravel and boasts upwelling springs. Beaver dams limit the amount of clean gravel and access to some sections, or it would be a blockbuster. The Clack crew counted only 10 redds, but they were well-developed and each redd probably held thousands of eggs.

I counted lower Bowl Creek along with another crew member. We hiked up the Middle Fork a few miles to the mouth of the creek and began counting upstream. The redds showed up mostly in the first five miles of the stream, past Grizzly Park, to the junction of Basin Creek. This first day, we counted 18 redds and made plans to return the next day to count the remainder of the stream.

The next day, the other crew headed upstream to start counting Strawberry Creek; this would be a big, fourteen-mile, multi-day task on this large tributary that flows from the Continental Divide at Badger Pass.

Early the next morning back at Bowl Creek, I trekked up the trail from Grizzly Park about seven miles to the headwaters at Teton Pass. During these very first redd counts in 1980, we didn't know for sure which stream reaches the bull trout from Flathead Lake used, so we tried to count every section of stream that could possibly hold redds.

When I reached Teton Pass, I was surprised at the condition of the trail: a wide swath of bare dirt extended over the pass, obviously heavily used by parties entering the wilderness from the east. I backtracked off the pass and jumped into the tiny upper reach of Bowl Creek and began surveying downstream.

The stream was small and not well suited for bull trout spawning. It was steep at first, then eased to a moderate gradient over fairly large cobbles. Now and then, there were flatter sections. A few miles downstream, I was wading in the stream through the timber and broke into the bright sunshine of a nice little meadow. What I saw next surprised me.

There, sitting in the sun with her back against a log, was a young woman with long blonde hair, in long underwear, reading a paperback book right in the middle of nowhere. Her feet were propped up right at the edge of the stream. I walked down the stream right beside her, and I paused to explain what I was doing. It turned out she was a cook and wrangler for an outfitter camped nearby. A wise man once told me that, in the wilderness, you can never predict what you might see around the next bend. Looking for redds, I'd stumbled on a meadow pixie.

I continued downstream and finished the count by late afternoon. I met my partner and we compared notes. He'd been checking Basin Creek and found no bull trout redds there. We anticipated this result because the substrate was very small in Basin Creek, and it lacked chilly, upwelling springs. Also, that summer I'd seen lots of beaver dams in the drainage, making it hard for big bulls to access it.

I'd counted a handful of redds in upper Bowl Creek, yielding an overall total of 29 for the entire stream. That extrapolates to about 145,000 eggs deposited and fertilized by a total spawning run of an estimated 93 mature bulls. These super fish had run the gauntlet and had made the 120-mile run from Flathead Lake, surviving to spawn in their natal stream. I wondered how many of these stressed-out fish would survive the downstream migration back to Flathead Lake. At any rate, they fulfilled their eons-old duty, and because of them, many thousands of bull trout fry would be coursing in the Bowl Creek drainage the following spring.

Our next target was Trail Creek, a high-quality, large tributary of Strawberry Creek that joins about two miles upstream from Bowl. Trail and Bowl make a pair separated by the long ridge of Bowl Mountain. Bowl has Grizzly Park and Trail has Grimsley Park, with 6,917-foot Mount May in between. Trail Creek absolutely gushes into Strawberry Creek like it's hurrying to attract big bull trout spawners. We had high hopes for Trail because when I snorkeled it on August 5, I counted 18 juvenile bull trout and observed gentle stretches with upwelling springs. That was a pretty good count of young bull trout; because they hide in the rocks, they're underestimated in snorkeling surveys.

We set up camp at Grimsley Park, named after iconic outfitter Chick Grimsley. A few months earlier, a grizzly had walked around my tent here in the middle of the night and scared me scatless. Maybe it was Grimsley's ghost (for old-timer Chick's detailed story, see my 2018 book, *Rangers, Trappers, and Trailblazers*).

I found that bull trout from Flathead Lake had poured into this lower section of Trail Creek, leaving big, churned-up redds. The high-use section centered around Grimsley Park and extended upstream past the South Fork of Trail Creek. I found a few redds that were almost out of the water, exposed by dropping flows. When we finished Trail Creek the following day, we'd located 31 well-worked redds. That would add up to about 155,000 eggs deposited and fertilized in this stream.

Altogether, Trail and Bowl Creeks represent a blockbuster source of bull trout for the upper Middle Fork. These two streams must offer something special—so many adult bull trout from Flathead Lake swim about 125 miles and crowd into these two creeks to spawn. In bull trout spawning, as in many aspects of life and biology, success breeds success.

After finishing the upper basin redd counts, we all gathered back at Gooseberry Cabin. The other crew had walked about twenty miles, plus a lot of stream miles in Strawberry Creek, yet only found 17 redds.

Strawberry looked like a gorgeous spawning stream, but the redd densities were low.

After lunch, the whole crew hiked back to Schafer, and I headed for the big pool at the mouth of Clack Creek. We had noticed that the larger cutts we'd seen in the river had been concentrating in the bigger pools. I wanted to take advantage of that by trying to mark some bigger cutthroat and take scale samples from them. The fishing was hot. I first caught little sculpins (a small, bottom-oriented fish) and put them on a size-12 hook. The big cutts loved them. I took scale samples from about a dozen larger cutthroat from 12 to 15 inches, large by Middle Fork standards. I lost track of time, and by the time I'd finished sampling the hole and collecting the scales, the day was waning.

Mark Deleray releasing a bull trout in the South Fork of the Flathead River within the Bob.

I figured on meeting the crew at the Cox Creek outfitter camp about nine miles downriver and six miles this side of Schafer Meadows. I climbed out of the river and up to the trail, which traverses up the mountainside through open country in and out of the Winter Creek and Switchback Creek drainages. As dusk began to fall, I could still see well enough on the open slopes, but when the trail dove into the dark timber a few miles short of Cox Creek it was like a black curtain dropped. I couldn't see the trail, and I couldn't find my flashlight.

Resigned to my fate, I sat down just off the trail to wait until first light and then catch the crew just a few miles ahead. But to my delight, at about 10 P.M., the moon rose and bathed the trail and forest in a spooky light. I used a piece of lodgepole for a cane and watched and felt my way along the trail to the Cox Creek camp, which sat in heavy timber. By the time I arrived, my crew had turned in. I restarted the campfire to warm up, then turned in myself. The crew wasn't happy with me because I made them worry, but when they found out I collected scales from a dozen lunkers, I think they forgave me.

Back at Schafer the next day, we trekked downriver about five miles to count Lake Creek, lower Morrison Creek, and Lodgepole Creek. We found 1 redd in Lake Creek, 14 redds in Lodgepole Creek, and a number of redds in our partial count of Morrison. We would count the upper portion later from the Morrison Creek Trailhead.

Then we all met back at Schafer and prepared to fly out the next morning. We had spent eleven wonderful days on this trip, enjoying bright sunshine, cold mornings, and warm afternoons. It might've been the longest stable stretch of Indian summer that I've ever experienced. When we headed in, the larch needles were turning gold, and on our way out they were beginning to fall and cover the ground.

As of 1980, none of the Middle Fork tributaries within Glacier National Park had ever been counted, but talking to park rangers, it sounded like Ole and Nyack Creeks supported bull trout spawning runs from Flathead Lake. I thought we should at least get a foothold in the Glacier tributaries for as complete a count as possible on the Middle Fork. So, although my crew was done, I decided to count Ole and Nyack alone to start the dataset.

On a beautiful late October day, I drove back up the Middle Fork and parked at the trailhead near the Walton Ranger Station, planning to count Ole Creek that day. The sun shone brightly, and the day promised to be unseasonably warm as I headed up the trail. The first half mile follows a timbered bench, then the trail swings into the incised Ole Creek channel.

A small suspension bridge spans the clear, rushing stream. From there, the trail winds up the ridge and heads toward the Continental Divide more than a dozen miles upstream.

The first three or four miles of the stream are dominated by big rocks and cliffy stretches, unsuitable for spawning. A bull trout the size of a great white shark couldn't move that substrate to build a nest. But at about mile four, the gradient flattens, the valley widens out, and the trail drops back down to the creek. This section of Ole Creek is a bull trout spawner's dream. The clean gravel and small cobbles are loose and unconsolidated, so the water can permeate and flow through it easily. This portion also shows lots of upwelling. In fact, the upper end of this spawning reach goes dry. But as soon as the stream bubbles up, the bulls take advantage of the upwelling and build redds.

On this first-ever count of Ole, I was excited to see the first redds. The spawning area was right where the Glacier ranger told me it would probably be. I jumped into the stream in the middle of the flat section and began counting upstream first. I saw a few redds right away. I waded about two miles upstream to the dry section. I walked above it and kept looking, as the stream re-watered, but the substrate size increased, and it looked like the bulls hadn't gotten above the dry section before it dried up. I walked back down to the wetted section and sat down by the stream to eat a late lunch.

I had a couple of pieces of fried chicken that I bought in Hungry Horse on the drive up that morning. It tasted really good. But then I started looking around and I thought, "I'm alone, and this strong odor of chicken could attract a bear." I had worried about this earlier because of Ole's ominous reputation as a bad place for griz maulings. I finished eating the chicken, and then, rather than pack it out, I buried what was left underwater in the stream substrate and put a big rock on it.

A few years earlier, a grizzly mauled a park fisheries technician about six miles upstream from where I sat. The way I heard the story, the griz knocked the man down and sat on top of him, holding him partly underwater in the stream. The bear eventually left. The young man survived, but I can't imagine the terror he must have experienced.

I wasn't taking any chances today; I was heavily armed. Pepper spray wasn't in use in those days, but I had my freon boat horn that I'd carried all summer on the wilderness stream surveys. And I brought along the big artillery—a Bowie knife I'd bought at an Army-Navy store. Looking back, it was ridiculous to think that either would do any good. The horn would annoy the griz, and then he could pick his teeth clean with the knife after he chomped me. But all went well. I ended up finding 19 beautiful redds in Ole Creek that day. Even though I saw lots of grizzly tracks, I never encountered a bear.

Chris Downs, a Glacier National Park employee, near a bull trout redd in Ole Creek, Glacier National Park.

That night, I slept in the "Blue Bomb" FWP station wagon in a pull-off at the Nyack Siding off U.S. Highway 2. The next morning, I waded across the Middle Fork and hiked seven miles up the Nyack Creek Trail to the magnificent Nyack Creek Falls. The trail snaked through Nyack's deep, dark timber, away from the creek for most of its length. This drainage feels truly remote, and in later years we ran into wolves, elk kills, and other wild things. Like so many other places in the Flathead, it's burned now and doesn't seem so deep and dark.

From the falls, I dropped into the creek and headed downstream, surveying for redds. Soon, the large creek flattened out, fanning into huge upwellings and tons of clean gravel. I walked up to a treasure trove of enormous redds.

All told, I ended up counting 14 redds that day, some of them "double redds," twenty feet long. I walked down the streambed all the way back, nearly to the ford of the Middle Fork. That ended the 1980 Middle Fork redd count. I hated to see it go; all told, we'd found 300 redds throughout the drainage.

As the years went by, I was always lucky when doing redd counts. In those forty-plus years and 1,000 miles, I had only one wolf "encounter." It happened a few years ago counting redds on Morrison Creek. Unlike most stream-related trailheads that are found near the mouth, the Morrison Creek Trailhead is closer to the upper end of the drainage. Jon, Tom, and I split up to complete the drainage in one day. Tom entered the stream and started counting from the top, and Jon and I walked seven miles down the trail.

At the second creek crossing, Jon donned his hip boots, jumped in the creek, and started counting down from that point to the end of our survey section about three miles downstream. I was headed to Lodgepole Creek, so stayed on the trail for a few miles, then hung a left, crossing Morrison and heading up the Lodgepole Creek Trail to the Whistler Creek junction. There's a remnant of a cabin, thought to be one of Slippery Bill Morrison's, a legendary trapper. It's a remote spot, and I've always loved starting the Lodgepole Creek count from here. Over decades of counting this stream, I've never seen another human, but I always see grizzly bear tracks in the timbered, brushy bottom. I surveyed this lonely creek about three miles back down to where it joins Morrison. From there, it's about nine miles back to the trailhead.

I'd completed the Lodgepole count by 4 P.M., finding a dozen nice redds. I started hiking back up the Morrison Creek Trail, but I began to wonder. Jon should've finished his count long before me, and I should've been seeing his tracks in the muddy trail, but there was no sign of him. Something was up.

At the creek crossing where Jon had jumped in, Tom had left a note. He reported how many redds he'd found in the upper section and recorded the time, about 3 P.M., that he'd reached this point and headed back to the trailhead. Jon would have picked up this note if he'd passed here, so obviously he was still downstream. The question was why.

I decided to wait for Jon, although daylight would be fading soon. If he didn't show by dusk, I would start back down the trail to look for him, although he could've been anywhere and it would soon be pitch black.

After an hour or so, the dusk descended. I kept shouting his name, with no answer. Finally, I pulled out my flashlight and started back down the trail. Finding him in the dark seemed pretty hopeless. I started thinking about mounting a search in the morning. Hoping my flashlight would last till I got back to the creek crossing to start a fire, I turned around and just then was surprised and delighted to hear Jon's yell.

It turned out that he'd missed the last trail crossing, wading right on by and all the way to the Middle Fork of the Flathead River. He realized his error and hightailed it back up the trail, slowing a bit when his flashlight conked out. We had seven miles to hike back to the trailhead, our waiting truck, and a worried Tom.

It's a good thing that I had a decent flashlight, but two good headlamps would have been better. I wondered why I always seem to have good flashlights when I don't need them and poor ones when I do.

Jon and I hiked up the trail to the last trail crossing of Morrison Creek. From here, the trail jumps up the ridge and runs 5.5 miles through heavy timber to the trailhead. Beyond our little flashlight beam, it was black.

About a mile up the trail, a loud series of howls caught our attention, and the howls were close. Below us, in the creek channel, it sounded like a good-sized pack of wolves was following right along with us. Our light beam revealed lots of wolf tracks on the trail; they'd been circling the area.

That haunting sound of wolves howling and following us within sixty yards was really scary. We were a little worried that in this black of night, they might mistake us for deer or elk. Our one little flashlight was fading. I shined the light on Jon's face and took a photo. Later, when we looked at the picture, Jon's eyes looked as big as golf balls.

The wolves followed below us for at least a mile. Finally, they either veered off or just quieted down. We hoped that they wouldn't get above us and circle back on the trail to see what we were. We finally reached the low rise near the end of the trail and hurried back down the last mile or so in heavy timber. At 9 P.M., we burst out of the trees and into the open Morrison Trailhead parking lot. Tom was waiting patiently for us in the pickup with the engine running and the fog lights on. We'd done this long count in one day many times and he wasn't surprised that we were late.

You would think that with all the remote streams I've walked down in the past forty-two years, I would've seen lots of bears. Wading down all those miles and miles of remote channels, I've sure seen lots of griz tracks, and I've probably walked right by many bears, but I've had few real encounters.

True to Ole Creek's reputation, I did experience an up-close encounter with a grizzly while counting redds there. I had completed the count and was striding back down the trail toward the Walton Ranger Station. I rounded a bend in the trail and there was a medium-sized grizzly eating huckleberries, feeding right on the trail's edge about fifteen yards away (I paced it later). The bear saw me at about the same time, and without hesitation he charged. My pepper spray was in the pocket of my FWP coat so it was handy. Without even thinking, I had my pepper spray out and pointed at him as he rocketed toward me. At the last second, he swept to the right and veered down the bank and into the brush and trees of the Ole Creek bottom. It all happened so fast that I didn't even have time to be afraid. My chest felt a little tight though, kind of like the feeling you get when you almost hit a deer on the highway. I'm not sure if this was a bluff charge, or if the bear at the last second decided to dive past me and down the bank. I'll never know, but I'm glad the bruin did what it did.

The only other significant close-up bear scare I had while counting bull trout redds over the years was in Coal Creek, also in the Middle Fork drainage, during the mid-1980s. I was trekking down the trail toward the river in this lonely drainage after I'd finished counting redds. I'd surveyed all the way upstream about seven miles to Elk Creek, near the Fielding trail junction, a stunning spot below Cloudcroft Peaks and Mount Doody. I'd found only 3 redds.

Only two miles short of getting out, I hurried around a sharp turn in the trail that cut through heavy timber and right ahead of me stood a massive, dark-colored grizzly (almost black), not twenty yards away. He looked at me, I looked at him. He dropped down, spun, and dashed down the trail, in the opposite direction. When he ran, it sounded like a huge cow galloping and thundering along; I couldn't believe how fast he could run for such a huge animal.

I was glad that the bulky griz ran in the opposite direction. But as I reached his tracks on the torn-up trail, I realized I had to follow along in his path to reach the river. I walked warily ahead, and sure enough his tracks showed that he just stayed on the trail; I had visions of him waiting for me up ahead, ready to pounce. Luckily, I came to an abrupt switchback, and at that point I dove down through the timber, heading straight for the Middle Fork at top speed. I reached the river ford and crossed, then hiked up the other side and across the railroad tracks. Breathing easier, I promised myself I would stop doing bull trout redd surveys alone, especially in remote areas.

That promise lasted about a week. ◄○►

CHAPTER 10

My Dash through the Bob

Friends and acquaintances have often claimed that wilderness treks are more satisfying if you move at a slower pace. You notice more, they say. I don't think so. I believe you experience more and get more excitement by covering a lot of ground in a short time. It's like fast-forwarding in technicolor. My senses electrify when I'm dashing through the wilderness. I just revel in it.

In 1975, while taking classes at the University of Montana's Flathead Lake Biological Station at Yellow Bay, I planned a day trip into Jewel Basin around that strategy. The way I figured it, I could see eight alpine lakes in one day. I thought my friends would be as psyched as I was. But when I described the plan, one of them said, "I don't want to see eight lakes in one day. I want to go to one lake and fish." I explained that I would be fishing too, just not as long at each lake. He didn't catch on to it.

My wilderness treks have often centered on challenging myself physically and mentally. That's a good way to get in touch with your spiritual side, which for me was intimately connected with being in the wilderness. My friends sometimes would refer to these trips as "crazy" or "death marches." But really, the trips weren't that remarkable. To cover big distances, you just keep moving and rely on your best friend—time. None of my treks could hold a candle to the distances that ultra-runners cover nowadays, but back then that was just an emerging practice.

My philosophy pushed me to attempt a forty-two-mile day trip through the Bob in 1992. At the age of thirty-eight, I could feel the clock ticking. I was used to challenging myself, but I'd never hiked forty miles in one day.

I thought I should bag a forty-miler before I turned forty. Bob Marshall was my hero; I'd studied his life and read all about his long treks through the mountains. During the summer of 1928, Marshall, then twenty-seven, visited the wild Montana backcountry that would later bear his name.

In five days, he hiked an astonishing 182 miles in the South Fork of the Flathead River drainage. On one of those days, he covered 40 miles. (Read more about Marshall's 1928 exploits in my book, *Rangers, Trappers, and Trailblazers*, Farcountry Press, 2018.) Naturally, I chose the South Fork, which I knew well, for my own trek in the Bob Marshall Wilderness.

On July 3, 1992, my wife Dana and I drove down the Swan Valley from Kalispell to Holland Lake and the Owl Creek Packer Camp, a popular entry point to the South Fork of the Flathead and the Bob. Along on the drive was our two-year-old son, Kevin Marshall Fraley. We planned on camping at the trailhead. I would leave for my Fourth of July trek from there, planning on covering the forty-two miles up and over the Swan Range, down Big Salmon Creek, down the South Fork of the Flathead, past Black Bear, and out to the Meadow Creek Trailhead where I had left another car.

We set up our tent and joined some cowboys and packers around a shared campfire. Kevin's wide eyes stared at the fire. We roasted marshmallows. The packers took a liking to Kevin. I've often found that backcountry people love kids and are eager to treat them to wilderness experiences.

Enjoying the campfire with cowboys and packers at Owl Creek, July 3, 1992.

Kevin, Dana, and John around the campfire at the Owl Creek Packer Camp, July 3, 1992.

These men asked me about our plans and, when I told them, I heard the usual "You're crazy; at least take a sleeping bag in case you don't make it; forty-two miles is a helluva long ways, etc." I appreciated their concern, but I assured them that I'd done nearly thirty miles a few times, and twenty or twenty-five miles dozens of times, carrying a big backpack. This distance would be only twelve miles longer than thirty, and I'd be carrying a light daypack, so I'd be fine. I told them I'd be starting early; I mentioned that the whole thing sounded a lot harder than it would actually turn out to be. I was confident.

My wife listened to this, but she didn't really care; she knew I was nuts anyway, and she never worries until I'm at least a few days or more overdue from a wilderness trip. Besides, we had upped my life insurance coverage after Kevin's birth.

After sharing this wonderful fire with these great wilderness folks, Dana, Kevin, and I turned in. For some reason I barely slept; the insomnia would cost me later.

At 4:30 A.M. I was ready to head out. I tried taking a timed photo but, in the pitch dark, it didn't turn out. All you can see is the bright bulb on my headlamp. I jogged my first step at 4:35 A.M.

I moved through the trail switchbacks the first few miles up Holland Creek. At 5:30 A.M., daylight broke and it slowly got lighter. I felt nauseous, probably from the excitement, freedom, adventure, and daring that I felt.

At 6:15, after six miles and 2,100 feet in elevation, I reached Upper Holland Lake. The lake serves as a pitstop before jumping over two different passes into the wilderness beyond. Daylight was gaining. The morning dawned clear and beautiful; a mist floated above the lake's surface.

After a five-minute stop, I hoofed it one mile in twenty minutes on the fairly open trail over Pendant Pass, only 450 feet in elevation above Upper Holland Lake. Pendant offers relatively easy entry to the Bob. I'd already encountered significant blowdown, though, which slowed my progress and drained some energy.

I started jogging downhill on the South Fork side of the pass, hopping over downed trees. By 7:40 A.M., I'd covered ten miles. I reached the junction with Big Salmon Creek, passing the spot where I'd seen the bull elk in late September 1973.

Big Salmon Falls, July 4, 1992.

The trail carried running water, and even the small creek crossings were running strong. By 8 a.m., at mile eleven, I ran into two men and a woman camped at Big Salmon Falls. These folks were friends of Gordon Ash, the Big Prairie ranger and a fellow student from UM in the 1970s.

* * *

Bear with me on a short detour from my dash through the Bob to paint a picture of my friendship with Gordon. It's a small world back in the Bob, and I knew Gordon well. He was already a legend in backcountry management. People liked Gordon; he was good-humored and known as an over-the-top practical joker. I'd been the butt of more than one of his pranks, including the time he put three live mice in my dry suit before I snorkeled a section of the South Fork. Once or twice, though, I got the better of him. Two of these retributions came during my annual June visit to Spotted Bear Ranger Station to train Forest Service employees on fish identification and fisheries management. As an added bit of fun, each year Gordon and I would face off in some misguided competition.

Our first battle was an eating contest, held outside the mess building. It made no sense, since I'm about five feet, seven inches and 135 pounds, while Gordon is at least six foot four, a couple

Big Prairie ranger Gordon Ash.

hundred pounds, and big boned. His stomach volume is probably twice mine. No doubt he thought it would be a cinch to destroy me in an eating contest, and it should've been. But I had an advantage: I could outsmart him.

We began the contest in the early evening, after our training seminars ended. A mildly interested group of spectators looked on; they didn't really see the point, since it seemed so one-sided.

I'd brought along a fish scale to weigh the food we ate as the battle progressed. We designated a trail crew member as an unbiased judge to weigh the food and tally the totals.

Things looked to be going all Gordon's way at first. He ate three steaks, two baked potatoes, lots of bread, beans, and I'm not sure what else, as we went through our first plates. He was up to about three pounds of food to my two and a quarter. He was beating me badly and gloating about it. I needed to shake things up or it was over.

I've always loved watermelon and there was plenty of it on the serving table. Gordon was avoiding it. When I started eating watermelon slices, he protested, saying that, sure they weigh a lot, but you don't eat the rind, which comprises the majority of the weight. He argued that I should be disqualified for the watermelon.

But unbeknownst to Gordon, I had worked it out with the judge to subtract the weight of the rind when I was done with each slice. Instead of eating more heavy steak and filling bread like Gordon did, I downed the less dense, water-rich melon, and my totals skyrocketed. Think about it: just a quart of water weighs two pounds. In the end, I thrashed Gordon, downing 5.2 pounds versus his 4.5 pounds, and I did it with my brain, not my stomach.

The next year, we planned a 7.5-mile race for our Bob Marshall competition. I figured this one would be an easy win for me, given our size difference. Sure, Gordon was a big strong guy and in great shape, but how fast could he run with his body type? Plus, he spent a lot of his time on the back of a horse. At the starting line, he wore hiking boots; I felt pretty superior as I looked down at my ten-ounce running shoes.

This time, a small crowd of bemused employees was on hand to watch the contest between two over-the-hill guys. The truth was, nearly all of them would've left us in the dust if they'd entered the race.

We left the starting line at the Spotted Bear Lake Trailhead not far from the ranger station. We started up the well-worn trail snaking through the forest and a smattering of beargrass blossoms. When we crossed the first old road, we hung a right and followed a series of roads that eventually looped back to our starting point.

Gordon ran surprisingly well; despite his size, he was light on his feet. I stayed with him for a while, and we exchanged the lead a few times. We were moving at a pace of about 7:15 minutes per mile. I'd never suspected he'd be able to keep up that pace uphill and down. At the midway point, I stopped trying to race him and trailed along just behind him so I could be sure to stay on course and save up for a final kick. As we reached the last part of the route, I surged ahead and covered the last half mile pretty quickly. Nearing the finish line, I could hear a few people cheering, which surprised me because I thought everyone would be rooting for their fellow Forest Service employee.

Gordon came puffing in like a freight train only about 300 yards behind me. One person said that I looked fresh, and that Gordon was red-faced, huffing and puffing. Actually, I barely beat Gordon, even though I had all the advantages. I tried not to gloat and to be as magnanimous as possible. But I was starting to get him back for his practical jokes.

The third part of our trifecta unfolded the following year. The two previous competitions seemed pointless and silly, but the next contest was the worst idea of all. We decided to battle it out in an eat-*and*-run contest, something I'd never heard of before or since. I think it was my idea and I will always regret it.

We assembled for dinner at the picnic tables outside the ranger station mess hall. The menu for the evening included baked ham, potatoes, beans, salad, and pie. We agreed to eat a "substantial" meal, and then race up the trail to Spotted Bear Lake and back, a round-trip of about 3.5 miles with about 400 feet of elevation gain. This time, Gordon was crafty. He goaded me into eating too much. I obliged him because I was ahead 2 to 0 in our personal Bob Olympics, and I was confident that my stomach, always reliable, could handle it. I found out later that Gordon hid how little he ate, and on top of that, he turned out to have a rock-solid stomach.

We lined up at the trailhead, with maybe a dozen bored spectators looking on. This time Gordon wore running shoes. We bolted up the trail, and I confidently took the lead, thinking I could run under 7 minutes per mile on this short course.

At about a mile in, I began to feel, let's say, incredibly sick. I slowed down despite my best effort and Gordon passed me, grunting in satisfaction as he went by. He reached the lake and turnaround point and started back down; at that point he probably had a few minutes on me. I looked at the lake, surrounded by meadows, when I reached the shore, but its beauty was completely lost on me. My pace progressively slowed, while Gordon sped along well ahead of me.

With about a half mile to go, I reached a small, pretty meadow and had to stop. I was suffering by far the worst nausea of my life, and I've never felt that sick since. I wanted to curl up and die. You can imagine what happened next.

When I finally got going again, I meekly jogged down the rest of the trail to the finish line. Gordon was sympathetic; he waited for me. All the spectators had left; they'd guessed what had happened. Nobody rubbed it in. My stomach remained sore for about a week, and it was a long time before I could eat ham again. That was our last competition; Gordon had gotten the better of me again.

* * *

Back at Big Salmon Falls on my daylong dash through the Bob, I bid Gordon's friends goodbye and loped down the trail. I reached mile fifteen at Albino Creek/Tango Camp and took my first rest, savoring the warm sunshine as I ate a snack and gulped water. I took stock of how I was feeling physically: my usually stable stomach was queasy, my legs felt tired, and my foot and left knee were sore. After a fifteen-minute rest, I proceeded on.

The trail through this stretch runs along the beautiful rocky banks and ledges of Big Salmon Creek, with several tricky creek crossings. I also encountered more blowdowns, forcing me to climb over large tangles of trees. I trekked past Barrier Falls, and then a short distance upstream of Big Salmon Lake I ran into a Forest Service crew that was clearing downed trees from the trail. What a relief—no more clambering over blowdowns.

169

John taking a break at Tango Creek on the morning of July 4, 1992.

At 11 A.M. I reached the lake, the biggest in the Bob, and bushwhacked through the willows and swampy backwaters to the inlet. After nearly twenty miles, my knees were bothering me, especially the lateral ligaments. But I didn't care, I was just happy to be in one of my most favorite spots in the Bob, or in the world for that matter. I sat down for a minute to soak in the sunny day with scattered clouds, in the center of paradise.

For probably thousands of years, the inlet of Big Salmon Lake has represented a vortex for native fish in the drainage. Here, the waters of Big Salmon Creek spill into the lake and flow for a few hundred yards. The westslope cutthroat line up to eat insects delivered by the current, and the bull trout line up to eat the cutthroat. In the spring, the cutthroat spawn upstream in the creek, and in the fall, the bull trout take their turn. It's a wonderful, timeless dance.

I dug out my telescoping fishing rod and cast a bubble and dry fly out into the current. A few cuts hit my fly, but they didn't seem very interested. I switched to a small spoon, made a few casts, and caught and released two bull trout and a small cutthroat, and that was plenty. My fishing was only ceremonial; I couldn't dash by one of the best fishing holes in the Bob and not wet a line, and it added another fun angle to the trip.

The westslope cutthroat caught and released from the inlet stream into Big Salmon Lake, July 4, 1992.

I sat there for a while, watching the cutts feed on bugs and the bulls feed on small cutts, remembering past trips. At noon, I made my way back over to the trail. I hiked the four miles along Big Salmon Lake to its outlet, picking a few strawberries and early huckleberries on the way. At the outlet, I ran into two llama wranglers who sang the praises of their docile pack stock.

I sat down and contemplated the stretch of wonderful, flat shoreline along the foot of the lake. For generations, Native Americans met and spent time here, chipping arrowheads and scrapers. I saw chips and one partly complete arrowhead in the gravel where I sat. I could almost picture the hunched tool makers skillfully working the stone into sharp edges. My trek was a lark; theirs was a way of life. I thought of how important this point of geography must have been to them, and how this exact spot on the Bob's largest lake served as a universally recognized landmark among the region's tribes. After a short rest, I headed down the outlet toward the junction with the South Fork of the Flathead River, just a mile away.

At the South Fork, I turned north and hiked a few miles downstream to the Little Salmon Creek footbridge. I walked down to the stream and bent down to get a drink (I never filtered water back then). Right at my feet at the edge of the stream lay a beautiful, mostly intact arrowhead. Another gem in the wild from long ago.

I was beginning to think that my upset stomach might stem from eating too much snack food, especially red licorice. I thought it would be better to stick to conventional food, like sandwiches, fruit, and maybe breadsticks. That's the menu Bud Moore, my wilderness mentor, recommended.

A couple hours later, at 4:30 P.M., I crossed Hungry Creek and swung around the bend in the trail, finally arriving at Black Bear Cabin, which was deserted. I'd left the packer camp trailhead thirty-one miles and twelve hours ago. I reclined sleepily in the sun, listening to the chirps of the Columbian ground squirrels and watching their little heads poke out of their burrows.

For a combination of reasons—trail conditions, blowdowns, rough stream crossings, no sleep—my knees were super sore. I had gone similar distances before without any problems. This trek, I had paced myself well and rested occasionally, so the pain surprised me.

I walked down to the bank and took a good look at the South Fork. It was flowing too high to stay on the west-side trail and then ford the river about a mile upstream of Black Bear Creek, even though that would cut a mile or two off the route. So, I crossed the big pack bridge and headed up the trail along the east side. I had eleven miles to go. But by the time I covered the four miles to Black Bear Creek, my legs had fallen apart, a new feeling for me. I was limping and favoring my right knee, and a sharp pain emanated from under my left kneecap. Unfortunately, the trail was muddy in this final stretch, and the squishy footing added a special kind of discomfort.

I reached Mid Creek (thirty-eight miles) at 7:20 P.M., and I couldn't imagine making it through the pain four more miles to the trailhead. A huge storm was gathering, and even in the long July daylight, the sky turned almost pitch black by 8:15 P.M.. But I marched on and finally reached the Meadow Creek Trailhead (forty-two miles) at 9:05 P.M. The last couple miles required a lot of willpower, as I dragged my right leg along. Looking back, I can't believe it was that bad; it shouldn't have been a death march, especially with my pre-dawn start. I took plenty of time to do the distance and was well prepared. But when I read my notes and relive it, yep, it was that bad.

An exhausted John at the Meadow Creek Trailhead, after covering forty-two miles, 9 P.M., July 4, 1992.

The storm clouds opened and lashed the landscape just after I crossed the footbridge spanning the South Fork; the river boiled below in its deep gorge. I trudged as fast as I could through the sheets of rain to the trailhead parking lot, my Honda sedan illuminated by the big flashes of lightning. It was so nice to finally be off my feet that I didn't care how bad the storm was.

Crazy lightning and pounding rain held my attention during the fifty-mile drive on the winding road around the west side of the Hungry Horse Reservoir. The weather gnomes threw everything they had at me, but I drove through it. When I finally reached home in Kalispell at midnight, it was still raining.

I opened the door and willed myself upstairs. My wife woke up and calmly watched me limp up the stairs, my right leg dragging. Dana shook her head, maybe in sympathy. But her face said, *You asked for it and you got it.*

But I had seen so much, such a big chunk of the Bob, in a very short time. I'd soaked in so much inspiration, so much profound beauty. I'd been immersed in the Bob, as if it had taken me into its arms. Nothing memorable comes easy, and a hard challenge like this usually brings joy in the end.

This whole trek had started from our tent near Holland Lake, followed a circuitous route through America's best backcountry, and finished back home in Kalispell, all in twenty hours. A long but wonderful day.

A few days later, Dana, Kevin, and I were in Bigfork and we ran into my good friend Mike Enk, who worked for the Forest Service. He noticed that I was limping, so we were talking about my trek. He said that first of all, it was stupid, and secondly, I would sustain permanent knee damage from the ordeal.

I'm happy to report that he was wrong on both counts. ◄○►

CHAPTER 11

Following the Fur

Winter surveys of wolverine, lynx, marten, and more in the heart of the Great Bear

In winter, an active world inhabited by scurrying furbearers goes mostly unseen in the depths of the wilderness. The dozen or so species of mustelids, canids, felids, and more are mostly nocturnal, but they leave their signs in the snow for those who can read them. That's why winter track surveys work so well for monitoring these seldom seen critters.

If you care about furbearers, such surveys are important—and they are a heck of a lot of fun.

In the early 1990s, biologists in western Montana wanted more information about lynx, but also about marten, wolverine, and others. There wasn't much data available on wilderness furbearer populations. FWP's Region 1 carnivore biologist, Shawn, asked my advice about setting up a survey area deep in the Great Bear Wilderness. I'd been the fisheries biologist for the area, lived it in my heart, and had counted bull trout redds for years from one end of the Great Bear to the other. I guess I was the go-to guy.

I told Shawn that my idea was to mimic the old-time trappers and their traplines. You have a central hub, and branch out like spokes on a wheel. That way you have a good, representative sample of a variety of elevations, aspects, and vegetation and forest types.

I suggested that we stage out of Schafer Meadows, the heart of the Middle Fork of the Flathead drainage. At Schafer, a sturdy ranger station cabin and bunkhouse graced the only active airstrip in the Bob, grandfathered in decades ago. Plenty of furbearer habitat stretched upstream to Dolly Varden, Schafer, and Cox Creeks, and downstream to Miner, Morrison, and Lodgepole Creeks, and the Three Forks area where Morrison Creek joins the Middle Fork. Throw in Lodgepole Mountain and Porter Creek, and you've got a pretty good sample. Schafer was the hub, and the drainages were the spokes.

The only problem was that this area was deep in the wilderness, far from the nearest trailhead. In winter, fixed-winged aircraft couldn't land at Schafer because the airstrip would be buried in snow. We'd need multiple ski travel days just to get in before we even started our survey spokes. No problem, Shawn said, we can use a helicopter. That sounded good to me.

Using a helicopter gave our team access to the Middle Fork Flathead country to track furbearers in winter.

Shawn always was a smart guy. He later left FWP to get his PhD at Cornell University. He even took a course there from Carl Sagan. Shawn then enjoyed a long professorship at Michigan State University. When we started the survey, his career was just starting to skyrocket. But his helicopter idea showed he would go far.

Furbearer surveys aren't complicated. You identify and record the tracks that cross your survey route, and you complete a set route length, the same place, same time, each year. That way you get a pretty good idea of species presence and whether they are rare, common, or in between.

Our First Survey in the Great Bear, 1993

It was March 3, 1993, by the time we got the sampling trip underway into the Great Bear. We coordinated with the Forest Service to use the Schafer Ranger Station as our base of operations.

I'd surveyed the entire Middle Fork drainage from a helicopter in the early 1980s as part of my fisheries biologist work. But the ride into Schafer in winter was an entirely different experience. It seemed that we were sneaking into a silent world empty of any human beings, but full of life.

Luckily the cloud ceiling stayed high and we could overlook the drainage, complete with the heavy snow depths, the snowed-in peaks, and mostly frozen river. In my data book I recorded the portions of the river that were frozen and open based on drainages and landmarks. The river was open in the gently flowing reach at Schafer Meadows, probably due to upwelling springs there. I could see good portions of open water on Schafer and Dolly Varden Creeks, where we'd begin our surveys that morning after landing.

Two chopper trips brought four of us and our gear into Schafer Meadows. The station hadn't seen visitors all winter, except for maybe a Forest Service patroller once or twice. The chopper took off, blasting us with the rotor wind. We'd see it again in four days. Besides Shawn and me, our group included Brian, who was FWP's statewide furbearer specialist, and another biologist. We split into pairs to cover all the spokes of the wheel, with Brian leading one pair and Shawn the other.

I was one of the lucky ones to go on the first survey on the morning we landed. Our plan was to cover the 4.5 miles from the ranger station up Schafer Creek to the Capitol Mountain Trail junction and then ski back down to complete our day.

We set off at 11:30 A.M. and skied upriver along the main trail, noting tracks of hardy elk that were wintering in the meadows area, along with moose and deer. The snow depths in the valley weren't great, maybe a couple of feet. We quickly covered the mile of trail through the lodgepole flat and skied down the bank to the river ford.

The area we surveyed was a sea of lodgepole, mostly younger stands, with scattered spruce and fir. A variety of critters have adapted to the monotony of the habitat.

One of the fur trackers fords the Middle Fork of the Flathead River, March 1993.

We had to pop off our skis and wade across the Middle Fork, which was mostly open water at the shallow ford. The water barely reached our knees. The air temperature hovered between 30 and 40 F., a really mild day, with occasional sunlight peaking through the late-winter clouds. We were lucking out—it felt like the banana belt.

As for furbearer tracks, we hit the jackpot. Just past the ford, where William Schafer, the first Middle Fork pioneer, had his cabin, we recorded a classic set of wolverine tracks. Instantly, the backcountry around us felt wilder. Wolverine always have been found in low densities, so seeing a great set of one's tracks was special and exciting. Maybe this *Gulo* was a reincarnated version of William Schafer. But it really gave our survey a jump start.

We started crossing sets of marten tracks in the lodgepole timber about one-third mile past the ford. By the time we'd covered 1.3 miles, we'd counted seven sets of marten tracks, pretty good for a "seral" stand of forty-year-old, relatively small lodgepole offering limited canopy cover.

In general, marten tend to select older-growth timber. Perhaps they feel more secure being protected from above by the dense canopy. They must live on constant alert for attacks from raptors like hawks and owls, although if you've ever seen an angry marten, you know it would be a formidable foe for a bird no matter how large and predatory it was.

As we skied along, we noticed an old cubby about thirty yards off the trail. Old-time trappers had built it from small logs to direct bobcat and lynx, and possibly wolverine, into it using various types of smelly lures. We imagined what it must have been like to trap these valuable furbearers in the wilderness: lonely and remote, but exciting.

The skiing was great. About three feet of firm snowpack covered the route. About three miles along our route, we forded Dolly Varden Creek. Here, the trees thinned out and we skied down the gentle bank and across the ice. In the last mile or so, we'd added nine more sets of marten tracks.

As we skied up the opposite bank, we made a truly riveting find: a set of massive mountain lion tracks. The lion may have been tending the elk that we'd seen evidence of wintering nearby. We imagined all the interactions that were going on in this forest system: the wildlife community here was vibrant, even in the depths of winter. Most of the action took place at night, but looking at the story in the snow allowed us to peer through a window into the inner workings of this remote wilderness ecosystem bound by the Middle Fork drainage.

We clicked off six more marten, a probable bobcat, and a number of ermine tracks as we continued skiing. The trail cut an arrow-straight path through the lodgepole. By the time we reached the Roaring Creek Trail junction, we were up to twenty *Martes americana*. We were surprised to see such track density in fairly open lodgepole. It was as if the marten decided to hold a convention here. Who knows why, but I'm sure they had their reasons, and with mustelids it's usually food. We were seeing lots of squirrel and snowshoe hare tracks.

We reached the Schafer Creek ford and right there the snow revealed that a lynx had walked along the creek, up onto the bank, and into the lodgepole. We were happy to see our first lynx track. The larger predators seemed to travel the creek drainages, which served as natural corridors.

We took careful measurements of the lynx track: it measured 4.75 by 4.5 inches. Much of the size of a lynx track is made up of the puffy fur around the paw. There isn't much chance of mixing up a lynx track with anything: bobcat are much smaller, wolverine have a much different gait and obvious claws, and mountain lion are much bigger and make heavier imprints in the snow.

When we had any doubt about track identification, we consulted our track bible, *A Field Guide to Mammal Tracking in North America*, by James Halfpenny. It was the go-to source on all things tracks, and we always kept it handy. We referred to the book simply as "Halfpenny."

Brian examines lynx tracks near Schafer Meadows.

The Schafer crossing comprised a kind of wetland and a stand of willow brush. Rising up straight before us was the ridge of Union Mountain. This 7,601-foot peak sits like a cap on top of open ridges that sweep down into the Schafer Creek drainage. The mountain sports beautiful ridges and cliffs where, reportedly, old man Schafer and maybe Slippery Bill Morrison hid loot in caves (as covered in my 2021 book, *Wild River Pioneers, 2nd edition*).

We followed the trail along the west side of Schafer Creek and across the base of Union Mountain as the canyon of the stream closed in. We noted about a half-dozen more marten tracks and picked up another lynx.

We had noted only seven ermine tracks. Also called the short-tailed weasel, they are maybe the most numerous carnivores in our forests. They only measure about a foot long, tip of snout to tail, but they're fierce and can bring down a snowshoe rabbit. Then again, an ermine makes a good meal for a much larger, three-pound marten. I suspected the ermine were lying low because of the marten convention. This route was probably not a safe place for short-tailed weasels to be running around just then.

We soon crossed Rouge Creek and ended our survey at the Capitol Mountain Trail, 4.5 miles from Schafer Cabin. It was just after 5 P.M., but on March 4, the days stretched longer and there was plenty of light.

We flipped our skis around and headed back down the drainage. What a joy to be skimming along through that remote wilderness corridor. But we looked at it in a different way now. Because of the stories in the snow, we knew a lot more about what was going on.

We re-crossed the Middle Fork ford in the dusk at 7 P.M., headed up the bank, and skied toward the lantern light in the windows and the smoke coming out of the stovepipe of the ranger station. Dinner would be hot and ample thanks to Schafer Cabin's cooking facilities, including propane. The basement was loaded with canned and "non-perishable food," but we had to be careful because some of the same cans had been there when I worked as the Middle Fork biologist a decade before.

The next morning, March 5, our crew planned to head up the Middle Fork channel, in part to cover riparian habitat. I love rivers, so I was glad to be included on this crew.

At 9 A.M. Brian and I skied upstream to the ford, then broke trail going upriver. The first tracks we ran into were those of a bald eagle that had killed a whitefish and dragged it across the snowy bank. Large whitefish scales lay scattered across the ice. It was fascinating to read the struggle in the snow.

Another quarter mile along, we could see a school of whitefish finning in the shallows in the tail of the run. Predators of all kinds had been drawn to them. We counted a number of mink tracks on the ice and saw a large mink scurry along the stream channel.

Just short of a mile along our route, we noted a large set of otter tracks along the river ice. We also counted lots of coyote and weasel tracks. It was clear that the river habitat supported a much different community of critters than the forested uplands.

The weather had warmed to near 40 degrees, and a steady drizzle fell. Tracks were beginning to lose definition, but we kept at it all the way to the mouth of Surprise Creek, and then on to Calbick Creek. We'd covered around four miles from the start and had waded the river or crossed the ice about four times along the way.

At Calbick Creek, we crossed the river again and climbed the ridge on the east side of the Middle Fork canyon. After about 400 feet of climbing, we joined the main trail that parallels the river. On the way back to Schafer, we noted lots of coyote tracks, a few marten, and even a moose. But the snow conditions deteriorated in the drizzle, and the survey quality plummeted. Even with Brian's expertise, we could no longer positively identify some of the tracks we saw. Winter track surveys are great, but snow conditions definitely affect results.

We rejoined the other crew at Schafer and warmed up with a fire in the woodstove. They had surveyed downriver along the main trail to Three Forks and on to Miner Creek. The next day, we counted tracks on upper Dolly Varden to Argosy Creek and in the Lodgepole Mountain area. Both crews noted multiple mountain lion tracks. Shawn was surprised to see so many lion tracks in an area where it was thought that few deer and elk wintered.

Another interesting find was many tracks of a lone wolf between the airstrip and the river. It appeared that a mountain lion had killed an elk, and then the wolf took possession of it. Each morning, we saw fresh wolf tracks at the elk carcass. When its print was a little melted out, it was almost as big around as my baseball hat.

All told, our efforts added up to six total track survey routes totaling thirty-five miles one way. We felt good about what we'd learned from this first track survey in the central Great Bear Wilderness. The warm weather and rain had hurt our survey quality, so we realized that we should survey in February. But we documented a vibrant furbearer community around the "hub" of Schafer Meadows. We'd seen wolverine, lynx, lion, wolf, and a ton of marten tracks. How do you beat that? What a privilege it had been to peer into the critter community deep in the Great Bear in winter.

The Best Laid Plans, 1994

The next year, we were all excited to build on our initial success, but the weather threw us some sliders. The first day, February 22, produced a decent count, but then heavy snowfall nixed our luck.

After landing in the chopper and unloading gear, Rick, Menno, and I skied the route from Schafer to the Capitol Mountain Trail. Right from the start, we could tell that the fresh, deep snow would be a challenge. Not only were the tracks less defined, but snow filled in many of them. We would only be able to see the most recent tracks. But it was deeply quiet, and snow hung on every lodgepole and fir. The Middle Fork was as pretty as it gets.

Even with the new snow, we counted marten tracks regularly along the route, so that was exciting, and snowshoe hares were out and about. When we reached the Schafer Creek ford, we skied along the bank for a half mile before crossing the creek below a big spring. In the gravel at the tail of a run, I showed Rick and Menno a three-by-six-foot bull trout redd, still visible from the previous September's spawning run. Bull trout have been spawning below this gushing spring for thousands of years. It was humbling to contemplate this as we stood in the quiet solitude.

We noted a set of moose tracks and a probable lynx. We rejoined the trail and continued up the drainage for a mile. Right at the end of a meadow, we noted another marten track, making fourteen for the route at that point.

At the Capitol Mountain Trail junction, we thought we had a trophy. Rick said that the track was either a Boone-and-Crockett marten or a fisher. We measured it and consulted our Halfpenny track guidebook. Based on the track, stride, straddle, and leap, it measured out as a fisher, so we recorded it as such. Thus began a debate that lasted for years: were there really fisher in the upper Middle Fork, or can their cousin, big male martens, make a track that large?

At Capitol Creek we ended the survey, swung our skis around, and headed back down the trail in the soft light of a snowy wilderness evening. By 7:30 p.m., a while after dark, we made it back to Schafer, and the warmth of the woodstove felt wonderful.

We woke up the next morning, the 23rd, to two feet of fresh snow. Brian and I skied the Morrison-Lodgepole route, and Rick, John, and Menno skied the Lodgepole Mountain area. Between the two crews, we surveyed eleven miles and counted only a handful of tracks that we could positively identify. The powder that fell the night before had erased any chance of a good count, but the day produced no more snow.

That night, we celebrated my fortieth birthday. I don't drink alcohol, so the party consisted of a large homemade chocolate chip cookie with a stick in it for a candle. It was a noteworthy year for John as well; he had recently turned thirty. We looked forward to exciting and challenging surveying the next day.

On February 24, John and I got an early start because the Scott-Miner route was a long one, totaling eight miles out and eight miles back. We knew that we had to cross the Middle Fork four miles downstream of the station, and we hoped it was iced over. The fairly deep snow would be taxing, but at least it had been a day since any new snow. This also gave us hope that the critters would be out and moving and we'd get at least some kind of count.

I felt so full of life that morning. I'm not sure why, but I felt super-charged and ready to break trail forever. From the beginning, we could see that the track count would be marginal in this deep, new snow, and there'd been only about twenty-four hours for animals to make tracks. But it was better than the day before. We started seeing good numbers of snowshoe hare and a marten track as we crossed the airstrip and headed down the trail through the lodgepole.

We skied for four miles along the lodgepole bench, then hung a left on the side trail that drops to the mouth of Morrison Creek on the Middle Fork. The deep snow really slowed our pace. At the ford, we crossed the river on snow and ice bridges that seemed safe. After we started up the Lake Creek-Miner Creek Trail and gained the bench, John began feeling sick. We never did figure out if it was something he'd eaten the night before, or exhaustion from the deep snow, or both.

We knew we couldn't complete the route at the pace we were moving, so about a mile short of Scott Lake, we decided that John would stop and rest, while I would survey up past the lake and outfitter camp, and toward Flotilla Lake a short distance. To keep warm, John could follow slowly in my trail, and we'd meet as I skied back down.

I reached Scott Lake and skied through the outfitter camp. I felt so fortunate to be able to take part in this deep-wilderness survey in the dead of winter. It seemed so free and stirring, so isolated. My enthusiasm surged and I didn't feel tired at all. I guess turning forty agreed with me.

I noted the fresh tracks of lots of snowshoe hare, five marten that had dashed across the snow surface that morning, and a few coyotes. I skied about three-quarters of a mile on toward Flotilla, then figured I'd better turn around.

The ski back down the trail through the soft, fluffy backtrail was invigorating. No, that doesn't come close to describing it; maybe spiritual is a better word. As I skied down a steep straight section of trail though the lodgepole, I could see John skiing up to meet me. We caught up with each other and compared notes. He had seen a large male marten track that crossed my backtrail and then followed in the furrow for a while. I wished one of us could've seen him. I wondered what the wilderness critter thought of such a strange, odd-scented creature carving a deep trail through his territory. What a nice reward for us having skied way up into this wonderful drainage.

We turned around and skied back to the river ford, crossing it as dusk began to fall. I was glad we at least got across the river safely before dark. We still had about five miles to go to reach the station. But as we proceeded, John deteriorated.

Each mile was a struggle for my poor companion. When we reached the Lodgepole Mountain Trail junction, his nausea worsened. We would ski along for a few hundred yards, and then he would be on his hands and knees, retching. We finally made it back to the ranger station and our worried colleagues by 8 P.M., long after dark. Thankfully, John awoke the next day fully recovered.

Big Cats, 1995–1996

The 1995 trip had its highlights. Eric and I had a pair of lynx on our backtrail on Lodgepole Mountain. We missed seeing them by less than an hour. On my birthday, Brian and I did an eight-mile upriver route up to Cox Creek and Wapiti Park and noted a number of mountain lion track sets. That remote area seems to draw the lions and coyotes because a small herd of elk apparently winters there. In the dead of winter, the wildness of the place is an inspiration.

In 1996, we saw more lion sign on that route. In fact, a pair of them gave me a spook. John, Leonard, and I headed upriver on February 28. The results of that survey covered five pages in my data book; we saw such a variety among the hundreds of track sets and stories in the snow.

After leaving the flats at Schafer, we followed the trail high above the river, crossing timbered and open hillsides. We saw lion and coyote tracks to Surprise Creek, tending the small ungulate herd. Then we skied into the timber past Calbick Creek and found the trail littered with prey tracks. We measured two beautiful sets of lynx tracks. By the time we'd reached Cox Creek, at about mile 6.5, we'd measured four widely spaced sets of lion tracks and a lynx along the way. The cats were really moving. And so were their prey—we'd counted a few hundred

Measuring mountain lion tracks in the Great Bear Wilderness.

dred snowshoe hare, many squirrel, and scattered ungulate tracks.

Tim and Brian measuring furbearer tracks deep in the Great Bear Wilderness.

We continued north up the Cox Creek Trail, finally stopping for lunch at 2 p.m. with a light snow falling. We were excited about all the tracks we'd seen. John and Leonard decided to head back to the station, but I relished the chance to explore alone for a while and wanted to check out Wapiti Park, another mile up the trail. I'd have a broken trail to follow back to Schafer, and dinner would be ready when I returned.

As I skied toward Wapiti Park, I crossed lots of snowshoe hare and squirrel tracks, along with some deer and elk. The park itself was beautiful and remote, and I was drawn to keep going.

Then I ran into a very fresh line of lion tracks coming from the timber on my right and onto the trail, I followed them for a quarter mile. Despite the light snowfall, the tracks were fresh and clean—the lion had just joined me. The prints measured 4.5 inches across, and the cat's stride spanned up to 53 inches. It felt a little spooky to follow the cat up the trail.

Then it got spookier. Out of the open timber on my right, another set of super-fresh lion tracks, with prints also measuring 4.5 inches and stride lengths from 24 to 45 inches, joined the trail of the first lion. Based on the angle of the tracks, this lion might have been walking parallel to me in the timber and then, at a bend, got ahead of me and crossed the trail to join the other lion. Both tracks left the trail and led side-by-side down into the creek channel. I thought of how close these lions were, and how far into the wilderness I was. A bit spooky, yes, but also thrilling.

I sketched a diagram of the tracks and made notes in my data book. Then, with evening coming on and a nine-mile ski back to Schafer, I swung around and headed back down the trail.

The next day, Leonard, Menno, and I skied the downriver route, bound for Three Forks, Scott Lake, and Miner Creek. We ran into a perfect set of wolverine tracks with textbook measurements: 4.5 by 4.5 inches, with a straddle of 9 inches, and a stride of 18 inches. These critters are built like little bears. We could see the pads and toes in the imprints. We were excited, and I wrote WOLVERINE!!! in the data book.

As we dropped off the lodgepole bench and headed downhill toward Three Forks, we crossed lots of coyote, weasel, snowshoe hare, and squirrel tracks, with a few marten and a lion thrown in. Excellent tracking conditions made the identifications easy. I was looking forward to the river crossing and the route to Scott Lake and Miner Creek, where I knew we would see tons of tracks.

But it wasn't to be. When we reached the Middle Fork, there was a mix of open water and jumbled ice jams, making it almost impossible to cross. I wasn't ready to give up, though. I searched downstream and found an ice bridge about a foot above the churning water. I thought we could get a good start and surge across the narrow part. Leonard and Menno both said no way.

I skied to the edge of the ice, planning to slip across and show them it could be done. Then I skied back to them one more time, psyching myself up, and said, "I'm going to do it, I'm going to do it." They shook their heads and were dead against it.

I turned back toward the river again, and Leonard said, "Hey John, how old are your kids again? Isn't Troy's first birthday coming up in about a month?" Leonard, a senior hunter education coordinator, has always been a wise mentor to me. This time, his questions may have saved my life.

Moose Tracks: Not Just an Ice Cream Flavor, 1998

The year 1997 ranked as one of the biggest snow years on record, which meant almost impossible tracking conditions, so we didn't even try to conduct a survey. But 1998 greeted us with excellent conditions. After landing at Schafer, we rejoiced in the solid snowpack with a few inches of soft snow on top, perfectly suited to hold tracks. The forecast called for stable, moderate temperatures with mostly clear skies. We figured that this survey would be one for the ages.

We had a bolstered crew of five FWP experts, Menno from the Forest Service, and me. All signs pointed to three days of great data collection.

On February 17, I accompanied Brian (the statewide fur coordinator) and Tim, our top furbearer biologist as well as a moose and bear expert. I was excited to spend a day with these experienced wildlife biologists as we examined hundreds of tracks from Schafer all the way up Dolly Varden Creek to Argosy. The canyon narrowed after the Chair Mountain Trail, but the bottom remained relatively flat and gentle through the lodgepole, closely following Dolly Varden Creek all the way.

Furbearers were really on the move in this lodgepole-dominated drainage. We counted 4 lynx and 16 coyotes. Lots of prey tracks littered the snow surface, including 244 squirrel, 182 snowshoe hare, and a dozen grouse. Mustelids included 22 weasel or ermine, and a stunning 43 separate sets of American marten tracks. Many of the marten tracks threaded around a small area in the flats near the junction with Argosy Creek.

We were all surprised to see such a high density of marten in stands of mostly lodgepole pine. Their tracks were everywhere, apparently ignoring the territorial distancing they're known for, perhaps tolerating other marten to take advantage of an abundance of prey. We all had to ruminate on this for a while.

After skiing seven miles, just past Argosy Creek, we called it for the evening and enjoyed a scenic ski back down the trail. Dolly Varden is a gorgeous drainage with big avalanche paths on both sides. To the east it is bound by Chair Mountain and the Gable Peaks complex. To the west rise Argosy Mountain and its associated high ridges. Argosy Creek itself is an enchanting, seldom-visited drainage coming in from the west side of the main canyon. We reached Schafer long after dark, our late return rewarded with dinner waiting for us.

On February 18, I was excited for the next survey route to the remote country around Scott Lake, on the west side of the river. I'd be going along with Harvey, the FWP wildlife manager, and Jerry, a wildlife biologist, moose expert, and fur biologist.

Every once in a while, a backcountry trek throws a real surprise your way, the sort of situation that gives you a glimpse of the pearly gates sooner than you expected. I didn't know that this feeling would flash through my mind later that day, as Harvey, Jerry, and I skied away from Schafer that morning.

We skied downriver on the trail, skimming along on the deep but firm snowpack. A few inches of soft snow on top served as a perfect matrix to hold clear prints. We headed for Three Forks and what we expected to be a challenging crossing of the rushing, boulder-strewn Middle Fork. Luckily, we found a solid enough snow and ice bridge to cross, so we didn't have to try wading the river.

We humped up the trail on the west side of the river and topped out on the flat bench leading to Scott Lake and Flotilla Lake. We noted a lion track and a lynx. But what really surprised us was the density of marten tracks; we'd discovered another "pod" of marten. In a little more than a mile, we sorted out nearly forty separate marten track sets.

We mused about why marten were so concentrated here, similar to what we'd seen near Argosy Creek. In a lodgepole forest like this, voles and mice move up and down around the straight trunks, in and out of the snowpack. The marten must watch for that movement, or they smell their prey, and pick off the rodents when they emerge from the snow. In some places, shrubs and downed trees created open pockets under the snowpack where the marten could hunt. We tried to imagine this unseen, subnivean world, and the marten dance floor made more sense.

A biologist once told me that a marten's sense of smell is so acute that they mainly smell the critters, signs, and landscape, rather than see them. Maybe they follow an olfactory map in their heads. That might explain how they hunt so well at night or under the surface of the snow.

Before we ended our survey, we counted 133 separate snowshoe hare track sets, another marten food source. Apparently, marten will abandon their solitary habits to feast on a profusion of food.

We skied past Helmet Point on our left, and continued up through mixed lodgepole and spruce in the gentle Lake-Miner Creek drainage toward Scott Lake. We noted lots of weasel and squirrel tracks, a few coyote, scattered ungulate tracks, and a half dozen grouse tracks. These were likely made by the Franklin's grouse or "fool hen." If there's such a thing as easy prey, they are it, at least from a human's perspective. The fact that these trusting birds still exist is tribute to their ability to fly into a tree or over the ridge if they sense a natural predator closing in. After all, coyotes can't climb a tree and martens can't fly.

We reached the Scott Lake outlet after about four miles of the route. We skied along a little ridge where the creek leaves the lake near the junction with Miner Creek, coming in from the south. I surveyed the creek bottom toward the outlet, while Harvey and Jerry skied along the ridge thirty yards above me.

Looking upstream, I received a wonderful gift: a moose calf standing in the unfrozen outlet of the lake. I thought how hard it must be to raise a young animal in such a place—so much deep snow and mountain lions around every corner. Moose must be great at taking care of their calves. I was fascinated, and I wondered where the adult was. Just then, Harvey shouted at me; he seemed alarmed. He said, "Moose! Do you see that moose?"

And I said, "Yep, I'm looking right at him. Cute calf; he's up to his belly in the water."

Harvey shouted again, and he sounded really urgent this time: "No, I mean *that* moose. Look downstream!"

A very angry, very big cow moose was set to mount a full charge upstream straight at me. I realized that I was between her and her calf. I was wearing skis and carrying poles, so was not able to move quickly. I only had one choice: I had to plunge backward into the thick alder and hope she didn't stomp me. I took the foolish chance to snap a photo. My chest felt full and my heart raced, and I thought, *No, I don't want to get injured way in here.* I could imagine blood on the snow.

The angry cow moose just before she charged.

The cow galloped my way, sending snow and rocks flying. Five days short of my forty-fourth birthday, I was having a meet-your-maker moment. She looked mean and mad. But lucky for me, she made the right decision: she rushed by and ran to join her calf. If you've never seen a moose sprint with those long legs, you can't imagine how fast they pick up speed, and it sure looked like she was going to take me out. She could have, but she didn't. With his view from above, Harvey thought I was a goner.

The photo? It was a good one, and she sure looks mad. It all happened so fast that I didn't really have time to be scared. Well, maybe a little. That was probably the closest call and biggest excitement we ever had during the decade of Middle Fork fur surveys.

We continued past the frozen lake, taking in a view that almost no one else ever sees in winter, and skied on toward Flotilla Lake. We saw lynx and lion tracks, plus more marten and coyote.

We had penetrated deep into the Great Bear in winter and the feeling was just overwhelming. We were peering into a special world: a community of critters that rarely if ever see a hominid in the depths of winter. By the time we hit our turnaround point, about five miles from the Middle Fork, we'd counted the following track sets: 133 hare, 50 marten, 39 squirrel, 11 coyote, 9 weasel or ermine, 2 lynx, and 2 mountain lion.

Oh yeah, and two moose. And those tracks were super fresh.

Short of Flotilla Lake, we flipped our skis around and swished back down our packed trail. It was getting late and the light was waning. I was reluctant to leave because I might never again get such a special opportunity to spend a winter day in this wonderful place.

The ski down the gentle drainage below towering Wild Rose Mountain took our breath away. Back at the Middle Fork, we were relieved to see that our snow and ice bridge had held. We knew it would be dark before we got back to the station, but that was okay.

The next morning, Harvey, Tim, and I headed back downstream on the trail to the Morrison Creek Trail junction. We would start from there and do our survey up Morrison Creek to the second creek crossing, then back down and up Lodgepole Creek for two miles to Whistler Creek. This is country I knew intimately, having done fisheries surveys and bull trout redd counts there for years. Slippery Bill Morrison's old cabin site sat along Whistler Creek, so the area is rich in Middle Fork history.

Tim was a recognized furbearer expert. I learned a lot about measuring stride length and straddle in the lynx tracks we saw to positively identify them. We skied along the bottoms of Morrison Creek on the trail, passing through stands of large spruce and more lodgepole. On our five-mile Morrison route, we counted the track sets of six lynx, a pretty good density for this cat. We recorded hundreds of snowshoe hare, squirrel, and grouse tracks, so there was plenty for the lynx to eat. Living alongside these critters were twenty-one coyotes and a few martens and weasels.

On the way back down Morrison Creek, we swung up Lodgepole Creek, a major tributary. It can be confusing to get on the trail here in this big wooded flat, but I'd counted it so many times for bull trout redds that I knew exactly where to go. We found elk tracks up the drainage, confirming that a band of elk winters here, deep in the heart of the Great Bear Wilderness. Lion tracks showed that these big cats tended this elk herd closely. We also identified another lynx and lots of weasel tracks.

Tim and Harvey turned around and headed back down Lodgepole Creek, but I skied another half mile to Whistler Creek. I wanted to touch bases with old Slippery Bill Morrison. The ruins of his cabin and maybe his storage cabins would be covered by the snowpack, but I knew how to find them, right along Whistler Creek just downstream from the trail crossing. In fact, the standard topo map marks the spot with a little square. In the waning light, looking at another lion track, the area felt wild, remote, and spooky, exactly how I like it. Just imagine spending a whole winter in here alone as Slippery Bill did.

Soon, I turned around and swished back down the trail that I knew so well, and eventually caught up with the crew on the way back to Schafer. It would be another after-dark return to the ranger station.

The other crews had noted good numbers of tracks on their routes as well. In fact, during the whole 1998 survey, snow conditions remained excellent. We were pleased to document forty-three lynx in the thirty-seven miles of routes we surveyed. Later that same year, federal wildlife officials proposed listing lynx as threatened under the Endangered Species Act, and the listing was finalized in March 2000. Montana FWP opposed the listing, but it went through anyway. By 2018, the feds admitted that the Canada lynx didn't warrant listing in the Lower 48 after all, and should be delisted. Predictably, the decision is still tied up in the courts.

Year of the Lynx, 1999

We were all excited to get back to the Middle Fork in 1999. Perry and I skied in from the Morrison Creek Trailhead off Skyland Road after an eleven-mile snowmobile ride from U.S. Highway 2. (Days later, on the way out, the chopper gave us a lift back to the snowmobile.) Starting at the Morrison Trailhead would give us ten miles of survey route down to the main Middle Fork Trail.

The furbearer tracking crew at Schafer Ranger Station, 1999.

We enjoyed skiing down the Morrison Creek Trail, which passes through stands of old-growth spruce, along with fir and lodgepole. It was looking like the year of the lynx. On that stretch, we counted six sets of lynx tracks widely spaced from one another.

The lynx were probably hunting the abundant snowshoe hare. We documented an amazing 221 sets of hare tracks, along with 132 squirrel. We counted 21 sets of marten tracks and 37 ermine, so they were in on the smorgasbord too. Add in a few coyotes and the cast was complete. We were sharing the woods with a thriving set of critters in an age-old dance.

We skied forty-five miles of route on the 1999 survey, covering all the spokes and then some. We had a total of 998 snowshoe hare, 423 squirrel, 263 weasel, 72 coyote, 56 marten, 9 mountain lion, 4 wolverine, and a few otter. With so many hares, it would make sense that lynx numbers would also be high, but we were still astonished to document 38 lynx.

The Final Survey Year, 2001

The 2001 survey offered plenty of exciting moments, and the results were pretty similar to other years. It was a boom year for marten, with 162 sets of tracks. Snowshoe hares were surging; we counted well over 1,000, along with their shepherds, 16 Canada lynx.

On February 20, Jerry and I helicoptered into the Morrison Creek Trailhead again. From there, we skied a ten-mile route to the junction with the Big River Trail, four miles from Schafer. Jerry and I surveyed the trail

John near Schafer Meadows in 2001.

down Morrison Creek with good results, including thirty-nine marten and a couple hundred snowshoe hare. Around dark, we arrived at the ranger station and rejoined the crew that had been helicoptered all the way in. They had done routes that day as well.

On February 21, I joined the crew to survey Dolly Varden upstream to Argosy. We hit the jackpot again, skiing into another marten convention of fifty-one track sets. The pod of wintering marten in this drainage is starting to get predictable. I guess we should stop being surprised by it and try to figure out what the marten are telling us.

On the last survey day, I accompanied the crew on the upriver route to Cox Creek. We counted six lynx and a bunch of marten. This eight-mile upriver route leads into the remote upper river drainage where few if any people go in winter. It was an old haunt of mine when I was the Middle Fork fisheries biologist in the early 1980s. Nostalgia washed over me in the winter silence of the Great Bear.

A Decade of Furbearer Data

During the decade of surveys, I'd sit in the Schafer Cabin each night, recopying my notes for the day and asking the other crews for their day's numbers. I've always been kind of a stats guy. This may or may not be the official count, but here's what I have for the annual average over the years on our thirty-five to forty-mile hub-and-spoke area: 676 snowshoe hare; 345 squirrel; 84 weasel; 74 marten; 45 coyote; 15 lynx; 5 mountain lion; 2 wolverine. Other critters: wolf, otter, mink, beaver, bobcat, eagle, raven, several possible fisher, deer, elk, moose, whitefish, cutthroat trout, bull trout.

Imagine this thriving community of native species coursing around the landscape, over the snow, up into trees, under the snowpack, and back and forth across the streams. You have to imagine because you rarely see them, the predators at least. Sometimes you see blood or fur or feathers on the snow's surface. But most of the action happens under the cover of night or in the subnivean darkness, under the deep snowpack.

These predators are like ghosts. The late Alaska naturalist, Richard Nelson, described the winter mysteries of these hunters in his classic book, *Make Prayers to the Raven*. "They share with humanity the gift of cunning,"

Nelson wrote. "They are quick and agile, inquisitive of mind, always restless. They move at the open edge and the precipice, rush suddenly upon errant prey, then vanish like shadows, leaving flecks of blood to soak into the snow. They are the predators."

Skiing all those hundreds of miles, we never actually saw many of the predators except for a few otter, weasel, or mink. It's amazing how much you can learn about a system just based on tracks in the snow. I felt good about the surveys because the counts covered a variety of snow conditions, track quality, annual variations over a decade, and diverse routes and habitat.

The snowshoe hare and red squirrel form the animal base of this food chain or trophic pyramid. You would have to include the fir and pine needles that the hares eat and the seeds the squirrels eat. If you charted all of the relationships and interactions, you'd end up with a complex diagram. A few of the predators occasionally eat each other. And you can't leave out the scavengers, like the raven.

When it's all said and done, I'm betting that the collective numbers we found over the decade are probably reflective of what actually occurs in the wilderness landscape on average. And to think this existing species complex has been thriving here for many thousands of years. It's humbling, and a testament to the protection afforded by wilderness designation.

On February 23, 2001, the last day of that year's survey, I turned forty-seven. What a birthday present! I was lifted out of the Great Bear via helicopter on the last flight, and I watched the Middle Fork canyon speed past below me. The magnificent, snow-covered peaks of the Lewis Range stretched into the distance. I didn't want to leave but couldn't figure out how to stay. I didn't know it then, but that was my last Middle Fork fur survey. ❧

CHAPTER 12

Villain in Velvet

In wilderness, the American marten reflects a collective soul

When it comes to wilderness trapping and many other things, I am a student of Bud Moore. Bud was the expert of experts on trapping pine marten, also known as the American marten, *Martes americana*. His passion and love for fur trapping in the wilderness beamed strongly from his soul when he talked about it, especially when he was counseling me on how to do it right: practically, ethically, and spiritually.

Bud, who passed in 2010 at age ninety-three, was a long-line wilderness trapper in the Lochsa when he was a young man, operating a trapline eighty miles long, arranged in a circle using way-cabins. Much later, he relived long-line trapping in the Bob Marshall Wilderness when he was pushing seventy just to show it could be done, and done right (for more of that story, see "Bud Moore's Wilderness Experiment" in my book, *Heroes of the Bob Marshall Wilderness*).

His forty years with the U.S. Forest Service and thirty-five years in a second "career" as a conservationist earned Bud wide acclaim and total respect from all sides. The University of Montana awarded him an honorary doctorate in science for his contributions to forest leadership and ecosystem and fire management. Being a federal forester had its rewards, but Bud relished his later opportunities to think outside agency constraints. "Get out of government service while you still have the energy to make a difference," he once said. "Working for the government sort of neutralizes you as a person." Bud lived that advice.

Humility is the number one trait you need in the backcountry, Bud told me, especially if you are going to trap fur. "You can always cross that pass the next day," he said.

Bud Moore at his cabin home in the Swan Valley.

Like fairy dust, Bud sprinkled me with humility, because I think he sensed I really needed a big dose. I looked at wilderness travel as a challenge and a chance to prove something to myself, or maybe to him. I'm sure Bud picked up on that.

There's a utilitarian side to trapping, just as there is with hunting and fishing. No one makes their entire living by trapping, not even close. So obviously, there's something much deeper going on. Bud placed a lot of importance on this practical side of fur trapping, seeing it as producing a renewable value from the land. But he also reveled in the spiritual side of trapping marten in wilderness.

After you've interacted with this mustelid in the backcountry, no other furbearer matches up. Old-time Glacier Park ranger Clyde Fauley, who, like other rangers, trapped marten in the park, called the big weasel the "Villain in Velvet." Intensity and curiosity are the trademarks of *Martes americana*, and like other members of the weasel family, they're vicious and full of verve. If you've been caught by its laser stare, you know what I mean. The face is triangular, with forward-pointing, cat-like ears, and the body is supple and muscular. They have killer claws. Males, around thirty inches long with tail, are larger than females. A large male can weigh more than three pounds.

Marten are known for their speed in trees. Once, I was hiking along a trail in the Great Bear when a snowshoe hare came dashing around a bend in front of me and literally ran right through my legs at top speed. A large marten rounded the same bend heading right at me, going as fast as the rabbit. The marten saw me and in one motion pivoted and rocketed up a broken snag without branches. He stared, growled, and scolded, then dashed right back down the tree head-first and melted into the timber. The marten likely wasn't too happy that I had foiled his hunt.

If you're trapping marten, it's important to strive for a quick, clean dispatch. Bud's no-trace wilderness peg-sets worked well, and I used those for my first few years. But modern conibear traps (named for Frank Conibear, the Canadian who invented them) do much better and dispatch the marten very quickly. That's good for both your soul and the marten's.

The pelts of this carnivore are light, elegant, soft, and most beautiful. They can be used to make hats, gloves, shawls, scarves, coats, and much more. Marten and their fur are a renewable resource, in contrast to say polar fleece, which is made from petroleum products. Marten pelts are valuable, and there is a good market for them. Their silken fur is similar to sable. Tanned marten pelts and mounts also make attractive home decorations.

In his book, *Make Prayers to the Raven*, the late conservationist and anthropologist Richard Nelson noted that the Koyukon people of Alaska held the marten in high regard for its fur and its spiritual power. In their tradition, when Raven created the world, he was wearing a marten-skin hat. The Koyukons called the marten *sooga*, brother of the wolverine, to which it's closely related.

To the Koyukons, Nelson said, the wild sees with a "forest of eyes." It's a watchful world that is sensate and able to be offended. All living things have spirits, and humans must treat them with reverence. In this world, things in nature have a special kind of life, and when you enter wilderness, you enter the realm of the spiritual. To the Koyukons, there wasn't much separation between the natural and the supernatural.

The Koyukons accept the killing of marten or other furbearers if the animal is respectfully taken and treated properly. For example, after pelts are removed, the carcass should be returned to the wild to cycle back into the system. I think that's a fine idea, and I always adhere to it.

There's been a millennia-long dance between these powerful animals and the hominids that have pursued them. In distant times, people used log deadfalls and snares to catch this valuable furbearer that represented warmth and survival. Now, we have the opportunity to relive this wild tradition.

My daughter and I have shared this heritage in the wilderness for decades. Heather has a shawl made from marten and ermine. This attractive scarf is designed after the fur tippet that Cameahwait (Sacagawea's brother) gifted to Meriwether Lewis in the Big Hole a few centuries ago. Heather's marten-fur pixie hat blends right into her dark brown hair. From time to time, we sold a few marten, so she's also experienced that kind of value that can come from this critter.

Heather Fraley with a large male marten taken in the Great Bear Wilderness.

So much communication is expressed through eyes: ours and the marten's. Once I watched Heather's eyes as we moved through the timber and approached a wilderness marten set. I saw a sparkle in her eyes, and I knew we had a marten. I looked ahead to our set and saw a gorgeous, dark male perfectly caught; it obviously died very quickly and without a struggle. It was a wonderful thing to share. This started us talking about people living in the woods thousands of years ago. That intelligent eye-glow of humans is nothing new. We mused about it and realized how intelligent those ancient people must have been about the landscape and everything in it.

In my mind, while humans have an individual soul or spirit, marten have a collective soul. Let me explain. Over the millennia, for thousands of marten generations, these weasels have thrived in the big open. That they're still thriving reflects the long, unbroken line of their hereditary magic, their special DNA sequence that makes a marten a marten. This tenuous DNA strand has physically passed through generations over time out of mind without interruption; if it's broken, the species is finished. The molecule is a double helix with a sugar-phosphate backbone and paired nucleotide bases coupled in a unique sequence. This special chemistry is what makes a marten all that it is, and all marten share that singular quality of "martenness." If you pursue marten, keep this weighty concept in mind and think about treating the species with respect for the sake of their soul and yours.

Marten likely don't share our aesthetic enjoyment of a snowy forest floor glowing in the moonlight. But its collective soul is inside each individual, and that should be honored and respected. Also, bear in mind that human DNA and marten DNA are far more alike than they are different; even a mouse's DNA is 92 percent similar to a human's. The basic building blocks are the same, and the genetic differences that distinguish a human from, say, a pine marten, are a small fraction of the whole. We share a remarkable connection with all life.

Some people wonder how you can kill an animal that you respect and love. In part, the answer is in how humans evolved. We are omnivores, with teeth and digestive systems adapted to eating meat and plants. We've also long depended on hides and furs to protect our bodies from the elements. Place yourself back in time 20,000 years, standing on the wide savanna or in a deep boreal forest. Imagine the gratitude you would feel for an animal that gave its life to feed and clothe you. From time immemorial, our ancestors have shown great respect and love for the animals they relied on to survive. Even today, many indigenous peoples follow rites of gratitude for the animals they hold as sacred. Members of Pheasants Forever, the Rocky Mountain Elk Foundation, Ducks Unlimited, and many other organizations and individuals demonstrate similar respect for game animals while participating in their responsible harvest.

When you keep in mind that the eyes of the wild are watching everything you do, it makes you a better, more conscientious trapper. Bud Moore understood this in his own way. He counseled leaving no trace, making a quick kill, and getting the highest value from the marten's beautiful pelt.

My own trapping started out as a way to emulate Bud's experiences, and to know the wilderness during a season where you rarely saw another person. I soon found that it felt like freedom and suited me perfectly. In fact, it was more exciting than hunting. I could revisit my high-country mule deer spots after everyone else was gone and follow up on marten tracks that I'd seen earlier. All the bears are asleep, so I didn't have to worry about attracting one with marten lure. I could wander around the woods all night; there's no "shooting hours" as with hunting.

"Anticipation," Bud said, "is the spice of trapping." I soon understood what he meant. It's a thrill to learn the habits of the animal, make your set, and then return to see if it worked. With hunting, you may or may not get an opportunity on a given day. With trapping, you know that your set is just around the bend, you look forward to checking it, and you have a chance to find something special.

The Koyukons and others felt that marten trapping was particularly dependent on the vagaries of luck. You would be successful with this wanderer if you did everything right and if you pursued the marten in a certain way. Bragging about catches was a sure way to lose your luck and, once lost, it's very hard to get it back. I try to follow this guidance and, call me superstitious, it seems to work.

Marten lead all parts of their lives with a fierce energy. They breed in summer, and courtship can last fifteen days while the pair wrestles, growls, screams, and chuckles. The male grabs the female's neck with his teeth and drags her around for thirty minutes or more before copulation, which can last for another hour. The fertilized eggs are inactive through the winter, then attach to the wall of the uterus in what is known as "delayed implantation." Young are born in April and reach adulthood by late summer. They are sexually mature at about eighteen months.

Marten pelts harvested in the Great Bear Wilderness.

Pursuing marten offers a great chance to learn their hidden habits. Their tracks reveal their movements and success at preying on red squirrels, voles, and snowshoe hares. Marten are supposed to be nocturnal, but I've seen them out and about during all hours. Once, after setting a five-mile trapline in the Great Bear, my son Kevin and I headed back out in the late afternoon and retraced our path. During the four hours we were out, it snowed steadily. For whatever reason, this little blizzard was a call for the marten to move, and we crossed a half-dozen sets of fresh tracks.

For me, marten tracks always engender excitement. Paired and offset, their surprisingly large prints show that marten bound up and down terrain, hanging broad rights and lefts as they glide along. They rarely leave walking tracks like a bobcat, mountain lion, or lynx. All mustelids leave similar tracks. A set of short-tailed weasel tracks looks like tiny versions of the marten's.

None of those marten stepped into our traps that day, but two days later when we crossed the river and skied the line to check the half-dozen sets, we had caught several: one large, dark male, a lighter male, and one ermine (that is, a short-tailed weasel). Crossing the Middle Fork of the Flathead River in waders, in winter, cast a remote and adventurous feeling to this trapline.

Each marten displays a throat patch, but these vary in size, shape, and color. The dark male we caught that day sported a yellowish-orange patch that seemed to glow. The second male's throat patch had a very different pattern, with a duller orange color but no less beautiful.

This remote, short trapline dipped a few miles within the wilderness boundary. Crossing the river in winter sure was exciting, and it cut down on any possibility of running into anyone. But it also added a layer of risk. My son Kevin and I ran this same trapline one cold, clear December day. Kevin was a big nine-year-old at the time, but he wasn't strong enough to wade the river on his own. I carried our packs, skis, and hip boots across the river and dropped them on the bank, then went back to carry Kevin on my back. Safely on the other side, we stepped into our skis, hefted our packs, and began skiing up the ridge high above the river. I left my waders on the bank under a tree.

We skied along the trail as it crossed in and out of avalanche slopes illuminated by brilliant sunshine. We checked each of the first six or so sets with no luck. I was beginning to think that the marten had forsaken us. After about five miles, we reached the last trap-set, in a small grove of spruce along the bench just above a tributary drainage. I looked ahead and saw a brown beauty, covered in fluffy snow, hanging frozen in our set about four feet off the ground. Kevin skied up to the set and found the marten, and boy was he excited. We brushed the dry snow off the frozen animal and admired its beauty and soft pelt. Its color was classic—medium brown with a large, unique, star-shaped orange throat patch. I took a photo of Kevin holding the marten backed by a snowy scene. We felt lucky and privileged to have caught this mustelid in such a remote setting. I had hoped that Kevin would experience the thrill of finding a marten that day. We felt like wilderness trappers or hunter-gatherers from a bygone era.

Running the line and breaking trail had taken us longer than expected. As we headed back down through the trees, it was already late afternoon and the temperature was dropping. We checked each set on the way out, which took extra time because they were well off the trail.

When we finally arrived at the ford, the light was fading fast. During that morning's crossing, the water hadn't crept much above my thighs, so

Kevin Fraley with a marten in the Middle Fork of the Flathead River drainage.

my hip boots kept me dry. But despite the cold, the river had risen.

As I removed my ski boots and pulled on my hip waders, I considered the situation. Obviously, I should've planned to reach the ford before dusk. And chest waders would've been wise in case the river came up, as it clearly had. Most importantly, I had brought my young son on a remote trek with a sketchy river ford in subzero cold. I regretted all these things, but there was nothing I could do about it.

I got out my headlamp and took a closer look at the river. I could see through the glass-clear water why the level had risen. A layer of "anchor ice" had formed on the streambed. As small particles of ice (known as "frazil") form and float in the water column, they can sink and anchor to the bottom. This reduces the volume of the channel, so the water has nowhere to go but up. Anchor ice looks spooky, but it isn't solid, just mushy. I'd waded through it many times and never struggled with slippery footing.

Kevin hopped on my back and we began wading across the river. The boots of my hip waders sank about six inches into the soft anchor ice. When I was about a third of the way across, I realized that I was in trouble. Even trying to walk on my tippy-toes, the water was topping over my hip boots and filling them up, making them really heavy. When I reached the deepest, swiftest point of the stream (the "thalweg"), I pushed though and made it to the other side, depositing Kevin on the snowy bank. I took off the waders and dumped out the water, but I was wet to my waist. Already, my legs were numb, especially my feet. Nevertheless, I pulled the waders on again and crossed to the far side to retrieve our packs and skis. I emptied the waders again and waded back across to my waiting son. I dumped the waders yet again. By this time, my entire lower body felt like a lead weight.

We still had a quarter mile to our car, and we had to cross a smaller tributary stream, with me back in the waders, carrying Kevin across and then going back for our packs and skis. From there, we slogged through the snow to reach the car. Everything below my waist was numb, so I was anxious to thaw out.

I started the car and turned the heater on full blast. Kevin was dry and warmed up quickly. I took a bit longer, and my big toes were still numb. In fact, they stayed numb for months. My knees were worse. Slogging through the river in the water-filled waders, and then through the snow, must've strained the ligaments in my knees. But the cold had numbed the pain.

Over the coming weeks, my knees ached. That continued for a few years whenever I skied or ran or hiked. Going downhill was especially tough. My doctor suggested considering surgery, but I just popped anti-inflammatory pills. I figured this was my new normal and I would just live with it. Eventually, the pain eased a bit and then finally, surprisingly, went away.

In hindsight, I realized how irresponsible it was to have taken my young son on such a trip. In the mountains, you don't always see that things are getting bad until they're bad. But all's well that ends well, I guess. My son was unharmed, which was the most important thing. Most of my wilderness trapping adventures were not this intense. And overall, my luck with marten has been pretty good. Maybe the marten's collective soul senses how much I respect and value this species.

It's surprising every time you catch a marten on your way back down a trapline that you had just set. What a thrill to find a marten in your set just hours after you left it. Sometimes you see a new track and follow it right to your trap-set. For a trapper, it doesn't get any better.

A few years back, my son Troy and I snowshoed back down our short wilderness trapline after checking the last trap at the head of a little canyon. We angled through the old-growth timber, happy to be out in such superb marten habitat. We checked every set as we went, to make sure they were operating, and finally returned to the first set we'd made that morning. Troy mushed through the timber and downfall to check it. I brought up the rear. As Troy neared the set, he looked back at me with that excited light in his eyes.

"Well, how does the set look?" I asked. "It looks good," he said. "It has a nice male marten hanging in it."

Troy Fraley with a beautiful pine marten.

We felt joy on this father-and-son day because everything had worked perfectly, and we were able to share the experience together. I joined my son at the set. We admired the dark brown, thirty-two-inch marten, still a little warm on this very cold day. What a beautiful, heavily furred animal. Like some other local males, this marten bore almost no throat patch, perhaps a genetic trait peculiar to the marten in this drainage.

We put the marten in a protective bag, loaded him in my pack, and headed down the trail to our car. We would remove his pelt that night and return his carcass to the deep woods of the trapline a few days later. This marten would be a perfect one to use in the shawl I planned to give to my wife. ◄◦►

CHAPTER 13

A Long Walk with Bud Moore

Well-known conservationist Bud Moore was a driven man who spent much of his life in the wilderness. A highly respected forty-year U.S. Forest Service veteran, Bud stood as a beacon to show the way for generations of younger folks, many of whom he hosted at his place down the Swan that he named "Coyote Forest." If Bud wasn't immersed in the wilderness, he was talking about it or thinking about it.

When he trekked through the backcountry, Bud's mind formulated the meaning of what he was doing and how it related to wilderness preservation and management. His landmark 1996 tome, *The Lochsa Story*, is a classic in wilderness literature and stands as his soul-felt masterpiece. Bud and I recorded many radio shows together about the book's message and showcased his masterful storytelling.

As my most important wilderness mentor, Bud honored me by reviewing the manuscripts for each of my first two books. He gave me great advice, and he wrote endorsements for the books.

Bud mentioned that, as a Forest Service administrator stationed in Missoula, he'd walked through the Middle Fork before it became designated wilderness and wrote down his thoughts, though he never published them. He offered to look for his notes so I could use them in my writing about the area. In 1998, he found those notes and gave them to me with a letter of permission to use them. I gave a copy of the notes to his son, Bill. Bud was a gifted writer and philosopher, and I was excited to finally bring his thoughts to the forefront, and to repeat and retrace his Middle Fork trip nearly a half century later. As I worked with Bud's words, written long ago, they seemed as fresh as the rushing waters of the upper Middle Fork on a sunny September day.

Bud's 1972 trek forms the first half of this chapter. His trip, and the words and ideas from his journal, inspired me to retrace his route in 2018; this is the chapter's second half.

Bud, Kenai, and Kyukuk Hoof It Across the Bob, 1972

Note: Bud's words appear in italics.

Bud's sixty-mile trip through a big swath of the Middle and South Forks of the Flathead River reflected his constant focus on wild lands. From September 6 to 10, 1972, Bud and his two trusty malamutes, Kenai and Kyukuk, forged through this lightly traveled country to look at current management practices, and to evaluate parts of it for wilderness designation. On the trip, he gathered facts and impressions about the proposed 286,000-acre Great Bear Wilderness area, which he strongly supported. Bud's trip ended up contributing to the establishment of the Great Bear six years later, and certainly helped focus and improve federal management of these lands.

Along the way, Bud wrote down ideas for management improvements and many ideas for writing about wilderness. His mind never rested. For example, when he looked around the Cox Creek outfitter camp in the upper Middle Fork, the impacts bothered him. He noted in his journal:

Idea for writing—How to Enjoy and Care for Wilderness.
    a. Man, Part of the Ecosystem
    b. But with Capability to Modify it Unnaturally
    c. All the Rules of Conduct
    d. Build Around Anecdotes

The weather was wet and cool during their trek in 1972. Johnny Robinson, likely a Forest Service employee, dropped Bud at the Morrison Creek Trailhead, reached via Skyland Road west of Marias Pass. Snow dusted the peaks. Bud wrote:

Winter hovers near in this remote land of water, timber, and wildlife.
All across Montana school started yesterday. The kids are back at their lessons. And like them, I too have returned to Nature's school where here in the upper reaches of the Flathead drainage on Morrison Creek the grouse, the martens, the elk, and the Great Grizzly bear, though they know it not, await the Forest Service decision on the Continental Divide Wilderness Candidate Study.

My first lunch fire along the trail 8 miles beyond the Morrison Creek Road's end is small but nourishing for cold rain poured down from the menacing cloud all morning to chill both mine and the malamutes' bones. . . . Up there at road's end Johnny watched while I packed the dogs in the cold drizzle, then swung up my pack to hike through mud across bogs and through the creek several times to reach this spot where the small fire dries chill from my bone, while I munch jerky Thuringer and bread.

Bud finished his lunch and headed down the Morrison Trail, full of the excitement of exploring new country with a purpose. His companions shared his happiness:

While I sloshed along, those faithful malamutes stuck at my heels, muddy, happy, not that this was such an unusual woods but it is wild and that's all they ask. Hungry to explore this legendary country, that's all I ask, too.

As Bud hiked through Morrison's old-growth timber that wet September day, he lamented that road construction down Morrison Creek would be an ill-conceived project that would open the terrain to erosion, contribute to land slips, negate the possibility of including this land in the proposed Great Bear Wilderness, and maybe affect the proposed river's Wild and Scenic designation, noting:

In all this there's one common denominator, Damn few people want the Middle Fork roaded-up.

Bud couldn't be more direct in his opinion. He hiked the last few miles of the Morrison Creek Trail and joined the "Big River" or the main Middle Fork Trail, which he derided and described as such:

More aptly put, Middle Fork Boulevard. Built by a dozer some 15–20 years ago, this trail slashes through the Middle Fork's landscapes, its 16-foot width with long straight tangents desecrating the land's pristine conditions. . . . This obviously choice mountain country shouts for wild classification but how much better it would have been had those trail builders risen above callous disregard for the wild, natural values crumbling under their dozer blade.

Bud and his malamutes covered the last four miles of trail to the Schafer Meadows Ranger Station: *With the trail a full quarter mile above the river on a lodgepole pine covered bench, the hike to Schafer Meadows was easy, pleasant but by the fourteenth mile chill rain had stiffened up my muscles. . . . the snug log Schafer Station looked welcome as the dogs and I trudged along the airport fence while two horses and six mules eyeballed us as intruders.*

At Schafer, Bud met the ranger, Jay Deist, station guard, Oke, and several other Forest Service folks, as well as outfitter Chuck Ray. Bud hit it off with Jay. He felt that the area was in good hands and headed in the right direction. Jay was glad to see a high-ranking Forest Service manager from the Missoula office and was happy to talk wilderness philosophy and share his plans for the area with Bud, whom he urged to sleep inside the station. Bud wrote that the crew wished their supervisors would visit more often to give them some guidance and see what they were accomplishing.

So instead of under a dripping fly, I slept upstairs in the log administration building where pole rafters and cedar shingles warded off persistent rain outside. Secure beneath that down sleeping bag, it didn't take long for the rain's drone on the shingles to lull me into deep sleep.

The next morning, Bud and the crew rose early. *With daylight, over Oke's hotcakes the Schafer cabin window framed the mountain, its treeless crest painted fresh with snow.*

Bud jotted down notes about the great channel damage wrought by the 1964 flood, the poor fishing, and the scarcity of game and bears. Bud looked forward to the spellbinding scenes of his destination, the Middle Fork's headwaters.

Bud packed his gear, loaded the packs on the malamutes, and left the station. As he moved upriver, he took inventory of the condition of this proposed wilderness.

After breakfast Jay and his crew got at their work while the dogs and I hiked easily up the Middle Fork trail. By noontime, we'd covered 6–7 miles and explored the Cox Creek commercial packer's camp. A neat, heavily-used place but with its hitch racks, tables, stovepipes and storage cabins an obvious wallop on the wilderness scene. In contrast to the law, here man's impact is substantially noticeable and it's getting more so as each year these outfitters pack in or build more facilities. Horse impact will be hardest to manage. . . . Obviously these commercial outfitters either do not understand or do not subscribe to a true wilderness ethic. Since wilderness is apt to be their bread and butter, they not only should fully understand it but should be missionaries to train their customers as well. And it's time that the Flathead crew got at the job of converting these entrepreneurs to the cause. Parties might have to be smaller in the future with fees higher. And why shouldn't they be? After all, wilderness itself is a near priceless resource.

Bud Moore in the Selway-Bitterroot Wilderness with his dogs. PHOTOGRAPH COURTESY OF THE MOORE FAMILY AND ARCHIVES AND SPECIAL COLLECTIONS, MANSFIELD LIBRARY, UNIVERSITY OF MONTANA.

Bud hiked from Cox Creek into the more open country from past wildfires near Winter and Switchback Creeks, noting browse lines from deer and elk on the conifers and willows along the benches above the river and the scour from the 1964 flood, the most devastating for at least 100 years:

No tributary escaped it for even the smallest stream channel overflowed as heavy rains poured on the rocks and open slopes above, then rushed down to overload and scour the channels. The dogs and I plodded along through this fascinating wilderness . . . we are weary and the mood is changing for those clouds now yield sky space to the sun and its warmth on the moist willow and companion shrubs stir musk-like smells along the trail. Whenever I smell wet willow warming in the sun I always think of beavers. Similarly, with hot sun on ceanothus comes visions of big mule deer bucks. It's a great world.

Bud was a well-respected expert on fire management. He moved the Forest Service away from declaring that fire was public enemy number one. He inventoried the proposed Great Bear for fire history as he hiked along.

From the time we left Morrison Creek's old growth timber at Star Creek we've travelled through young timber from 40 to 60 years of age. A 2-mile-long mature old-growth stand below Schafer and a similar 2-mile-wide block near Surprise and Calbick Creek[s] provided the sole exception . . . wildfire is most apt to spread in pockets of timber missed by these early fires. Some of these are ecologically ready to burn. Once the destiny of the Middle Fork is determined through land use planning, it will be most interesting to arrange complementary fire management priorities. And these will obviously be something different from the present practice of putting fires out at all times under all conditions.

As Bud traveled the trail upriver, he looked for a campsite. But from a few miles past Cox Creek to Gooseberry Park the trail stays high on the mountainside, much of it passing through old burns and grassy slopes. Just short of the Gooseberry Park Ranger Station, the trail finally descends to the river channel. Finally, Bud had his campsite. He set up camp at a nice spot along the small, rushing Middle Fork just a mile downstream from Gooseberry.

My leg muscles ached and my mind numbed with weariness so much it was hard to assimilate the delightful scenes along the way. Those two dogs were so tired too that even the occasional fool hen along the trail failed to stir their curiosity. At 1745 hours we staggered in to a delightful campsite on the Middle Fork's bank where wood, poles, and water were adequate. Across the river an open vista extended from the valley to the first peak where half way up I saw two elk graze near an alder patch. When I pulled their packs, the dogs curled up and never moved all evening. But I built a fireplace, pitched the fly, cooked, dried my socks around the fire, then crawled into the bag for welcome rest. Comfort was not the objective here, only the priceless luxury of stretching out on the good earth, boots off, aching joints at last relieved of upright stance, with the river's song penetrating my mind and soul. A full galaxy of stars shone through the fly front as I crawled in but these soon went out as sleep gripped me and the malamutes.

Bud never short-cut his routine on these wilderness trips. He just loved being out in the backcountry with its rituals, challenges, and discomforts. He believed in a good breakfast and was a champion morning person. He recognized that an early start and a ground-eating stride made all things possible in the mountains.

To jump out into that frost at daybreak proved a first-class wilderness challenge softened soon, however, by a crackling fire started with lodgepole kindling I'd whittled the night before. And I soon warmed up inside with hotcakes, bacon, oatmeal, and coffee. While I broke camp, the sun crept down the slope across the river, its golden rays in sharp contrast to the frost-crisp shade along the river.

After a short, fifteen-minute hike, Bud strolled into the openings around the Gooseberry Park Ranger Station, having covered twenty-nine miles so far on his trip from the Morrison Creek Trailhead. He met trail crew members Dick and Eric, who were helping Oke pack his mules for a trip back down to Schafer. The workers told Bud that they were heading out for the year, and he was disappointed: *They'll leave the country to the elk, the bears and the outfitters. I wonder if we have anyone up here in the fall teaching wilderness philosophy to these outfitters. From the non-wilderness character of their camps, I doubt it.*

Bud relaxed at Gooseberry for a few minutes and visited with the crew. Then he and the malamutes forded the clear-running, cobbly Middle Fork, at this point a very small river, and headed up the spectacular Clack Creek drainage. As Bud hiked along, he could see the massive limestone reefs up-drainage, framed by openings in the spruce and fir forest.

Clack Creek flows down from Pentagon Mountain and the Trilobite Range high on the divide between the Middle and South Forks of the Flathead. The watershed spans from Cruiser Mountain and Trilobite Lakes to the north to Switchback Pass to the south. Clack is one of the most diverse drainages in the Middle Fork, with old-growth timber and beaver meadows in its lower reaches to high reefs along its headwaters.

About a mile up, the valley opened in to a large willow flat where Beaver Town, Middle Fork, floated behind two husky dams. From here on we hiked though old-growth timber where an occasional cat track—Lynx I think—added interest to the trail.

At Trilobite trail junction, the valley opens into a large open flat covered by some species of sage. Then above this half-mile-long flat we entered dense alpine-type timber growing in deep soils dumped back through the ages from the limestone cliffs above. Here in this lush forest, numerous fresh track along the trail showed elk to be abundant and nearby. Each small brook we crossed was in itself a wonder, its course blinking red argillite, limestone chips and chalky brown sedimentary rock. Time caught up with us, so at one of these purring brooks we stopped to lunch on Thuringer, cheese, bread, oranges, and candy bars.

Shortly beyond our lunch site, we began climbing a series of switchbacks. Slow though our pace, we seemed to burst at once from the spruce forest into the alpine basin where those giant cliffs towered so high we had to lean back to see the rim above.

From there the trail turned south along the shelf-like basins at the foot of 1,000-foot-high limestone cliffs above. On this lush north slope we sensed a closeness, yet at the same time a bigness where one might meet at short distance some far-ranging animal like a giant grizzly . . . pastures of hellebore and wild parsnip seemed a likely place. Though we watched diligently, we saw no game.

As a forester, Bud paid special attention to the condition of the alpine vegetation. Like many of us, he held a special admiration for the classic symbols of the high country, alpine fir and whitebark pine: *Those alpine firs are true trees of the wilderness. At the base of the reefs along this shelf where soil is deep, they send their spiral-like tops towards the sky with vigor unmatched by any alpine vegetation. Though some whitebark pine along the way reach near 3-feet diameter breast high, they cannot match the alpine firs for height, grace, and beauty.*

The nine miles of trail Bud walked that day traced the drainage to its headwaters at Pentagon Mountain; at its base, Bud would camp at Dean Lake, maybe one of the most unique and spectacular settings for an alpine lake in the Bob, or maybe anywhere. According to my GPS, Dean Lake sits at mile thirty-nine on the trek. The elevation over the shelfs challenged even Bud, who was beginning to feel his age, although he was only fifty-four and still a force in the mountains.

Wind I have plenty of, but my leg muscles and joints ached as the dogs and I plodded along the bench to reach scenic Dean Lake at 1800 hours. There, shaded by massive Pentagon Mountain, we settled camp. Time collapsed. I laid up the fireplace here near the top of the world with stones formed of mud from prehistoric sea bottoms. If sea mud can get up here, then those alpine firs will likely march right over Pentagon Mountain to meet their partners coming up the other side. While I worked camp, the malamutes curled up in the beargrass on a point above camp to rest and guard our little Shangrila from varmints like Canadian Jays, chipmunks, bears, or squirrels. As they rested, only their fur tips showed above the coarse, green beargrass clumps, but at the slightest sound two heads would pop up simultaneously, ears erect, alert, ready to charge any suspect movement. In the Malamute Kingdom it must be a fine line between fast asleep and wide awake.

As Bud dozed off, he looked forward to viewing and photographing Dean Lake and its alpine setting in the bright morning sun, but it was not to be. Rain pelted his tent all night and when dawn broke, he looked out at swirling snow. Bud tarried around breakfast for an hour or so, hoping that the clouds would lift. Instead, they settled in with more dense fog. At 10:15 A.M., on Saturday, September 9, 1972, Bud broke camp and headed up the trail that followed the ridge around the head of Basin Creek, a large tributary of the upper Middle Fork, an area Bud noticed had been "rarely visited" by fire.

Bud strode along the couple of miles from his Dean Lake camp along the shelves to Switchback Pass at mile forty-one of the trek. Alas, clouds and fog prevented Bud from seeing very much of arguably the most spectacular pass in the Bob.

That turned out to be a tough climb. At the pass, the terrain caught up with the cloud base and we went over in swirling fog and spitting snow. That pass must have been named from the Spotted Bear side for we dropped down innumerable switchbacks through whitebark pine forests, some Douglas-fir, then into dense spruce, lodgepole pine at Pentagon Creek's forks. . . . Further down we broke out from the delightful wilderness setting into a widely cleared, heavily built trail with contrast like leaving a pleasant country road for a modern freeway. Why would we build such a massive trail up into this country?

When Bud reached "shabby" Pentagon Cabin at mile forty-nine of the trek, he lamented the condition of the structure and its surroundings. Rather than showing the wilderness way to others, it set a bad example. Bud jotted down a writing idea, inspired by this and other poor examples of management: "Wilderness: What is it. What it's for and How not to use it." But Bud noted that there was hope for the wilderness complex, recalling his meeting a few days earlier with the Schafer ranger: *Yet in men like Jay Deist lurks the finest sort of wilderness ethic. How proud he was of opening, rough wilderness style, several old sick trails locked with windfalls for so many years. How quick he was to favor the Great Bear Wilderness.*

Bud continued with more optimistic observations:

But we're making progress too. Consider how man's hand must have laid on the country 30–40 years ago when the fresh impact of a new telephone line traversed Trilobite shelf and the basins echoed dynamite blasts as those early Forest Service men hacked out trails like Switchback Pass. . . . [A] long blaze shown like new paint throughout the ridges and basins, all necessary actions in their time. One wonders what the grizzly bears thought of all that.

Except that more of us visit here, the country's quieter now. The oldtimers' once bright blazes are now dimmed by 3 inches of new growth. Shrubs have closed in along the trail, and most telephone lines have been gone so long it takes a trained eye to spot the old tie trees.

The next morning, Bud left Pentagon and hiked down the wild Spotted Bear River, a modest-sized stream that flows through several canyons on its way to its confluence with the South Fork of the Flathead near the Spotted Bear Ranger Station. At 11 A.M Bud walked by the sign marking the wilderness boundary, where he saw a young man puttering on a motorbike who "buzzed happily down the trail, his exhaust fumes spreading low in the valley's cool air."

Here again is decision land, to extend this wilderness or leave the land for bikes and roads is the central question. I guess that'll take some doing, but the decision wouldn't be hard for me alone.

Bud soaked up some encouragement from two men he met over the final miles.

It's a pleasant hike down Spotted Bear because the trail, though well built and heavily used, winds naturally through the country and its clearing [the brushed-out corridor] hugs the trail in pleasant intimacy. At the mouth of Dean Creek, I found Jack Addison, guide for Spotted Bear Resort, cutting tent poles along the trail. We'd barely exchanged greetings when Jack slid down the bank, hauled his 60-year-old frame up and said: "I hope they don't push more roads back into this country." At least I know where Jack stands. I pushed on to Silvertip Cabin. . . . District Engineer Bill Armstrong came in to report that road's end is only 1-1/2 miles away. Well, I'd like to rest here, then hike up through the Silvertip Basin but that'll have to wait some future time. For now, it's time to go back to the Monday morning staff meeting.

Bud hiked the last couple of miles to the Silvertip Trailhead, closing out the sixty-mile trek. As always, Bud waxed philosophical in the end, knowing it would be a long struggle to preserve wilderness and wilderness character. He'd been immersed in an internal back and forth over it for five days and sixty miles, his mind never letting it go. Bud had a lot of hope, and it eventually paid off for him and the land as he retired from the Forest Service and carved his own way as one of Montana's most prominent conservationists. In closing, Bud delivered a dose of philosophy in a metaphor about the importance of fighting for wilderness over the long-term:

Engineer Bill Armstrong, as did Jay and his crew, told of problems to satisfy wants of those entering wilderness who pick a wide trail with good signs in contrast to trailways that rest lightly on the land or no trail at all. If we can lead them a bit—through wilderness experience with understanding—America might mature to rise above the efficiency ethic to full quality of life. There is no need to cry to the Gods if one's strength gives out on a switchback or when trapped by a snowstorm in some high basin. The mature approach is to dig in, wait it out, and enjoy it.

The Re-Wilding of the Middle Fork:
Retracing Bud's Steps Nearly a Half Century Later

From August 8 to 11, 2018, my son Kevin and I retraced Bud's footsteps through the Middle Fork country and looked at how things had changed and what had stayed the same. We followed Bud's route, studied his notes along the way, and found some surprises. In his intense but very human way, Bud brought the land and its management alive for us as we re-experienced the country this great man had trekked through.

We began our trip from the Morrison Creek Trailhead, a major entry point into the Middle Fork country in what is now the Great Bear Wilderness. As Bud had, we would emerge from the wilderness at the Spotted Bear River Trailhead after hiking sixty miles. On the drive to the trailhead forty-six years earlier, Bud had lamented the clear-cuts and even-age management of the forest along Skyland Road. I know how he felt; in the 1980s as a fisheries biologist, I'd tried to convince the Forest Service not to clear-cut this area because of the unstable soils and the high-use bull trout spawning reaches in Granite and Morrison Creeks. I wasn't successful, but the outcome wasn't as bad as I'd feared, for the bull trout at least. They've mostly held their own, especially in Granite Creek.

My wife, Dana, drove us to the trailhead and walked a few miles down the trail with us before turning back. My daughter, Heather, would pick us up four days later near Spotted Bear. Right from the start, the weather was hot and hazy, with smoky skies. In fact, it turned out to be the hottest week of the year and nearly broke the all-time heat record for the area. What a difference a half century makes.

Forty-six years after Bud's trip, Kevin and I were on his trail. Nine miles along, we ate lunch—pita bread, peanut butter, granola bars, and Nutella— at the same spot, near the lower Morrison Creek ford. But instead of the cold dripping rain that had pelted Bud, nothing but heat and the haze of wildfire smoke greeted us.

Kevin during the lunch break on lower Morrison Creek.

I'd passed this way many dozens of times over the years, studying local fisheries beginning in 1980, and surveying bull trout redds in Morrison and Lodgepole Creeks ever since. I thought of the wolf pack that followed me and a co-worker one night, howling as we went. I'd also brought Kevin

The Middle Fork Trail at Morrison Creek cuts a straight, wide swath through the forest. Bud called it a "boulevard."

hunting here when he was young. I'd come to think of the drainage like a good friend. But following Bud's footfalls from decades earlier added a special feeling to the day.

Kevin and I crossed Morrison Creek and joined the Middle Fork Trail, which still looks like the straight, wide boulevard through the lodgepole Bud described. In all my travels through the Bob, I've never seen a longer, more direct stretch of trail.

We reached Schafer at 2:45 P.M. on that first day, having covered the same fourteen miles. We walked along the airstrip, and, as Bud did, met mules and horses in the station yard. A young man, Jake, was filling in as station guard. The temperature hovered between 90 and 95 F., extremely hot and unheard of for this country. We asked Jake about trail conditions in the headwaters, but all he knew was that trail crews were working in the area.

We hiked over to the willowy Middle Fork near the raft put-in to cool off and swim. We caught a few small westslope cutthroat, but as in Bud's day, the fishing at this point in the river is generally poor. The fish were so small that we had to go with size 20 midges to catch anything. It was fun to see some whitefish finning along the bottom of the gravelly runs, but they calmly refused any fly we offered.

Rather than spend a night at Schafer as Bud had, we headed upriver, bound for Cox Creek camp. This would let us enjoy more time in the upper

Kevin at Schafer Meadows Ranger Station.

Middle Fork while it was bright and sunny on this long summer day. As we moved upriver, the trail climbed hundreds of feet, winding more than a mile away from the river. I love this more out-of-the-way portion of the trail, full of memories from summer work and winter furbearer surveys. Finally, after passing Surprise Creek and Calbick Creek we reached Cox Creek at mile twenty of the trek. That's when we ran into it: the re-wilding of the Middle Fork.

Bud had described a heavily impacted outfitter camp at Cox Creek, and I remembered a very similar condition when I was the area biologist in the early 1980s. My crew and I had camped at Cox Creek a number of times. Back then I remembered seeing the same tables, bare ground, massive fire rings, hitching rails, and so on, scattered over a wide area. But now, little or none of that remained. The elk hunting had declined, wilderness designation and awareness rose, and the country healed. I couldn't believe how lightly impacted it looked, right down to a surprisingly untrammeled trail that once showed heavy impacts from horse travel.

We camped along the creek in a little flat. Just past our campsite stood a swath of old-growth spruce and fir where we hung our food high in the air. After a dinner of freeze-dried stew, we fished for small cutthroat in the creek. I'd once collected a sample of twenty Cox Creek cutthroat, and genetic testing proved them to be indigenous and pure. The ones Kevin and I caught that evening were small but pretty, and it was nice to know they reflected the original genetics. Their ancestors had lived in this tributary of the upper Middle Fork for thousands of years.

At 6 A.M. on August 9, our second day out, we awoke to a beautiful, cool morning. We didn't mind the cold air, though, because we knew that soon the day would become one of the hottest of the year. Kevin went to lower the food bag while I boiled water for oatmeal and cocoa.

When Kevin returned, he had a tale to tell. He'd walked into the old-growth timber, looked ahead, and saw what looked like a brown shape lying on the trail. When he reached the spot, he saw two back quarters from a young mule deer smack in the middle of the trail, near the tree that held our hoisted food.

I followed Kevin back to the site and I was floored by how perfectly these quarters were separated from the carcass, which was nowhere to be seen.

They looked like they'd been carefully quartered by a hunter. One was mostly consumed. The other had the hide intact and looked amazingly pristine.

Then Kevin told me the best part. He'd peeked around a tree and saw a salt-and-pepper colored wolf striding through the woods, paralleling the trail and apparently returning to the kill site. Kevin calmly addressed the canid by saying, "Hey, Pup," which got the animal's attention. The wolf ran off. The wolf didn't concern him, but he said that he was glad he had pepper spray with him when he went to get the food bag, just in case.

We returned to our camp along the creek, aware that we'd just had a priceless wilderness experience. While we'd slept, this wolf, likely as part of a pack, ran down and killed this young mule deer less than

Near Cox Creek, Kevin looks at the mule deer leg left in the trail by a wolf.

forty yards from our camp. We sure felt grateful that we were a part of this ancient wilderness dance, and that it took place in a formerly heavily used and impacted site that was now mostly pristine.

Life doesn't get much better: indigenous westslope cutthroat trout, wolves, and mule deer; this spot was back to being wild.

We broke camp and by 9 A.M. were four miles up the trail. We reached Winter Creek, where the trail crosses a nice flat fairly close to the water, an exception on this upper river trail. From there the trail climbed high and moved in and out of little drainages and the larger Switchback Creek. The smoky haze limited our view of the mountains across the canyon but not as much as we feared it would. It was a fine, fine day in the upper Middle Fork, and headed toward a record temperature in the 90s.

We walked the trail high above the river, winding in and out of side drainages. I'd forgotten how beautiful and remote this drainage really was. About a mile short of Gooseberry Park we finally dropped to the river and Bud's second camp. We enjoyed the same scene he'd described forty-six years earlier and took the same fifteen minutes to hike up the trail to Gooseberry Park.

Kevin on the trail high above the Middle Fork of the Flathead River, hiking toward Gooseberry Park.

In recent decades, big wildfires had consumed large tracts of the timber in the Strawberry and Bowl drainages, so we walked through a much different landscape than what Bud saw. Gooseberry Park itself was almost completely nuked. Burned snags lay across the trail, and jack-strawed burned logs made access to the river a challenge.

It had been a bad year for blowdown around the Bob, and I worried that the trail over Switchback Pass and the remainder of our trip would be plagued by downfall. While Kevin checked out Gooseberry Cabin, I crossed the Middle Fork and walked upstream on the Clack Creek Trail about a half mile. I was relieved to see that the trail crew had cleared downfall up the drainage. In fact, the trail looked more traveled here because of the traffic going over the Continental Divide National Scenic Trail.

Above: Kevin at Gooseberry Cabin.

Right: Kevin fishing the Middle Fork near Gooseberry Cabin.

I returned to Gooseberry and relayed the good news to Kevin. We stopped for an hour or so to fish the river, here only about twenty yards wide so near its headwaters. I remembered the good fishing just upstream during the 1980s and later near the junction of Bowl and Strawberry just a little over a mile upstream, but today, the cutthroat weren't interested.

Kevin caught one cutthroat. We ate lunch and hiked up the Clack Creek Trail.

Bud said that this drainage, with the backdrop of the Trilobite Ridge reefs, was stunningly beautiful and it still is. The lower reach had mostly dodged the fires. Kevin pointed out a Franklin's grouse hen looking us over while her young brood hopped around the base of a big spruce. With all this beauty and a cleared trail ahead of us, all was fine in lower Clack Creek.

John tries his luck at the beaver ponds on Clack Creek.

We paused again to fish and caught about ten small cutts above one of the big beaver dams. As Bud noted, these beaver meadows are so big and pretty. This could be the most scenic fishing hole anywhere. We wondered if migrating bull trout from Flathead Lake would breach the dam and fin their way to spawning areas upstream.

We reached the trail fork to Trilobite Lakes and hung a left, bound for the Clack Creek headwaters about six miles away. We trekked up the narrowing drainage, moving through shady spruce and fir, passing classic waterfalls along the way and enjoying their coolness on this sweltering,

90-degree day. We filtered lots of water and savored it, gulping ice water in the heat. One waterfall plunged 100 feet in a couple of drops and, as I stood looking down the drop, blasts of cool air rose up and enveloped me. Kevin had hiked ahead, and when I caught up he was standing in the transition zone at the beginning of the rock reefs and cliffs of the Trilobite Range. As Bud had said, the transition here from timber to alpine happens in an instant.

The trail to Dean Lake abruptly breaks into the alpine zone with scenic views of the Trilobite Range.

We continued along the base of the reef, bound for Dean Lake at the foot of Pentagon Mountain. We met the first travelers since we'd left Schafer Meadows, a man and a woman who were hiking the Continental Divide Trail. They informed us that the trail past Dean Lake and over Switchback Pass to Pentagon Cabin was cleared and in good shape. The trail crew deserved a reward.

Kevin and I hiked south on the high trail, winding through burned and gnarled skeletons of alpine fir and whitebark pine. Far below us, we could see thousands of acres that had burned the previous year in the Scalp Creek and Basin Creek drainages. Some copses of green trees had escaped the fire, but they were limited. In sharp contrast to Bud's description of the lack of fire, the landscape was scorched, the result of a shift in management policies to allow backcountry burns to run their course. With longer, hotter fire seasons, however, and large tracts of drought-stressed timber, some fires have grown into huge conflagrations.

We reached a beautiful, unburned valley on a shelf at the base of Pentagon Mountain. I was hungry and tired enough to camp, though we were still two miles short of Bud's campsite at Dean Lake. But we were also a day ahead, so Kevin humored me and we dropped our packs at mile seventeen for the day, and mile thirty-seven for the trip so far.

With Pentagon Mountain looming above, we were surrounded by some of the Bob's finest alpine scenery. The sun dipped behind the mountain and a soft light descended on our camp. Our tent perched in the glorious beargrass and alpine fir. Nearby, a small stream murmured through the flat valley. We filtered some water and enjoyed our freeze-dried beef stew and cup-of-soups. Following the steps of a legend had led us to this slice of paradise.

The next morning dawned sunny and cloudless. We broke camp and hiked two miles beneath the backbone of the Trilobite Range to stunning Dean Lake, nestled at 7,363 feet in the arms of Pentagon Mountain. Fire had claimed much of the timber around the lake, but Dean retained its alpine beauty. Forty-six years earlier, Bud had awakened here to stormy weather, but Kevin and I enjoyed a clear, sun-washed morning.

We climbed the last two miles to Switchback Pass, weaving in and out of rock formations and sparse alpine fir, some of it burned. Spooky rock shapes and imitation Stonehenges cast an unreal feel to the pass. By 10:30 A.M. the day's heat was already building. The little flat pass offered a nearly 360-degree view of mountains and more mountains, with Kevan and Table Mountains to the south, the rocky ramparts of Pentagon to the north, and the Elk Ridge reef to the west. What a classic mountain pass, maybe the prettiest in the Bob.

Kevin and I dropped our packs to savor the view and look for any artifacts we might find at this unique and likely spiritual point of geography. I felt satisfied just relaxing there in the sunny heat, but my son, as usual,

Pentagon Mountain looms behind beautiful Dean Lake.

was always looking for the next peak. He persuaded me to hang our packs and climb 8,412-foot Kevan Mountain. The last thing I felt like doing was tackling a big climb with exposure, but the twenty-minute ascent to the summit was easy, relaxing, and well worth it. A few snowfields added spice to the trek.

Our view from the top of Kevan Mountain was phenomenal. Lake Levale sat below us in a charming valley, and 8,259-foot Signal Mountain rose to the east. I felt that we stood above everything. From this point, creeks flow to the upper Middle Fork, the Sun River, and the Spotted Bear River. Sadly, Bud missed all this on his trip due to the soggy weather, but I was grateful for our good fortune on this clear, hot day.

We left the pass at 11:30 A.M. on the hottest day of the year, and maybe the all-time hottest day in the annals of the Bob. Striding down the twenty or so switchbacks on the East Fork of Pentagon Creek, we finally reached

Kevin and John celebrate atop 8,412-foot Kevan Mountain, with the Bob stretching into the distance.

main Pentagon Creek. The heat forced us to stop and filter water when we could find an easy place to access the stream. Temperatures in the upper 90s are not something you expect in the upper reaches of the Spotted Bear River.

After a couple miles, our trail met the main Spotted Bear Trail at the junction of Pentagon Creek and the Spotted Bear River. Here, our view of Pentagon Cabin differed from Bud's in a big way. In 1972, Bud camped here on his last night, and he openly complained about the condition of the grounds, the junk, the messy look, and the shabby cabin. In 2018, Kevin and I found the cabin freshly stained, the wood pile tidy, and no junk in view. Bud would have been pleased: the Forest Service was doing all right.

At the cabin, we encountered the second party of our trip, a couple with their five solid and happy children, ages nine to fourteen. They had entered the Bob at Benchmark on the east side of the divide, hiked over the pass, and descended the Spotted Bear Trail. This happy crew had covered a lot of ground. Kevin and I were glad to see them out enjoying such a big piece of the wilderness.

We sat beside the Spotted Bear River in the heat and filtered water to quench our thirst. We fired up the stove and cooked ramen for a snack. Tallying our daily distances, we found that we'd covered forty-nine miles following Bud on the trek so far. In the early afternoon, we started down the trail along the Spotted Bear River, heading for our third and final campsite in the big trees at the junction with Dean Creek.

John at Pentagon Cabin.

The next morning, we fished the Spotted Bear pretty hard, but inexplicably couldn't find a cutthroat. On that morning, at least, we had a beautiful river but stubborn native fish.

Silvertip Cabin.

We headed down the trail, bound for the Silvertip Trailhead, stopping at Blue Lakes to catch a few small cutthroat. We passed Silvertip Cabin, finding it just as neat and tidy as Bud had in 1972. I'll admit that I was happy to see the trailhead emerge from the heat and haze at 11:45 A.M. on our fourth day out, completing our sixty-mile, Bud retrospective trip. After a few hours, my daughter, Heather, picked us up and we headed to Spotted Bear Campground for the night.

In Bud's footsteps, we came to realize firsthand the value of wilderness and how close some of this country came to being roaded in his own time. Visionaries like Bud and many others fought to preserve this unspoiled landscape and made it possible for future generations to enjoy the freedom and solitude of wilderness. How diminished the Bob would have been without the remote and roadless Middle Fork of the Flathead and Great Bear Wilderness.

Thank you, Bud. ﹡

CHAPTER 14

Renewal

When I walked away from Terry's plane crash site in the Welcome Creek Wilderness that last time on September 1, 2019, I felt comfort and closure. We'd left the memorial in Terry's seat in the jumbled remnants of the plane on that forty-fifth anniversary of the crash. We headed up the ridge and began the long walk through the downed timber back to the truck.

It had been a meaningful day. We'd accomplished our goal, and my daughter had found a special gift, a beautiful moose antler shed. We marveled at the bull elk rub on the little pine just above the crash site. It was a beautiful and peaceful scene, and I felt that I'd finally done all I could do.

I knew I'd never come back. For me, it was over.

But it wasn't to be.

On August 23, 2020, I called Les Marcum in Missoula to ask if he had any past photos of himself in the Welcome Creek elk study area. More than anything, I just wanted to hear his voice. It's lonely writing about a tragedy, especially one so close to my heart, and Les is one of the few people left who knows the intimate details of Terry's story and deeply cares about it.

I left a message and received a call back on August 26; it was great to hear the drawl that I'd come to appreciate over the years. Les was mourning the loss of his wife, who had passed away after hospice. I hadn't spoken to him in months.

"Hey, John, I suppose you're calling about the fire." I didn't know what he meant and asked, "What fire?"

Les told me that a lightning-sparked fire had flared up in the Cinnabar-Carron Creek area within the Welcome Creek Wilderness a week before. The Cinnabar Fire had built to more than 2,000 acres and made a hot run directly up the ridge toward Terry's plane. Les said that after studying the photos and map of the fire on the Forest Service website, he concluded that the fire swept across the crash site, over the top of the ridge, and through the clearing that the smokejumpers had cut forty-six years earlier. The active flames and heat of the inferno likely vaporized what was left of the plane and the modest memorial we'd left there.

I sat there stunned at the odd timing. We'd visited the site a year earlier, left a memorial, and felt closure and relief. The site had sat there peacefully and virtually unchanged for nearly half a century with zero fires or other disturbance. It seemed like a strange coincidence that the area went up in smoke in what almost appeared to be a targeted conflagration. I guess I should stop being surprised about fate and irony as this story twists and turns.

By August 31, 268 firefighters were working to suppress the fire, which stood at 2,144 acres. Many of them worked along the Bitterroot Divide at the head of the drainage to stop the fire's growth over the top of the ridge and out into the Bitterroot Valley. On the USFS InciWeb website, photographs showed the fire torching up the ridge toward the plane site.

Other images on InciWeb showed the aftermath of the flames and the jack-strawed, black trees along ridgelines toward Cleveland Mountain. The fire-line that crews dug to contain the blaze snaked along the Bitterroot/ Rock Creek Divide Trail #313, which runs along the divide above the ridge where the plane rests.

I thought of the likely scene at the crash site. I've seen the aftermath of many intense fires, and I imagined that the area is now gray and denuded of trees. Likely, it would be hard for me to recognize the landscape or figure out exactly where I was.

The crash site had held traces of Terry before the fire. The trees, beargrass, and brush certainly cycled elements of his DNA. What now? Now, the inferno had likely released his essence as energy into the atmosphere.

To reach the crash site again, the route would be dangerous, hard to follow, and impassable after such a fire. I thought of those long ridges with big downed timber and brush leading to where the lodgepole dominated.

I had to accept it. The fire swept the ridge and crash site and renewed the landscape to start all over again. The traces of the tragic story are likely all gone now, and I'm not sure what I think about that.

Over the decades, the smokejumpers had never been far from my mind. They seemed like mythical, intrepid heroes who jumped into the sky over the tragic plane crash, hoping to find life. I tried to track them down through the Forest Service but always ran into dead ends. Finally, it all fell together.

On January 23, 2022, I was talking to Rick Trembath, a colleague at FVCC who teaches fire management, and I mentioned my long, fruitless search for the jumpers. He suggested that I call Tim Love, who I'd worked with decades ago on wildlife management plans in the Bob Marshall Wilderness. Tim had retired as the Seeley Lake district ranger, one of the best. Rick said that Tim was connected with the smokejumper fraternity. I called Tim and explained my quest. He called Barry Hicks, a retired smoke-jumper. One common thread among us: we all had known and admired the late Bud Moore. Barry contacted Roger Savage, a retired jumper and a keeper of the jump lists. Within days, Tim called me and said, "Have you looked at your email?" Incredibly, Barry had found all four jumpers and told me they could possibly set up a Zoom call. I contacted the youngest of the four jumpers, Rick Cunningham, and found out that he was my age, six-ty-eight, and has lived in Kalispell, less than ten miles from me, for decades. He remembered seeing me in the media as spokesman for FWP.

The jumpers had gone on to storied professional careers, and they were scattered across the west. Curiously, they had recently been in contact with each other and had wanted to get together on a call and compare their memories about the 1974 jump. Jumper John "Doc" Lammers wanted to refresh his memories and record them in a "Letters to Otto" for his grandson before the story was forgotten. The other jumpers were Art Morrison and Luther "Luke" Lemke. Luke was the lead EMT of the group; Art was also jumping as an EMT. At the time of the jump, these men were young to be on such a complex mission: Rick was twenty, and the other jumpers were twenty-four or twenty-five.

I was overwhelmed with emotion as these men appeared on my Zoom screen. As an added twist, Rick told me that a paragraph about the 1974 crash had just appeared in the January 2022 issue of *Smokejumper*, a maga-zine published by the National Smokejumper Association. In the magazine, Art Morrison mentioned the plane crash mission and the jumpers who were along with him. Rick probably figured that's why I'd called when I did, but I hadn't seen the piece. After all these years, the serendipity was amazing.

On the Zoom call, the jumpers took me back to the events of that night of September 1, 1974, and through the morning into September 2. Most of their information confirmed what we heard at the time, but it was good to hear some of the details from the first responders and to find closure to the tragedy. Luke couldn't attend the Zoom call, but he sent us a great summary of his recollections, supported by his jumper log book.

Late that afternoon of September 1, the search helicopter had finally located the downed plane in the Carron/Welcome Creek drainage. Rick and Art were first on the jump list; Luke and Doc were added as EMTs because of the nature of the search and rescue mission, which was being coordinated by the Missoula County Sheriff's Office. Luke served as lead jumper. The sheriff department loaned a radio to jumper dispatch, which Luke carried for the mission.

According to Luke's jumper log book, the Twin Beechcraft with the jumpers and spotter Jim Cyr aboard, left the airport in Missoula at 5:50 P.M. They circled the area of the crash and made several passes, but because of the dense timber and the almost vertical angle that the plane entered the canopy, they couldn't relocate the site. The helicopter had to return and hover over the area of the crash, delaying the jumps at least an hour.

Finally, Cyr located the crash and prepared to launch the jumpers from about 1,200 feet above the canopy. They planned on making "timber jumps," with their chutes deliberately hung in trees. Given the density of the lodgepole, they had no other choice.

Doc said that if it went well, a timber jump could be easy and safe. The jumper goes into the canopy leaning back, almost upside down with feet in the air, sticks breaking as the branches adjust under the descending chute. Then when the parachute hangs up firmly in the tree or trees, the jumper unbuckles and lowers to the ground via a 100-foot or longer let-down rope.

Luke said that, with the decreasing daylight, Cyr would drop the other three jumpers above the crash a few hundred feet on top of the ridge where they would gather and cut a heliport. He prepared to jump Luke right on the plane. Cyr tapped Luke, indicating that it was time. According to Luke's jumper log, he jumped out of the plane at 8 P.M.

"I was first out," Luke said. "Almost immediately on my parachute opening I was able to see the aircraft between the trees. I steered for a tree landing just uphill from the crash in order to mark the spot for the pilots. The rest of the team was dropped at the saddle." Rick Cunningham remembered that Luke landed almost on top of the plane. The jumpers could aim their jumps so effectively because they had steerable slots on their parachutes.

Luke did a "letdown," rappelling from his tree landing. He unsuited, and went immediately to the crashed plane, which had crashed nose-in and impacted the ground violently, although the fuselage was mostly intact. He entered the cockpit and saw that both seats had sheared their floor mounts, and the pilot, passenger, and seats had compressed against the instrument panel. He did a careful check for vital signs on both men but found none. It appeared that they had died on impact through head, chest, and internal trauma. Luke said that he radioed up to the plane that both occupants were deceased. When the bodies were extracted from the crashed aircraft, little external trauma was evident.

Doc remembered Luke kneeling near him and asking him, "How do I tell Cyr that they are both dead?" He said that Luke had his finger on the radio talk button, so Cyr heard him. None of the jumpers remembered who relayed the information back to jumper dispatch in Missoula.

Both Doc and Art remembered that the plane looked as if it had rolled almost into a ball because of the violent impact. When they inspected the close-in crash conditions, Luke noted one lodgepole top was broken, a second tree sheared off above ground level, and the engine hit the ground nearly vertically at the base of the third tree. He believed that the left wing caught the tree and rotated the plane nearly straight into the ground. The jumpers felt that the small two-seater Champion seemed underpowered to be flying to locate elk in such steep terrain. Art said that the plane's dry weight probably barely exceeded 1,000 pounds.

Cyr had dropped two cargo loads, so the jumpers had chainsaws, water, and tools. Wearing bright headlamps, they began cutting the helipad on top of the ridge at about 2 A.M. and finished two and a half hours later. Rick had gathered the chutes from the trees so they could wrap up against the cold.

In September 1974, the helicopter comes into the small clearing cut by the smokejumpers. PHOTOGRAPH BY SMOKE-JUMPER RICK CUNNINGHAM.

He said the night was "eerie." Imagine cutting a helipad in dense lodgepole in the middle of the night. These guys knew what they were doing.

Some sheriff's deputies hiked into the site, and the chopper came in the next morning to evacuate the bodies, which had been placed carefully in protective bags, and to retrieve the gear. The jumpers didn't remember for sure, but they probably hiked out with the deputies.

The jumpers had completed their tasks with great skill, but they didn't view it as unusual, and they didn't consider themselves heroes. Rick said it was like a military operation and they were doing their jobs. They had jumped frequently in 1974, so they were well-practiced. But this was the only plane crash rescue they had jumped on, which had to heighten tension a bit. To a man, they viewed it as part of their mission, and they didn't mind working over the Labor Day weekend. Smokejumpers are nothing if not professional, as were the sheriff's deputies, pilots, and others involved in the search and recovery.

Smokejumper Luke Lemke guides the helicopter pilot to a landing in the small clearing, September 1974. PHOTOGRAPH BY SMOKEJUMPER RICK CUNNINGHAM.

I'm so grateful that the jumpers were willing to search their memories and relive their experiences of nearly half a century ago; it helped me reach closure on this tragedy. I will always look up to them and be thankful for them.

To unwind after the mission, everyone gathered at the sheriff's house for a steak dinner with the crew. They later received a thank-you letter for their work from the Missoula County Sheriff. They sure deserved it.

* * *

I keep thinking back to that September day in 2019 when my son, daughter, and I walked away from the plane, hiked a few hundred yards to the top of the ridge, and lingered at the small, old clearing cut by the smokejumpers more than four decades before. We had stopped for a moment to marvel at that nice elk rub, and we thought of the big bull that must have created it. We didn't know that in a year the rub would be incinerated in a wildfire.

I wonder about the bull's fate. Gosh, I hope he survived the fire. ◄◦►

Terry McCoy using an antenna and receiver to locate elk. PHOTOGRAPH COURTESY OF ROBERT KRUMM.

Sources

Chapter 1: My Wilderness Life

Everyone who cares about wilderness should read two landmark articles by wilderness icon Robert Marshall: "The Wilderness as a Minority Right" (1928) in the *Forest Bulletin*, and "The Problem of the Wilderness" (1930) in *Scientific Monthly*, Vol. 30, No. 2.

Chapter 2: Spirit Elk of Pyramid Lake

Conversations in the summer of 2019 with Dr. Robert Beall, retired FVCC forestry professor, who conducted the UM elk study on the Threemile Game Range in the early 1970s.

Coordinating Elk and Timber Management: Final Report of the Montana Cooperative Elk-Logging Study, 1970-1985. Authored by a state and federal research committee. Les Marcum was lead author for the UM Forestry School portion. January 1985.

NTSB report on the August 31, 1974, plane crash that killed Terry L. McCoy and the pilot. Aircraft: CHAMPION 7GC, registration: N8092E

NTSB report on the May 26, 1964, crash of the same Champion aircraft in Collegeport, Texas.

Plane description and performance data are from industry online specs: The standard Aeronca Champion had a wingspan of twenty-one feet, a thirteen-gallon fuel tank and a range of 279 miles. It had a maximum speed of 95 miles per hour and a stall speed of 38 miles per hour. Maximum capacity was one pilot and one passenger. The craft was designed to compete with the Piper Cub.

Many interviews and conversations during spring and summer with Dr. Les Marcum, retired U of M forestry professor emeritus, Les was the PhD student who conducted the 1972-1973 elk-logging study in the Welcome Creek watershed and surrounding area.

Chapter 3: Heart of the Scapegoat

Dodge, Tom. "Weekend Warriors." *Missoulian*, February 17, 1980. Article featuring Dr. Forrest Thomas, UM chemistry professor, about his volunteer service at Snowbowl Ski Area near Missoula. Thomas was one of the best UM profs, very popular with students in spite of the difficult subjects he taught. He inspired me to embrace chemistry, which is important in a host of wildlife concepts. My plant ecology professor, Dr. James Habeck, another stellar UM prof, knew Thomas and forwarded this article to me.

Transcripts, John Fraley, 1972–1973 academic year, University of Montana.

Chapter 4: Skiing the 'Roots

USDA Forest Service, Bitterroot National Forest. *About the Selway Bitterroot Wilderness.* Accessed through fs.usda.gov.

Chapter 5: The Impassable Canyon

Territory Magazine, Summer 2019. "Solitaries: choosing to go it alone in the Salmon River country."

Knudsen, Ruthann, et al. "A Cultural Resource Reconnaissance in the Middle Fork Salmon River Basin, Idaho, 1978." Cultural Resource Report Number 7, U.S. Forest Service, 1982.

Interview with Dr. Maurice Hornocker, University of Idaho researcher and professor emeritus, April 21, 2020.

Interview with Dr. Cathy Ream, April 11, 2020.

Chapter 6: Second Chance in the Scapegoat

Lincoln Backcountry Protective Association. Designation of the Scapegoat Wilderness, association records, 1963–1972. The Scapegoat Wilderness, where I was hunting during this story, was included in the early backcountry elk season. It was a citizen-based wilderness finally designated in 1972 after a long effort. https://archiveswest.orbiscascade.org/ark:/80444/xv75243.

Chapter 7: White River Interlude

Fish and Wildlife of the Bob Marshall Wilderness Complex and Surrounding Area, Limits of Acceptable Change in Wilderness. 1987. Montana Department of Fish, Wildlife & Parks in cooperation with Region One, U.S. Forest Service. Working Document by Jim Posewitz, Gayle Joslin, and John Fraley. This document pulls together detailed survey information for aquatic and terrestrial resources and served as the first draft of the fish and wildlife management plan for the complex.

Fisheries Management Plan for the South Fork of the Flathead River Drainage. May 1991. Montana Department of Fish, Wildlife & Parks. In cooperation with a citizen committee and the U.S. Forest Service. John Fraley, coordination and lead author.

Montana Fish, Wildlife & Parks, South Fork tributary file box, raw data and original survey forms from the 1981 trip. This file even contained the helicopter flight reports I made for each stream in July 1981 in preparation for the trip. On these flights, I visually divided the tributaries into reaches for our on-the-ground surveys. The file contains fish numbers and all physical data on the South Fork of the Flathead River reaches we surveyed as well as all the tributaries. I was delighted that fisheries biologist Leo Rosenthal was able to locate this forty-year-old file.

Chapter 8: Cutthroat in the Wild

Fraley, John and Brad Shepard. 2005. "Age, Growth, and Movements of Westslope Cutthroat Trout, *Oncorhynchus clarkii lewisi*, Inhabiting the Headwaters of a Wilderness River." *Northwest Science*, Vol. 79, No. 1.

Fraley, John, Heather Fraley and Troy Fraley. May 2011. "Age, growth, and genetics of westslope cutthroat trout, *Oncorhynchus clarkii lewisi*, in the South Fork Flathead River headwaters." Comparisons of 2010 results with the results of a study conducted from 1985–1996. Open file report, Montana Fish, Wildlife & Parks, Kalispell. Submitted to Leo Rosenthal.

Various authors in Montana Fish, Wildlife & Parks, including John Fraley, Mark Deleray, Jim Williams, Lee Anderson, Neil Anderson, and Perry Brown. January 27, 2016. "Genetics and size of westslope cutthroat trout, *Oncorhynchus clarkii lewisi*, in the South Fork Flathead River headwaters." Open file report, 2015 results compared to previous above studies.

Journal books and notes, John Fraley, 1985–1996, westslope cutthroat study in the South Fork of the Flathead River headwaters. Montana Fish, Wildlife & Parks and personal books. All data summarized in first source above.

Chapter 9: Travelin' Trout

Fraley, John. Data books and personal notes from bull trout redd counts, 1979–2020. Montana Fish, Wildlife & Parks, Kalispell, MT. Bull trout redd data summaries.

Fraley, John. "Further Adventures of a Traveling Fish." *Montana Outdoors*, May/ June 1994, Montana Fish, Wildlife & Parks.

Fraley, John, and Brad Shepard. "Life History, Ecology, and Population Status of Migratory Bull Trout (*Salvelinus confluentus*) in the Flathead Lake and River System, Montana." *Northwest Science*, Vol. 63, No. 4, 1989.

Posewitz, Jim, Gayle Joslin, and John Fraley. "Fish and Wildlife of the Bob Marshall Wilderness Complex and Surrounding Area, Limits of Acceptable Change in Wilderness." Montana Department of Fish, Wildlife, & Parks in cooperation with Region One, U.S. Forest Service. Working document, 1987.

Chapter 10: My Dash through the Bob

Typed notes from my July 4, 1992, trip from Owl Creek Packer Camp to Meadow Creek Trailhead. I made these notes in my journal during the dash, then typed them out a few days later. They consist of two typed pages and include the times of sixteen different points along the way on the dash, from 4:35 A.M. to 9:05 P.M.

U.S. Department of Agriculture. Bob Marshall Wilderness, Flathead and Lewis and Clark National Forests map, 1973. The 1973 map contains good information on Robert Marshall and his long wilderness jaunts.

Chapter 11: Following the Fur

Fraley, John. Journal books, Middle Fork of the Flathead drainage, wilderness winter fur surveys, 1993–2001.

Halfpenny, James. *A Field Guide to Mammal Tracking in North America*. Johnson Books, 1986.

Nelson, Richard. *Make Prayers to the Raven: A Koyukon View of the Northern Forest*. University of Chicago Press, 1983.

Chapter 12: Villain in Velvet

Fraley, John. *Montana Outdoors* Portrait: Marten. Vol. 41, 2010.

Moore, Bud. *The Lochsa Story*. Mountain Press Publishing, 1996.

Moore, Bud. Numerous personal interviews and conversations with Bud, 1994–2008.

Nelson, Richard. *Make Prayers to the Raven*. University of Chicago Press, 1983.

Chapter 13: A Long Walk with Bud Moore

Fraley, John and Kevin. Notes made while retracing Bud's hike. August 8–11, 2018.

Moore, William R. "Bud." 1972. Flathead River hike, "Me, Kenai, and Kyukuk." September 6–10, 1972.

USDA Forest Service. Northern Region fire history map 1984–2018. Flathead National Forest and Glacier National Park.

Chapter 14: Renewal

InciWeb, U.S. Forest Service website on fire reporting. Cinnabar Fire, Welcome Creek Wilderness, August 2020.

Interview with jumpers via zoom call, February 16, 2022. Jumpers are: Rick Cunningham, Art Morrison, John "Doc" Lammers. Written summary provided by Luther "Luke" Lemke.

Additional conversations with Rick Cunningham.

Morrison, Art. "The Bad Old Days." *Smokejumper*. National Smokejumper Association, January 2022. In this lengthy article, Art delves into his personal and other smokejumper history, and mentions the other jumpers on the 1974 mission. ◂◦▸

Index

Page numbers in **BOLD** indicate photos.

About the Author

John Fraley came to Montana as a teenager and received fish and wildlife management degrees from both Montana universities. He retired after a forty-year career with Montana's wildlife agency, mostly spent in northwest Montana's Flathead country. John wrote regularly for *Montana Outdoors*, and he has written articles on the Flathead's history and other topics for *True West*, *Montana: The Magazine of Western History*, *Western Wildlands*, *Wild Outdoor World*, and other magazines. John's other books include *Wild River Pioneers*; *Rangers, Trappers, and Trailblazers*; *A Woman's Way West*; and *Heroes of the Bob Marshall Wilderness*. He lives with his wife, Dana, in Kalispell.

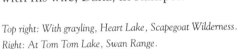

Top right: With grayling, Heart Lake, Scapegoat Wilderness.
Right: At Tom Tom Lake, Swan Range.
Below: Atop Kevan Mountain, in the Bob.

More Farcountry Press Books by John Fraley

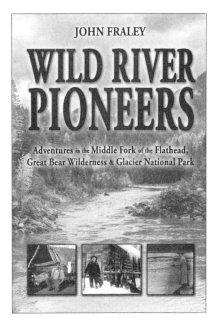

Wild River Pioneers
Adventures in the Middle Fork of the Flathead, Great Bear Wilderness and Glacier National Park
New and Updated Edition

Author John Fraley brings alive the history of Montana's wildest river by telling stories of some of its most riveting historical characters in the new edition *Wild River Pioneers*. Take a front-row seat to shootouts, murders, a hanging, a train robbery, marauding grizzly bears, lost graves, gold prospecting, and an ice cream-eating pet bear.

Rangers, Trappers, and Trailblazers
Early Adventures in Montana's Bob Marshall Wilderness and Glacier National Park

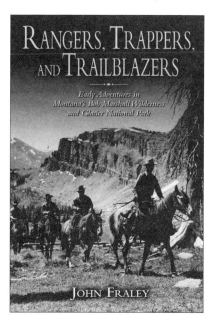

These are the true adventures of people who earned their living in the unsettled wilds of Glacier National Park and the Bob Marshall Wilderness Complex in the 19th and early 20th centuries. Tragedies and near-misses are balanced with tales of courage, endurance, and remarkable personal achievement.

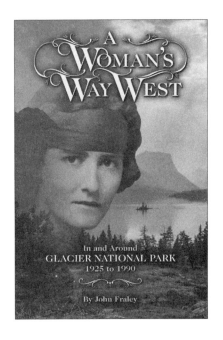

A Woman's Way West
In and Around
Glacier National Park, 1925-1990

Doris Ashley left her Iowa farm in 1925 after a string of personal tragedies, riding the train west to Glacier National Park. This is her story—her love affair with the wild Crown of the Continent, the rugged landscape, and equally rugged inhabitants. Romance, grit, and wit abound.

Heroes of the Bob Marshall Wilderness

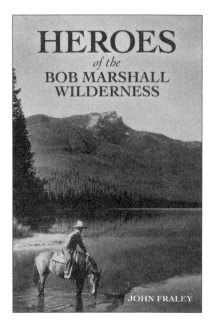

Come along and celebrate with author John Fraley as he traces the contributions, challenges, and fun times of past and present heroes of the Bob Marshall Wilderness. Over the past century, these heroes have ridden, packed, and hiked thousands of miles from one end of the Bob to the other, and they've helped make the wilderness what it is today.